Education

in Asia

A Comparative Study

of Cost and Financing

D0731621

WORLD BANK

REGIONAL AND

SECTORAL STUDIES

Education

in Asia

A Comparative Study

of Cost and Financing

JEE-PENG TAN

AND

ALAIN MINGAT

The World Bank
Washington, D.C.

LB
2826.6
.A78
T36
1992

© 1992 The International Bank for Reconstruction
and Development / The World Bank
1818 H Street, N.W., Washington, D.C. 20433

All rights reserved
Manufactured in the United States of America
First printing April 1992

The World Bank Regional and Sectoral Studies series provides an outlet for work that is relatively limited in its subject matter or geographical coverage but that contributes to the intellectual foundations of development operations and policy formulation. These studies have not necessarily been edited with the same rigor as Bank publications that carry the imprint of a university press.

The findings, interpretations, and conclusions expressed in this publication are those of the authors and should not be attributed in any manner to the World Bank, to its affiliated organizations, or to the members of its Board of Executive Directors or the countries they represent.

The material in this publication is copyrighted. Requests for permission to reproduce portions of it should be sent to the Office of the Publisher at the address shown in the copyright notice above. The World Bank encourages dissemination of its work and will normally give permission promptly and, when the reproduction is for noncommercial purposes, without asking a fee. Permission to copy portions for classroom use is granted through the Copyright Clearance Center, 27 Congress Street, Salem, Massachusetts 01970, U.S.A.

The complete backlist of publications from the World Bank is shown in the annual *Index of Publications*, which contains an alphabetical title list and indexes of subjects, authors, and countries and regions. The latest edition is available free of charge from Distribution Unit, Office of the Publisher, The World Bank, 1818 H Street, N.W., Washington, D.C. 20433, U.S.A., or from Publications, The World Bank, 66, avenue d'Iéna, 75116 Paris, France.

Jee-Peng Tan is a senior economist in the Office of the Regional Vice President for South Asia in the World Bank. Alain Mingat is professor of economics at the Université de Bourgogne, Dijon, France.

Cover design by Sam Ferro

Library of Congress Cataloging-in-Publication Data

Tan, Jee-Peng, 1954–
   Education in Asia : a comparative study of cost and financing /
Jee-Peng Tan and Alain Mingat.
     p. cm.—(World Bank regional and sectoral studies)
   Includes bibliographical references.
   ISBN 0-8213-2098-X
   1. Education—Asia—Finance. 2. Education—Asia—Finance—
Statistics. 3. Education and state—Asia. I. Mingat, Alain.
II. Title. III. Series.
LB2826.6.A78T36 1992
379.5—dc20   92-11537
                                                  CIP

Contents

CONCORDIA UNIVERSITY LIBRARY
2811 NE HOLMAN ST.
PORTLAND, OR 97211-6099

Text figures

Foreword

This study on education in Asia by Jee-Peng Tan and Alain Mingat and the companion study on health by Charles Griffin were initiated in 1988 as complements to other World Bank studies on the social sectors. As chief economist in the Asia Region at that time, I launched these studies to help strengthen the factual and analytical basis of the World Bank's lending operations in the Asia Region in two sectors that relate directly to the Bank's broader concern with poverty alleviation.

Both studies provide an overview of sectoral development, with an emphasis on cost and finance issues. This focus was chosen because education and health outcomes depend critically on resource allocation in the sectors, and allocation, in turn, is influenced by policy choices affecting costs and finance. The studies share three aims: to document current patterns of costs, finance, and outcomes in individual Asian countries; to explore linkages between sectoral performance and policy choices; and to identify potential policy options to promote efficient and equitable sectoral development.

The studies rest on a rich data base compiled from varied sources. While some of the data can be found in widely available publications (such as United Nations Yearbooks), other data, particularly on cost and finance, are scarcer. For the latter, the authors have drawn on documents provided by governments in the context of the Bank's operational activity. In this task, the contribution of colleagues in the Asia Region has been critical, for their generosity in sharing materials acquired in the course of their own work made it possible for the authors to assemble as much data as they have. Beyond this, the studies have also benefited from extensive discussion among Asia Region staff, so that they are, in a sense, a product of collaborative effort among Bank staff to expand knowledge and understanding of education and health issues in the region.

Comparative analysis was the common approach in both studies, with countries rather than individuals as the unit of observation. This orientation allows the authors to examine the impact of systemwide policies—such as the extent of private financing in a system—on sectoral development. Asian countries, and probably countries in other regions as well, differ widely in policy choices as well as outcomes. The diversity permits assessment of individual countries' performance relative to others in the region, and sheds light on the possible range of alternative policy choices and options. It also invites exploration of the linkages between policies and outcomes.

Beyond specific findings relating to individual countries, several general themes emerge from these studies. On education, the authors conclude that the two most essential components of an effective policy package are greater attention to primary education and reduced public financing of higher education. Country-specific conditions and political realities matter, but the authors identify three strategies that warrant general consideration to make education more efficient and equitable:

Increasing public spending on education in selected countries. This option is intuitively appealing but has to be analyzed in the context of the shares of total spending on education as well as the composition of the spending. In some countries, including Bangladesh, Nepal and, until recently, the Philippines, both total spending and spending on primary education (relative to GNP) are much below the Asian average. In such countries increasing spending channeled to primary education is justified.

Freeing up resources for primary education. In some other countries total spending on education is not below the average but a very high proportion for primary schools. For example, although India spends almost as much as Korea, Thailand, and Indonesia on education (around 3 percent of GNP), India's spending on primary education is only about half the levels in those countries. Systems with excessive bias toward higher education have invariably been less efficient and less equitable. To minimize these effects, three strategies in higher education, not mutually exclusive, have been used with success in several Asian countries: increased private financing in public institutions through user charges, promotion of largely self-financing private institutions, and low-cost distance education. These options should of course be examined in greater detail to identify ways to tailor them to conditions in individual countries.

Improving primary education. Regionwide, only 62 percent of first graders currently complete the primary cycle. This statistic suggests that improving primary education is a major priority and challenge in most Asian countries, particularly in view of the importance of basic education for social and economic development. Increased spending per pupil in primary education may, by raising the quality of schooling, make it more attractive and increase its holding power. However, the authors also stress that "throwing more money" at primary schools is not the answer—or not the whole answer. Using existing resources efficiently is no less important.

Beyond these broad messages, the reader will find ample information about Asian education in this study, as well as analytical support for the foregoing conclusions. It is my hope that the study's publication in an easily accessible form will contribute to a lively discussion among policymakers and others regarding future directions for the development of education in Asian countries, thereby encouraging consideration of policies to build on Asia's already remarkable progress in the sector.

Oktay Yenal
Chief, India Resident Mission
South Asia Region

Acknowledgments

Many people contributed to this study at various stages. When work began, we were greatly assisted by colleagues who generously made available to us data and resource materials collected for their own work. Among them we wish especially to thank Shigeko Asher, Richard Cambridge, Mae-Chu Chang, Nat Colleta, Rosslyn Hees, Elizabeth King, Jack Maas, Kenichi Ohashi, Andre Salmon, Thomas Schmidt, William J. Smith, Cecilia Valdevieso, Chia-Ling Yang, and Roberto Zagha. In collecting, processing, and checking the data we were assisted by three competent summer interns at the Bank: San Ling Lam, Andrea Madarassy, and Aleta Domdom. Their help was indispensable in completing this first part of the work.

The earliest draft of the study was read with great care and insight by Charles Griffin and Estelle James. They offered suggestions to refine the data and constructive ideas to improve the study's structure and analysis. We owe them thanks for overlooking the roughness of the initial draft and for making the effort to work through the material.

The study also benefited from the formal review process. We received valuable comments from, among others, Birgir Frederiksen, Emmanuel Jimenez, Martin Karcher, Elizabeth King, and Jandhyala Tilak. In addition, four anonymous reviewers appointed by the Bank's Publications Committee also offered detailed and very helpful comments. In the interest of facilitating our work in revising the manuscript, two of the reviewers, Andrew Rogerson and Donald Winkler, actually made themselves known to us. We are grateful for their decision to do so, as it proved to be a great help. We would also like to thank Douglas Keare, a member of the Publications Committee, for steering us through the review process.

Editorial and production support was provided by Katrina Van Duyn (editing), Mary Mahy and Kim Bieler (desktopping), and Kathy Rosen (graphics).

Our acknowledgment would not be complete without mentioning others who contributed behind the scenes. We are especially grateful to Oktay Yenal whose steady interest in the study offered much needed support through its sometimes difficult gestation. Thanks are also due to Alexander ter Weele, our immediate supervisor for this work. Last but not least, we owe a special word of appreciation to our families for creating the conditions for a fruitful collaboration.

1

Introduction

Education is universally recognized as an important investment in human capital. It contributes to socioeconomic development by endowing individuals with the means to improve their health, skills, knowledge, and capability for productive work. For societies as a whole, education enriches the political and cultural life of the community and strengthens the community's ability to exploit technology for social and economic advancement. Because the benefits are so broad and pervasive, the development of education is a key concern everywhere.

This study tries to document the progress of education in Asian countries. It is motivated by a desire to take stock of current conditions as well as an interest in exploring options for the sector's future development. Asia offers a particularly rich context for study because countries have such different education outcomes and sectoral policies. The comparative data give countries in the region a fresh perspective for examining their progress and policies in education in relation to their neighbors. And lessons of wider interest emerge to inform current debate about appropriate policies for education development.

Developing countries typically experienced rapid growth in education in the past two to three decades, accompanied by a parallel rise in government spending on education. The sector typically claims a large (in some cases the largest) share of the public budget, and governments are commonly the most important source of financing for the sector, even in countries where private education is well developed. So issues of education costs and financing attract special attention, particularly in an era of budgetary austerity. At a time when the demand for education is expected to grow relentlessly because of population pressures, governments are increasingly hard-pressed for resources—macroeconomic prospects are bleak and intersectoral competition for scarce public funds is intensifying. In this environment, an examination of education costs and financing is crucial for formulating appropriate policies for the sector's expansion.

Most Asian countries share this concern, but probably to a lesser extent than elsewhere. In many Asian countries external constraints are projected to ease considerably, with a slowdown in population growth and relatively bright prospects on the economic front. Of concern is not so much how to survive the present adverse environment, as how to improve on past achievements. That enormous resources are expended on education adds weight to the need for assessment. Evaluation is particularly relevant now as Asian countries enter a period in education development in which interest is likely to shift from expanding the system to upgrading the quality of available services.

Objectives, focus, and scope

The study has two primary objectives. The first is to document the main features of education in Asian countries. The second objective is to try to relate differences in policy choices—reflected, for example, in spending levels and allocations—to education outcomes. Because these choices affect whole systems, their effect is impossible to examine except in the context of cross-national analysis. Thus, although the high degree of aggregation in the data reduces precision in the analysis, the results nonetheless yield important information about the effect of different policies. At a minimum, the patterns that emerge offer a basis for formulating hypotheses for future analytical work.

The focus is on education costs and financing because these aspects of the education system reveal how resources are deployed in the sector. More important, because education costs and financing are key areas of government intervention, an assessment of priorities for future sectoral development must begin by examining current choices in these areas. Other aspects of education, such as management of the system, pedagogical practices, and cultural and political influences on education are also important to consider. However, they receive relatively little attention here because they are less amenable to economic analysis and are, moreover, difficult to quantify for comparative analysis. Because the treatment is selective, the study should be viewed as a complement to other comparative analysis (such as Unesco 1985) that considers the nonfinancial aspects of the education system in greater depth.

The study emphasizes cross-country analysis, highlighting differences among countries rather than details about individual countries. Special attention was paid to compiling data and indicators that satisfy, as much as possible, two requirements: comparability across countries and consistency within countries. The research and analysis is intended to complement more detailed studies of individual countries.

Comparisons among countries are based on indicators of the formation of human capital and the promotion of social equity. For human capital formation, the broad concern is the efficiency of investments in education. How do countries differ in resource allocation to the sector as a whole and within the sector? Do allocations maximize the returns to society, measured and unmeasured, of investing in educa-tion? To obtain better results, in what direction should countries shift their education policies?

For the promotion of equity, the principal concerns are distribution of resources and access to education. First because public spending on education is usually sub-stantial, its distribution is likely to have a significant effect on income distribution, and hence on some aspects of poverty. Second, a longer-term effect on equity arises because access to education (1) is a powerful vehicle for individuals' social and economic advancement in society and (2) is determined to a large extent by the pattern of public spending in the sector. So the study asks these questions: How do countries differ in the relative emphasis they place on the various levels of education, in relation to inputs, coverage, and financing arrangements? What are the patterns of access to and exit from the education system? What effect do these patterns have on the distribution of education opportunities and on public spending for education? And what policy options exist for improvement?

Limitations

To avoid misapplication of findings, the study's main limitations should be noted. First, it is a country-level study, meaning that countries are generally taken as the relevant unit of observation. Large countries, such as China, India, and Indonesia, are treated as single units, even though disaggregated data would reveal a more accurate picture of actual conditions. But having recognized this defect, note that each coun-try's education system operates under a common institutional and policy framework. Thus, as long as the focus remains on broad structural issues, the reliance on aggre-gated data is not as serious a shortcoming as might appear at first sight.

Second, the analysis is meant only to highlight policy issues of potential impor-tance. It does not substitute for more detailed studies that are essential in designing country-specific policy interventions. For example, if unit costs in a particular coun-try are significantly higher than those in neighboring countries, it does not immedi-ately justify a program to reduce costs; rather this finding signals the need for additional analysis to examine the reasons for the high costs and to evaluate the merits of alternative cost-reducing measures. As another example, comparisons of enrollment ratios may reveal that coverage in a given country is below that of other countries at comparable income levels. Again, this result does not immediately justify expansion of coverage; rather, it signals a potential problem that merits fur-ther assessment.

Third, not all aspects of education costs and financing are addressed in adequate depth. The study relies chiefly on secondary sources of data and suffers from the scarcity of resource materials on some topics. Moreover, some issues require survey rather than aggregated data for a meaningful analysis. For these reasons, the discus-sion on such topics as external efficiency, student achievement, and some aspects of equity does not go as far as necessary. Nonetheless, the existing data can yield useful insights. Aside from offering a broad overview of policy issues in the sector, the data help identify gaps in our present understanding, thereby suggesting the focus of future work. Thus, defining the analytical and research agenda is probably also an important product of this study.

Finally, the availability and accuracy of the data have been subject to some constraints. For most countries, statistics on the standard indicators—enrollment ratios, percentage of females in total enrollment—are readily obtainable. In contrast, financial data are scarce and often not comparable across countries even if reported in a single source. Most of the data were thus derived from basic sources, when these were available, including country sector studies, government statistical publications, and budget documents; these sources are described in more detail in appendix B. The data on a basic set of indicators were assembled for a core of 11 Asian countries (Bangladesh, China, India, Indonesia, Korea, Malaysia, Nepal, Papua New Guinea, the Philippines, Sri Lanka, and Thailand). For completeness of regional coverage, data for other Asian countries are also presented when available.

The data suffer from the disadvantage of having been generated mostly from secondary sources. This shortcoming was mitigated somewhat by special efforts to check for internal consistency in the data (in one or two instances with the originators of the data) and to ensure comparability in data definitions across countries. Thus, where broad orders of magnitude are sufficient, the statistics give a reasonably good basis for the overview approach adopted in this study. Although the statistics are robust enough to offer conclusions about general policy directions, further refinements are probably called for when assessing specific countries and policy options.

Overview of findings

At the broadest level, the study yields an overview of the current state of education in Asia and identifies major policy challenges. These conclusions are based on specific findings, which are summarized in the concluding chapter of the study.

Diversity across countries

Countries in the region differ widely in education outcomes, in external constraints on sector development, and in choice of sectoral policies. With respect to education outcomes, the spectrum stretches from Bhutan, with an adult literacy rate of only 15 percent and a primary enrollment ratio of 25 percent in the mid-1980s, to such countries as Korea and Thailand, where over 90 percent of adults are literate and where primary education has reached, or is approaching, universal coverage. Given current structures of the enrollment pyramid, the average grade attainment of future adults ranges from less than grade 5 in Bangladesh, Bhutan, India, Nepal, and Papua

New Guinea, to more than grade 9 in Korea, Malaysia, the Philippines, and Sri Lanka.

In part these differences in outcomes are the result of past external constraints. Low-income countries tend to perform less well than richer ones because of the twin pressures of rapid population growth and relatively slow economic expansion— problems that are often compounded by the high cost of education inputs, the weak demand for schooling, and the sparseness of institutional infrastructure. The squeeze on resources has been tight in countries with a high ratio of school-age population to adults (Bangladesh, Indonesia, Lao PDR, Myanmar, Nepal, Papua New Guinea, and the Philippines) because larger ratios imply heavier fiscal burdens for education finance. But the constraints were perhaps even tighter in countries where the economy grew more slowly than the population (Papua New Guinea) or only slightly faster (Nepal and the Philippines), because these conditions permit only a limited possibility of expanding coverage or upgrading services.

Perhaps more important, countries' achievements in education reflected the different choices they made in sectoral policies. For example, in the mid-1980s: aggregate spending on education varied from less than 2 percent of GNP in Bangladesh, Myanmar, Nepal, and the Philippines to 6 percent and above in Malaysia and Papua New Guinea; the share of public spending devoted to primary education, reflecting choices in intrasectoral emphasis, ranged from less than 30 percent in India to around 60 percent in Indonesia, Korea, the Philippines, and Thailand; the rate of cost recovery for conventional public higher education was as low as less than 5 percent in Bangladesh, China, India, Papua New Guinea, Sri Lanka, and Thailand, but was nearly 50 percent in Korea; and the mix of institutional arrangements to cope with excess demand for higher education encompassed low-cost distance systems (Sri Lanka and Thailand), private education (Korea and the Philippines), and overseas education (Malaysia).

Increasing efficiency and equity

Significant progress in education development has been made in many Asian countries, but striking inefficiencies and inequities remain. The unit costs of education are relatively high in some countries because of factors that include unexploited economies of scale and inadequate incentives for greater cost-consciousness among consumers and providers. Many education systems also suffer from poor internal efficiency; for example, dropping out in the first two cycles of education is an important mechanism of selection, although an implicit one, in a large number of countries. The problem is especially serious in primary education, with adverse implications for human capital formation and social selectivity. For the region as a whole, 91 percent of the population currently enter grade 1, but only 62 percent of the entrants reach the end of primary schooling. The situation is especially alarming in such countries as Bangladesh, Bhutan, India, Lao PDR, and Nepal, where survival rates are 40 percent or less. And girls' participation in schooling appears to be especially weak under such conditions.

Intrasectoral allocation of education expenditures in some countries reveals a decided bias toward higher education at the expense of primary education. This diversion results from failure to tap private sources of funding for higher education, despite evidence of excess demand. The subsector's large claim on resources is generated by the twin pressures of high unit subsidies and expansion of coverage to cope with excess demand. Evaluated by resource-intensity per student, extent of coverage, and degree of private financing across levels of education, the emphasis on higher education is especially strong in Bangladesh, India, and Papua New Guinea.

Substantial scope therefore exists for improving efficiency and equity in Asian education. In most countries, the external context for policy shifts is likely to be quite favorable, with the projected slowdown of population growth and generally bright prospects for economic expansion. The challenge in such countries is to avoid complacency and to focus on consolidating and strengthening past achievements through policies to increase spending allocations for education. But in a handful of countries—including Bangladesh, Bhutan, Lao PDR, Nepal, and Papua New Guinea—the demographic and macroeconomic conditions will probably remain difficult. For these countries, choosing the right policies is essential for progress, because the wrong policies can worsen present inefficiencies and inequities, and might even reverse past achievements.

Broad policy options

Given the diversity among countries in the region, the choice of precise policy options will differ according to initial conditions and sectoral objectives. However, few governments would disagree with the broad goal of alleviating poverty. Because education is an essential part of policies to effect social and economic advancement among the poor, this objective may be taken as a primary aim of policies in the sector. In some situations, promoting equity involves some sacrifice of efficiency, but the analysis in this report indicates an absence of conflict between equity and efficiency, at least at the aggregate level. Indeed, improving efficiency is essential if equity is to be increased, because inefficiency implies high costs, and these in turn shrink the pool of resources available for poverty-alleviating interventions. Given these broad goals, three major policy thrusts are indicated:

• Increased aggregate spending on education in selected countries. This option is intuitively appealing, but should be treated cautiously in light of the finding that appreciable changes in education outcomes result only with relatively large shifts in spending. The explanation is simple: outcomes are determined as much by the efficiency with which resources are used as by the aggregate amount of resources available. Thus, for most Asian countries improvement will result largely from promoting the efficient use of resources rather than from expanding the overall resource envelope. But in a few countries, such as Bangladesh, Nepal, and the Philippines, current spending levels are so low that an increase would relieve severe pressures on the education system. The increase should be directed as much as possible toward primary education, particularly in Bangladesh and Nepal.

• Improving access and retention rates in primary education. Primary education deserves emphasis because it affects social equity and the formation of basic human capital. In some countries (Bhutan, China, India, Nepal, and Papua New Guinea), a two-pronged approach is required because not all school-age children enter grade 1 and not all who enter survive to the end of the cycle. In the remaining Asian countries, with the exception of Korea and Malaysia, reducing the incidence of noncompletion is the main issue. The choice of specific interventions will differ according to local conditions. Increasing the level of spending per student is probably warranted in some settings, such as Bangladesh and India. But in view of extensive research evidence that throwing more money at schools does not in itself insure against low cohort survival rates, it would also be relevant to consider how resources are spent among school inputs. Assessing such resource allocation deserves priority in future analytical work.

• Freeing up resources for primary education. Shaping sectoral policies that favor primary education requires concomitant changes in other subsectors. Increased efficiency—say, by grouping schools to exploit economies of scale—is crucial as it would increase the resources available for reallocation to primary education. But reducing public subsidization of higher education is perhaps the most clearcut overall policy shift called for. There are several ways to do this, as indicated by the experience of several Asian countries with relatively low rates of public subsidization in higher education (for example, Korea, Thailand, and the Philippines): instituting cost recovery in conventional public institutions, encouraging the emergence of a largely self-financing private sector, and relying on relatively low-cost distance systems. The optimal mix of institutional and financing arrangements depends on unique country conditions.

Implications for policy dialogue

Study findings offer a basis for policy dialogue about education development in Asia. Data on the basic indicators facilitate assessment of individual countries in a regional perspective, thereby alerting policymakers to the relative strengths and weaknesses of their education systems. This information is especially relevant in shaping the broad objectives of future policies for the sector and in assessing the range of feasible options for accomplishing them.

The analysis also suggests several general assumptions that should underlie policy discussions in the sector:

• There is substantial scope for interventions to improve efficiency and equity in

Asian education. The conditions for such policy shifts are likely to be particularly favorable in the coming decade: the prospects for expanding coverage or upgrading services (or both) are bright for most countries in the region because of the projected slowdown in population growth and the relatively high rates of economic expansion envisaged.

• Choosing the right policies can make an appreciable difference in a country's performance in education, even though external constraints, especially demographic pressures, remain an important impediment. Poorer countries do not necessarily face a narrower range of feasible policy options, despite weaker administrative structures and, possibly, more fragile social conditions.

• Increasing aggregate public spending on education is an intuitively appealing but limited policy option for promoting education development in most countries. One reason is that although appreciable results can materialize with large increases in spending, such increases are nearly always difficult to provide—except possibly in countries where current levels of spending are relatively small—because of keen intersectoral competition for resources. A more important reason is that increased resources cannot overcome the effects of inappropriate policies within the sector, particularly those affecting the efficiency with which services are provided and financed.

• To the extent that poverty alleviation through education is a social objective, two interrelated components of education policies are essential: increased focus on primary education to improve the rate of cohort survival; and a concomitant reduction in public financing of higher education (through user charges in regular public institutions, through the promotion of a largely self-financing private sector driven by excess demand, and through low-cost distance systems).

• Increasing private financing for higher education to a moderately high level is likely to improve efficiency in public institutions (by reducing its relative costliness) and improve equity, both in the distribution of aggregate public spending on education and in expanded coverage of higher education.

Future research priorities

Although this study offers guidance to formulate policies in education, the detailed design of those policies would require additional research and evaluation to fill important gaps in the data and in our knowledge. Topics of interest include: assessment of the external efficiency of education by level and type; the appropriate regulatory framework for private education and decentralized control of schools; the cost and benefits of overseas higher education; and local centers of excellence. But from a regional perspective, the research priorities that stand out have to do with two problems that most countries in the region share.

First, further study is needed of the low cohort survival rates in many Asian education systems. To identify interventions to address this problem, research would need to assess the reasons for the current patterns of survival across population groups. Such research should distinguish between factors that are open to direct policy intervention (such as conditions of schooling) and those that must be taken as given in the short and medium term (such as poverty-related factors).

Second, further analysis of higher education is needed because of its vital importance in overall sectoral policy. Given the different alternatives for providing services, a central issue is the best mix of institutional arrangements across fields of study. Addressing this issue would require assessment of the labor market performance of people who have followed different careers in higher education.

Both lines of research require collection and analysis of individual-level survey data. This investment in further analytical work is probably worthwhile as it would strengthen the factual basis for policy dialogue on issues where existing knowledge is inadequate or nonexistent.

Organization

To place the analysis in context, chapter 2 highlights the main features of education in Asia in an international and regional perspective. Chapter 3 provides more detailed documentation of education costs and financing arrangements in Asian countries, focusing on such items as the pattern and level of unit costs across levels of education, the distribution of public spending, the contribution of private financing, and so on.

With the data in place, efficiency and equity are addressed in chapters 4 and 5. Chapter 6 offers conclusions based on the cross-sectional analysis and makes suggestions for future work. Taking account of the overall findings, appendix A gives a succinct description and comparative evaluation of the current status of education in individual Asian countries. Details on data sources and the corresponding core educational statistics are in appendix B. Figures and miscellaneous data referred to in the text and figures are given in appendix C.

2

Education Development in Asia:
Basic Characteristics

The education development of countries is compared in this study using such indicators as the schooling attainment of the adult population, which reflects past investments in education; the present structure of enrollments; the level of government spending on education; and the extent of private involvement in the sector. In what respects does Asia differ from other world regions? How do individual Asian countries compare with one another? What factors account for the differences among countries?

International comparisons

Education systems throughout the world grew rapidly during the 1960s and 1970s. The fruits of that expansion are revealed by the extent of literacy among today's adults and by their education attainment (table 2.1). In Asia the adult literacy rate in 1985 was about 65 percent, slightly higher than the average of about 59 percent for developing countries as a whole, but significantly below the average of 80 percent for Latin America. Schooling attainment for the average Asian adult is 5.3 years,[1] compared with 5.6 years for Latin Americans. The difference is smaller than might be expected, given the sizable gap in literacy rates. The reason might be that literacy is defined using stricter criteria in Asia; but it is more likely that the average-years-of-schooling statistic refers mostly to Asian countries with better developed education systems.[2] Note that even in such countries, women receive significantly less education than men—4.7 years compared with 5.9 years. The gap is much wider than in Latin America, but smaller than in Europe, the Middle East, and North Africa.

Among the current population of children and youths, participation in schooling is widespread throughout the developing world (table 2.2). In 1985, the average gross enrollment ratio for developing countries as a group was 90 percent, 37

10

Table 2.1 Education attainment of adults, world regions, 1980s

Region	Literate adults, 1985 (percent)		Average years of schooling			
			Males	Females	Both sexes	
Asia	64.6	(14)	5.9	4.7	5.3	(9)
Africa	47.8	(20)	3.5	2.6	3.1	(12)
Europe, the Middle East, and North Africa	48.2	(11)	5.1	3.7	4.4	(12)
Latin America	80.2	(12)	5.7	5.4	5.6	(16)
Developing countries	58.6	(50)	5.2	4.3	4.8	(56)
Developed countries	..	..	10.3	9.7	10.0	(12)

.. denotes not available in this and following tables.
Note: Figures in parentheses refer to the number of countries reporting.
Source: Data on percent literate are from UNICEF (1988). Data on the average years of schooling of adults are from Horn and Arriagada (1986).

percent, and 10 percent respectively in primary, secondary, and higher education.[3] On average, Asian countries have somewhat lower enrollment ratios than countries in Latin America and Europe, the Middle East, and North Africa; but if differences in level of economic development, as indicated by per capita GNP, are taken into account, they actually achieve better-than-expected coverage (figure 2.1).

The achievement in Asian education becomes all the more remarkable when levels of government spending on education are compared across regions (table 2.3). Expressed as a percentage of GNP, governments in Asia spend less on education than governments in all other world regions. This apparent paradox—high coverage despite relatively little fiscal effort—gives a first indication that as a determinant of education development, public policies in the sector are at least as important as the size of public spending. This idea is intuitive: government policies can affect both the extent of private involvement in providing and financing education and the efficiency with which public funds are spent; both outcomes influence the effective amount of resources available to the sector.

Table 2.2 Enrollment ratios, world regions, 1985

Region	Primary	Secondary	Higher	Number of countries reporting
Asia	92.0	42.9	11.1	16
Africa	77.8	19.5	1.5	30
Europe, the Middle East, and North Africa	2.9	46.9	14.2	16
Latin America	101.8	48.5	16.5	21
Developing countries	89.5	36.7	9.5	83
Developed countries	102.7	85.9	29.6	16

Source: World Bank BESD database.

The share of private enrollment in Asia (across the three levels of education) is not as large as the share in Latin America—an average of 20 percent compared with 27 percent (table 2.4). But the share rises from primary to higher education much more rapidly in Asia than in Latin America. In other words, in providing education directly, Asian governments concentrate more on the lower levels of education. (For

Figure 2.1 Relationship between gross enrollment ratios and per capita GNP, major world regions, around 1985

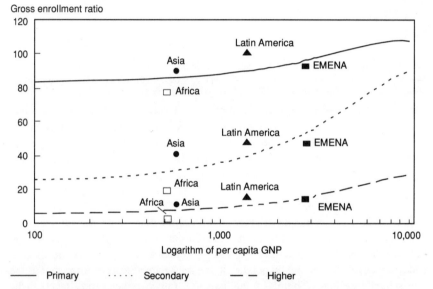

Gross enrollment ratio

Note: Per capita GNP is in U.S. dollars. EMENA is used for Europe, the Middle East, and North Africa.
Source: See appendix tables C.1 and C.2.

Table 2.3 Public spending on education, world regions, 1985

Region	Public spending, percentage of GNP	Number of countries reporting
Asia[a]	3.1	16
Africa	4.1	32
Europe, the Middle East, and North Africa	5.3	18
Latin America	3.5	21
Developing countries	4.0	91
Developed countries	5.7	21

a. Figure differs slightly from data in tables 1.1 and 2.8 due to differences in the sources of data.
Source: Unesco (1987).

Table 2.4 Share of enrollments in private sector, world regions, 1985

Region	Share of private enrollments (percent)			Number of countries reporting		
	Primary	Secondary	Higher	Primary	Secondary	Higher
Asia[a]	3.9	26.0	28.6	10	9	13
Africa	15.4	26.4	..	2	31	..
Europe, the Middle East, and North Africa	8.8	8.1	3.3	15	17	15
Latin America	17.7	29.1	3.6	19	19	7
Developing countries	13.1	21.8	17.0	77	77	31
Developed countries	17.3	19.3	..	20	20	..

a. The regional average for higher education differs from that in appendix table B1.4 due to omission of Lao PDR in that table. See also table 2.9.
Source: Data supplied by Unesco, supplemented for Asia by sources cited in appendix table B1.4; Europe, the Middle East, and North Africa (higher education) by Za'rour (1988); Latin America (higher education) by Winkler (1988b).

the extent of private financing, the data are only a rough guide, because no distinction is made between government-aided schools and those that rely mainly on private contributions.)

Variation across Asian countries

Asia encompasses a great diversity of countries, including some of the more advanced developing economies in the world, as well as some of the poorest. This diversity is reflected in the education characteristics of individual countries in the region. In 1985, literacy rates ranged from only 15 percent in Bhutan to over 90 percent in Korea and Thailand. This indicator improved rapidly for countries with low initial rates of adult literacy, such as Bangladesh and Nepal. But the improvement has also been dramatic in countries starting from a higher base, such as India, Indonesia, Malaysia, Papua New Guinea, and Singapore. Adults in Korea and the Philippines have significantly more years of schooling than their peers elsewhere in Asia—8.4 years compared with 6.9 years (table 2.5). In all Asian countries except Indonesia, the Philippines, and Sri Lanka, men receive at least one more year of schooling than women.

Education systems in Asia have made significant gains in coverage since 1970 (table 2.6). By 1985, most countries in the region have gross enrollment ratios in primary education that exceed, or are approaching, 100 percent. The exceptions are Bangladesh, Bhutan, Nepal, and Papua New Guinea, where despite past growth coverage still lags behind the rest of Asia. (Bhutan belongs in its own category, however, with a gross enrollment ratio of only 25 percent in 1985, compared with a range of 60-82 percent in the other three countries.) The expansion of coverage between 1970 and 1985 has been particularly remarkable in post-primary education;

Table 2.5 Education attainment of adults, selected Asian countries, selected years, 1970-85

Country	Literate adults (percent)			Average years of schooling, 1980s		
	1970	1985	Increase	Males	Females	Overall
Bangladesh	23	33	43	2.6	1.0	1.8
Bhutan	..	15	..	..	..	..
China	..	69	..	6.1	3.8	5.0
India	34	43	26	..	..	..
Indonesia	54	74	37	4.9	4.3	4.6
Korea	88	92	5	9.5	7.3	8.4
Lao PDR	33	44	33	..	..	..
Malaysia	60	74	23	6.5	4.9	5.7
Myanmar	71	..	..	..	..	..
Nepal	14	26	86	..	..	..
Papua New Guinea	32	45	41	..	..	..
Philippines	82	86	5	7.0	6.9	6.9
Singapore	69	86	25	6.0	4.9	5.5
Sri Lanka	77	87	13	6.1	5.5	5.8
Thailand	79	91	15	4.6	3.8	4.2

Source: For all countries, data on literacy are from UNICEF (1988a); except, data for Lao PDR for 1985 are from UNICEF (1987). Data on the average years of schooling of adults are from Horn and Arriagada (1986).

on average, the gross enrollment ratio for secondary education jumped from 26 percent in 1970 to 42 percent in 1985; in higher education it grew from 5 to 10 percent in the same period.

Asian countries differ in the amount they spend on education, as well as in the degree of centralization in those expenditures.[4] In most settings, the central government is the primary source of funds for education. Expenditures are usually channeled through the Ministry of Education but other ministries may also have substantial responsibility for the sector. In Indonesia, for example, the Home Affairs Ministry pays the salaries of primary school teachers. The major exceptions to centralized funding are India and to a lesser extent China. Because education is a state responsibility in India, it is financed largely from state budgets, augmented by direct contributions from the federal government. In China local governments finance the salaries of a large cadre of *minban* teachers in primary and secondary schools, thereby supplementing what the central government spends. And in some cases community resources are tapped by schools (as by the *barangay* schools in the Philippines until they were nationalized recently), but the amounts mobilized tend to be limited in most instances.

Public spending on education therefore invariably refers to central government spending in the data presented in table 2.7. However, when spending at other levels of government are significant, such as in India and China, they also include those expenditures. A general observation is that no country in Asia devotes more that 20 percent of total government expenditures to education. Below this limit, allocations vary widely, ranging from a low of 7.3 percent in Bhutan to 19.4 percent in Thailand.

The share of education in total government spending has, on average, dropped slightly, from 13.4 percent in 1975 to 12.5 percent in 1985. In most countries this trend is relatively stable; the exceptions are China, where the share of education increased significantly, and Sri Lanka, where the opposite is true. But in both countries the changes occurred because of unusual circumstances.[5] In general the education sector's claim on government spending neither expands nor diminishes dramatically as a result of intersectoral competition for public resources within each country.

Table 2.6 Gross enrollment ratios by level of education, selected Asian countries, selected years, 1970-85
(percent)

Country	Primary		Secondary		Higher	
	1970	1985	1970	1985	1975	1985[a]
Bangladesh	54	60	..	18	..	5.2
Bhutan	6	25	1	4	..	0.1
China	89	118	24	39	0.6	1.7
India	73	92	26	41	8.6	9.0
Indonesia	80	118	16	42	2.4	6.5
Korea[b]	103	96	42	75	10.3	31.6
Lao PDR	53	94	3	19	..	1.5
Malaysia	87	99	34	53	2.8	6.0 (8.6)
Myanmar	83	107	21	23	2.1	5.4
Nepal[c]	22	82	10	25	2.3	4.6
Papua New Guinea	52	70	8	13	2.5	2.0
Philippines	108	106	46	65	18.4	38.0
Singapore	105	115	46	71	9.0	11.8
Sri Lanka	99	103	47	63	1.3	4.6 (5.1)
Thailand	83	97	17	30	3.4	19.6
Trend average[d]	76	94	26	42	4.9	10.1

a. Figures in parentheses refer to the estimated enrollment ratio if students abroad are included. They are shown only for Malaysia and Sri Lanka, countries with sizable student populations abroad; see also table 3.7 below.

b. The data for secondary education in 1985 is lower than that reported in Unesco (1987) because it is the average over both subcycles of secondary education. The Unesco data refer only to the first subcycle.

c. The statistic for primary education for 1985 may be overestimated because of inaccuracies in official estimates of the relevant school-age population; see Smith (1988) for further details.

d. Excludes Bangladesh, Bhutan, and Lao PDR because data for these countries are incomplete. As a result of this exclusion, the averages for the region may differ slightly from the figures for Asia in table 2.2.

Source: See appendix table B1.2. .

Table 2.7 Public spending on education as a percentage of total government spending, selected Asian countries, selected years, 1970-80s

Country	1970	1975	1980	1985	Latest data Spending	Latest data Year
Bangladesh	..	11.8	8.5	10.3	11.3	1988
Bhutan	..	..	..	7.3	8.6	1987
China	2.9	4.2	6.1	7.8	..	..
India	..	14.5	14.5	13.7	13.8	1988
Indonesia	..	..	..	15.0	..	..
Korea	..	13.1	14.6	16.6	16.7	1987
Malaysia	..	19.4	13.2	16.0	18.5	1987
Myanmar	11.3	14.1	10.1	10.9	..	..
Nepal	..	12.0	9.5	9.6	10.4	1988
Papua New Guinea	..	..	..	17.9	15.4	1988
Philippines	..	..	11.1	11.5	..	..
Sri Lanka	14.4	11.0	7.8	8.1	7.3	1988
Thailand	..	20.1	19.8	19.4	19.1	1986
Trend average[a]	..	13.4	11.6	12.5	..	..

a. The trend average reflects the average level of spending of the nine countries for which data are available for 1970, 1980, and 1985.
Source: Same as appendix tables B3.6 and B3.8.

Across countries, however, there are striking differences in sectoral priorities.

The real level of public spending on education is discernable when expressed as a percentage of a country's GNP (table 2.8). Because total government spending has been rising as a proportion of GNP, public spending on education as a share of the GNP has also been rising, even though the share for education in total government spending has declined slightly. Bangladesh and the Philippines are at the low end of the spectrum in this statistic; Malaysia and Papua New Guinea are at the high end. It is noteworthy that very different outcomes in the development of education are possible with comparable levels of government spending: enrollment ratios in the Philippines far exceed those in Bangladesh, and enrollment ratios in Malaysia exceed those in Papua New Guinea. These results signal the strong influence of policy choices within an overall public resource constraint.

The private sector role in providing and financing education is one area where policy choices can affect education coverage. In looking at data on the share of private enrollments across countries (table 2.9), it is meaningful to distinguish between aided and unaided private schools. In Bangladesh, for example, the government provides subsidies for 70 percent of the cost of teachers' salaries in private secondary schools (World Bank-Bangladesh 1988b; King 1988); and private higher education enjoys similar large subsidies (Patwari 1987). So the sector is private mostly in the sense of being privately managed. In contrast, private schools in the Philippines receive little or no public subsidies and operate with a minimum of government intervention. This difference in policy may explain why, despite comparable levels of government spending on education, coverage is so much wider in the Philippines than in Bangladesh.

In India the financing arrangements for private schools are similar to arrangements in Bangladesh. The share of private institutions is 16 percent in primary education, 67 percent in secondary education (India 1980), and about 58 percent in higher education (Association of Commonwealth Universities 1987). However, nearly all the schools receive public subsidies. Consequently, the extent of private financing is limited, even though many schools might be privately managed. Among the remaining Asian countries private education is well developed in Korea and Indonesia.[6] In both countries private institutions are subsidized, but not to the extent as in India and Bangladesh. In Indonesia, for example, about 30 percent of teachers in private higher education are seconded from government service (World Bank-Indonesia 1988b), and at the lower levels of education, private schools receive some subsidies (Thomas 1987). In Korea, as in the Philippines, private institutions are mostly self-financing.

Sources of differences in education development

Education outcomes vary widely across countries, but so do constraints and policies. What is the relative importance of these factors in determining outcomes? If out-

Table 2.8 Public spending on education as a percentage of GNP, selected Asian countries, selected years, 1970-80s

Country	1970	1975	1980	1985	Latest data Spending	Latest data Year
Bangladesh	..	1.1	1.3	1.5	1.9	1988
Bhutan	..	..	..	3.8	4.0	1986
China	1.5	2.3	3.2	3.3	3.2	1987
India	..	2.7	2.7	3.0	3.3	1988
Indonesia	..	..	..	3.7	..	..
Korea	2.9	2.2	3.1	3.4	3.1	1987
Malaysia	..	6.1	5.4	6.0	7.3	1987
Myanmar	..	1.7	1.3	1.8	..	..
Nepal	..	1.4	1.4	1.8	2.1	1987
Papua New Guinea	..	..	..	6.9	..	..
Philippines	..	..	1.7	1.8	2.8	1988
Sri Lanka	4.2	2.7	2.8	2.8	2.2	1988
Thailand	3.5	3.9	3.7	3.6	..	..
Trend average[a]	..	2.7	2.7	3.0	..	..

a. The trend average reflects the average level of spending in the nine countries for which data are available for 1975, 1980, and 1985. The regional average for all 13 countries in 1985 was 3.3 percent.
Source: Same as appendix tables B3.6 and B3.8.

Table 2.9 Share of enrollments in private education, selected Asian countries, selected years, 1970-85
(percent)

Country	Primary				Secondary			Higher			
	1970	1975	1980	1985	1975	1980	1985	1970	1975	1980	1985
Bangladesh	..	4.1	14.6	11.0	..	..	93.0	..	..	..	58.7
Bhutan	..	..	..	..	..	..	0.0	..	..	..	0
China	..	..	..	0.0	..	..	..	..	..	..	0
India[a]	..	..	15.9	8.0	..	68.2	49.7	..	..	..	57.6
Indonesia	..	15.0	10.0	1.5	..	49.1	39.9	..	..	..	58.3
Korea	1.1	1.2	1.3	0.0	45.4	46.4	0.0	..	..	..	66.1
Lao PDR	11.3	..	0.0	0.0	0.0	0.0	1.7	..	..	..	..
Malaysia	..	..	..	0.3	..	..	..	..	..	..	11.0
Myanmar	..	..	..	..	..	..	..	..	..	..	0
Nepal	..	..	..	5.3	..	..	10.4	..	..	..	23.8
Papua New Guinea	63.0	..	2.0	0.5	..	..	..	..	..	..	6.3
Philippines	4.9	5.3	5.2	6.0	54.7	46.2	42.4	89.8	86.2	84.8	83.2
Sri Lanka	7.3	6.0	1.3	1.4	..	2.3	2.4	..	..	..	0
Thailand	14.2	11.1	8.4	9.0	31.7	18.9	20.0	..	8.6[b]	5.1	6.4
Regional average[c]											
With Bangladesh and India	..	..	..	3.9	..	..	26.0	..	..	..	28.6
Without Bangladesh and India	..	..	..	3.2	..	..	18.5	..	..	..	23.2

a. Data for primary and secondary education refer to the share in aided and unaided private schools as a percentage of all schools; the number for higher education refers to the share of privately managed institutions.
b. Figure refers to the share in 1977.
c. No overall trend average is calculated here due to the small number of countries for which the relevant data are available. Recall that private education in Bangladesh, India, and Indonesia are subsidized by the government, the subsidies being particularly large in the first two countries.
Source: See appendix table B1.4.

18

comes are primarily influenced by the system's constraints, little room exists for policy intervention; but if policy choices are also important, it is imperative to identify and promote choices that lead to better outcomes.

Demographic and economic constraints

Constraints on education development are determined largely by demographic and macroeconomic conditions.[7] An indicator of demographic pressure is the dependency ratio, defined here as the ratio of the school-age population (age 5-14) to the working population (males and females age 15-65). The smaller this ratio is, the lighter the fiscal burden on taxpayers, and the less binding the constraint on education development.

On average, the dependency ratio in Asian countries declined from 49 in 1970 to 42 in 1985, and is projected to drop to 36 by 2000 (table 2.10). The rate of decline was sharpest in the 1980s. Across countries there are differences in the variable's size and trend from 1970-85. In 1970, the school-age population in most Asian countries was close to half that of adults. By 1985, however, a more differentiated pattern had emerged: in one group of countries comprising China, Korea, Singapore, and Sri Lanka, the ratio was at or below 36; in a second group comprising Bhutan, India, Malaysia, and Thailand, it was moderately high in the 36 to 44 range; in a third

Table 2.10 Levels and trends in the dependency ratio, selected Asian countries, selected years, 1970-2000

Country	Population age 5–14 as percentage of population age 15–65[a]					Change in dependency ratio (percent)	
	1970	1975	1980	1985	2000	1970-85	1985-00
Bangladesh	55	56	46	49	42	-11	-14
Bhutan	46	47	44	44	47	-4	7
China	44	39	44	33	26	-25	-21
India	49	48	45	44	35	-10	-20
Indonesia	50	50	48	46	35	-8	-24
Korea	52	43	37	31	24	-40	-23
Lao PDR	45	46	60	53	49	18	-8
Malaysia	56	53	44	41	33	-27	-20
Myanmar	44	45	47	47	35	7	-26
Nepal	46	48	49	49	51	7	4
Papua New Guinea	47	48	53	50	40	6	-20
Philippines	53	55	48	47	37	-11	-21
Singapore	48	37	30	26	20	-46	-23
Sri Lanka	49	47	42	36	31	-27	-14
Thailand	56	55	47	41	29	-27	-29
Regional average	49	48	46	42	36	-13	-17

a. For this study this statistic is the dependency ratio.
Source: BESD database and Zachariah and Vu (1988).

group comprising Bangladesh, Indonesia, Lao PDR, Myanmar, Nepal, Papua New Guinea, and the Philippines, the ratio exceeded 44. These patterns imply sizable differences in the tax burden of financing education. For example, if China had had Bangladesh's dependency ratio, the tax contribution of each Chinese adult would have had to rise by nearly 50 percent to finance the current level of coverage in the education system, assuming that all else in the system remained unchanged.

In the future the fiscal burden on taxpayers will probably lighten in most Asian countries as the dependency ratio continues to drop. But in some countries it remains high (Bangladesh, Lao PDR, and Papua New Guinea) and may even rise (Bhutan and Nepal), implying that demographic pressures will remain a significant obstacle to the development of education.

Constraints on the education sector also arise because of the macroeconomic environment. In the last decade or so, most Asian economies have expanded in real terms at moderate to high rates. In every country in the region except Papua New Guinea, the rate of economic growth exceeded the growth rate of the school-age population (table 2.11). Thus, even with a constant share of education spending in GNP, resources were available for expansion (either in coverage or additional inputs per pupil) beyond what was needed to maintain current enrollment ratios. And in countries where education's share of GNP also rose, the pace of education development was even faster.[8]

Table 2.11 Population and real economic growth rates, selected Asian countries, selected years, 1975-2000

(percent per year)

Country	Population age 5-14		Real economic growth	
	1975-85	*1985-2000[a]*	*1975-85*	*1990-2000[a]*
Bangladesh	1.8	2.0	4.4	4.9
Bhutan	1.6	3.0	6.1	..
China	0.2	0.4	7.8	6.6
India	1.6	1.3	4.4	4.8
Indonesia	1.8	1.0	6.1	3.9
Korea	-0.8	0.3	7.4	6.8
Malaysia	0.8	1.4	6.3	5.0
Myanmar	2.4	1.0	5.8	3.5
Nepal	2.7	3.1	3.1	3.8
Papua New Guinea	2.6	2.0	1.5	5.1
Philippines	2.1	1.5	2.5	5.3
Sri Lanka	0.1	1.1	4.9	4.8
Thailand	0.6	0.5	5.8	6.0
Regional average	1.4	1.4	5.1	5.0

a. Projected.
Source: Calculated from population and GNP data in BESD database (UNESCOED and SOCIND); projected economic growth rates are from ANDREX database.

Although most Asian economies are projected to grow at moderate to high rates in real terms, averaging about 5 percent a year between 1990 and 2000, the school-age population is forecast to grow more slowly, by an average of 1.4 percent a year. The macroeconomic constraint is therefore likely to ease considerably. But the outlook is not uniformly bright in all countries. Nepal, in particular, faces much tighter constraints than other countries in the region because its economy is projected to grow only slightly faster than the school-age population; the scope for expanding education (in coverage or increased inputs per pupil) under these conditions is likely to be limited. Even in countries with a favorable outlook, the amount of extra resources that will be available for expansion depends on how education costs evolve with time and rising levels of per capita GNP. In most Asian countries some of those resources are likely to be absorbed by the natural rise in costs as a relatively young teaching force ages and moves up the wage ladder. Moreover, because costs also depend on sectoral policies, the favorable macroeconomic outlook does not guarantee future progress in education; it only makes it more probable.

Effect of constraints and sectoral policies

Using the aggregate data presented thus far, the effect of constraints and sectoral policies on education development can be assessed by regression analysis. Education development is here defined by the education system's coverage. Because the focus is not on any one level of education, but on the system as a whole, a summary indicator is needed to consolidate the data on enrollment ratios at the three levels. A simple approach is to compute the average education attainment of a school-age population passing through the system with its current structure of enrollments, and the average length of study at each cycle.[9] The result is a rough measure of the volume of human capital formation among the current generation of children and youth.

The independent variables in the regression include two proxies for the constraints on education development: demographic pressure (measured by the dependency ratio) and wealth. A priori, the larger the dependency ratio, the heavier the fiscal burden education places on taxpayers, and the more difficult it is to achieve a high level of human capital formation. A possible proxy for wealth is a country's per capita GNP,[10] but because of the variable's strong correlation with the dependency ratio, it is not used directly. Used instead are the residuals (RGNP) from a regression linking the per capita GNP with the dependency ratio.[11] A priori, RGNP is likely to have a positive effect on the dependent variable because, in relative terms, education inputs tend to be more expensive in poor countries: some books and equipment are imported at international prices, and teachers are in shorter supply (and therefore earn larger salaries relative to per capita GNP). These conditions effectively mean tighter market constraints on poorer countries,[12] which are therefore likely to achieve lower levels of human capital formation.

A third independent variable is the overall level of government spending on education, expressed as a percentage of GNP. It is less rigid a constraint than the demographic pressures facing a country, or the country's level of wealth, because appropriations to education are the result of policy decisions about intersectoral allocations of public funds. Moreover, appropriations are not entirely independent of choices about the financing arrangements within the education sector. Thus, although short-run shifts in spending may be difficult to achieve, they are possible within a longer-term perspective. So the level of public spending on education imposes a "fuzzy" rather than a strict constraint. Finally, another independent variable used in the regressions is the extent of private involvement in the education sector, proxied here simply as the average share of private enrollments across primary, secondary, and higher education.[13]

The regression results are in table 2.12. The first equation of the regression is based on data for 82 developing countries worldwide. The second is based on a subset of 15 countries in Asia and Latin America for which data are available on private enrollment shares. The coefficients on the first two variables—dependency ratio and wealth (RGNP)—have the expected signs and are statistically significant (at the 5 percent level of confidence) in both regressions, signaling their importance as determinants of human capital formation in a country.

For overall government spending on education, the coefficient in the second regression, which is based on data for Asia and Latin America, is statistically not different from zero. For the world sample, the coefficient is positive and statistically significant at the 10 percent level of confidence. Even so, the variable's effect on education attainment remains limited: an increase of one standard deviation in public spending, from a sample mean of 4.35 percent of GNP to 6.26 percent (which amounts to a 44 percent increase), raises the average grade attainment by only 0.44 years, from a sample mean of 8.47 years. The increase in the dependent variable is thus only 13.9 percent. This calculation shows that relatively large gaps in public spending on education account for only modest disparities in the volume of human capital formation. Figure 2.2 illustrates with Asian data the absence of a strong link between education expenditure and outcomes.

This startling result arises because countries differ in the way their education systems are organized and financed. The organization of education systems may differ in such areas as class size, teaching load, teacher qualifications and pay, use of multigrade teaching, and so on. Because some arrangements are more efficient than others, the same expenditure can achieve very different levels of education development. In financing, fee policies vary widely among countries, affecting the extent to which private resources are mobilized to supplement tax-based public funds for education, and therefore affecting the aggregate resources available for human capital formation. These considerations suggest that the development of education depends as much on policy choices within the sector as on the size of public funds devoted to it. This does not contradict the fact that in any single country—with a

Table 2.12 Ordinary least squares regression results using grade attainment of current population as dependent variable, world regions, mid-1980s

	(I)	*(II)*
Dependency ratio	-11.67[a]	-13.85[a]
	(4.55)	(2.01)
RGNP	1.16[a]	1.86[a]
	(4.10)	(2.49)
Education share in GNP	0.23[b]	-0.17
	(1.86)	(0.37)
Average private share of enrollments	-0.01	..
	(0.30)	
Asia	1.47[a]	0.34
	(2.21)	(0.37)
Europe, the Middle East, and North Africa	0.42	..
	(0.57)	
Latin America	1.83[a]	..
	(2.97)	
Developed countries	1.78[a]	..
	(1.76)	
Intercept	11.47[b]	15.05[b]
	(7.52)	(3.65)
N	82	15
R-squared	0.66	0.48

Note: Variable definitions are as follows: the average grade attainment is calculated by weighting the proportion of a cohort exiting the education system with primary, secondary, and higher education, by the length of schooling at each level; the dependency ratio is the ratio of the population age 5–14 to the population age 15–64; RGNP is the residual from regressing the logarithm of the per capita GNP against the dependency ratio; education share in GNP is public spending on education in 1985 expressed as a percentage of the GNP; average private share of enrollments is the simple average across primary, secondary, and higher education. The remaining are regional dummy variables that take on the value of one if a country is in the region, and zero otherwise. The omitted region is Africa in regression I and Latin America in regression II.
a. Statistically significant at 5 percent level of confidence.
b. Statistically significant at 10 percent level of confidence.
Source: Based on World Bank BESD database for data on enrollment ratio, dependency ratio, GNP; appendix table B1.1 for length of education cycles; and sources in appendix table B1.4 for private shares of enrollment.

given organizational setup and financing arrangements—the more the government spends, the better developed the education system.

The second regression also permits a preliminary assessment of the private sector's effect on the development of a country's education system. The coefficient on the relevant variable (average private share of enrollments) is statistically not different from zero, suggesting that the private sector exerts no influence on education development. This result, although puzzling at first, is to be expected. Because countries vary widely in their public subsidies to private schools and in the extent of cost recovery in public schools, the variable used in the regression is, at best, a poor proxy

Figure 2.2 Relationship between aggregate public spending on education and average grade attainment, selected Asian countries, around the mid-1980s

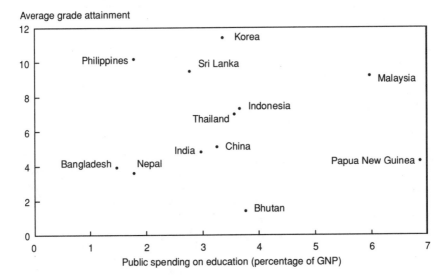

Source: Based on data in appendix tables B2.1 and B3.1.

for the extent of private involvement in financing education development. Put another way, the size of the private sector is not as important for human capital formation as are the pricing policies within the sector: pricing policies affect the contribution of private resources for education and therefore help determine the extent to which constraints on the public budget are eased.

Notes

1. In fact, it is more accurate to refer to grades rather than years of schooling, because allowances for repetition are made in reckoning the education attainment of the adult population.

2. The nine Asian countries in the sample are Bangladesh, China, Hong Kong, Indonesia, Korea, Malaysia, the Philippines, Sri Lanka, and Thailand.

3. The gross enrollment ratio is defined as the ratio of the number of students enrolled at a given level of education to the population in the corresponding age group. This statistic can sometimes exceed 100 percent because of the presence of overage (or more rarely, underage) students. When the numerator includes only students in the official age range for the cycle, the result is known as the net enrollment ratio. Data on this statistic are generally more scanty and are therefore not used here.

4. The degree of centralization in providing and financing education raises important policy issues about the effect of centralization on efficiency in an education system. It is

beyond the scope of this paper to discuss this question in detail: the subject is complex and the data needed for any analysis of the issues are scarce. See Winkler (1988a) for an overview of the subject.

5. In China the education system was being rehabilitated after the Cultural Revolution. In Sri Lanka civil unrest probably caused a diversion of public spending for military purposes.

6. In Thailand the private sector also enrolls a significant proportion of students in regular institutions. Overall, however, its share is dwarfed by the size of enrollments in open universities. In Malaysia government subsidies benefit only one private college, Tungku Abdul Rahman College.

7. Demographic and macroeconomic conditions are assumed to be constraints rather than variables because the first is not easily changed in the short run and the second cannot be affected in a predictable fashion.

8. This assessment is only a rough one, because no account is taken of the evolution of education costs over time. The comparison between the economic and population growth rates nonetheless gives a sense of the budgetary constraints on education development.

9. Suppose the enrollment ratio in primary, secondary, and higher education is P, S, and H respectively, and that these cycles of education last p, s, and h years. Among a cohort of people of the same generation, some will have more education than others. In particular, if P is less than 100 percent, then (100-P) will have no education. At the end of (p+s+h) years, H will have attained higher education, (S-H) will have attained secondary education, and (P-S) will have attained primary education. Weighting this distribution by h, s, and p, respectively, yields the average years of education attainment in that generation. In some countries the primary enrollment ratio exceeds 100 percent, in which case the calculation assumes that P is 100 percent. Because repetition is not taken into account here, the result shows the average grade attainment, not the average years of schooling of the population.

10. The rate of economic growth relative to the growth of the school-age population is not a suitable proxy because all the other variables in the regression are single-period indicators.

11. This procedure follows standard econometric method for addressing multicollinearity in regression analysis.

12. Note, however, that the prices of education inputs are not entirely exogenous; teachers, for example, often are part of the civil service, and their pay is determined as part of government wage policies. So this constraint may not be as binding as it first appears.

13. Because the cost of education rises with level of education, it may appear appropriate to weight the shares of private enrollments accordingly. However, the independent variable proxies the overall extent of private involvement, which depends equally on the volume of enrollments. Because the volume of enrollments is much larger at the lower levels of education, it partly offsets the effect of the rising cost pattern.

3

Costs and Financing of Education: Further Comparative Statistics

Variance in achievements in education stems in part from differences in policy choices that affect the costs and financing of education. This chapter documents the diversity among Asian countries in three areas: the allocation of spending among levels of education, the pattern of unit costs, and the extent of private financing.

Intrasectoral allocation of public spending

The pattern of allocation reflects the combined effect of a range of policies in the education sector: the structure of the enrollment pyramid, the structure of unit costs, the public-private split in providing and financing education, and so on. The pattern gives an early, rough view of a government's priorities in the sector. On average, countries in Asia allocate 48 percent of public spending to primary education, 31 percent to secondary education, and 19 percent to higher education (table 3.1). This declining pattern is similar to that in Latin America, where the corresponding shares of public spending are 51, 26, and 24 percent (World Bank 1986).

A cross-country comparison of the spending pattern for education reveals that nearly all the countries in the region make a strong fiscal effort in favor of primary education.[1] Countries showing the most pronounced emphasis on primary education include Indonesia, Korea, the Philippines, and Thailand—the subsector's share of the education budget in these countries ranges from 57 to 64 percent compared with the regional average of 48 percent. Except for the Philippines, the other three countries' overall level of education spending also exceeds the regional average.

The pattern of allocation reflects the combined effect of sectoral policies. In the Philippines, the existence of a mostly self-financing private sector in higher educa-

Table 3.1 Level and distribution of public spending on education, selected Asian countries, 1985

Country	Overall government spending on education (percentage of GNP)	Percentage distribution of public spending by level of education[a]				Spending by level of education (percentage of GNP)		
		Primary	Secondary	Higher	Other	Primary	Secondary	Higher
Bangladesh	1.5	49	34	15[b]	2	0.7	0.5	0.2
China	3.3	41	42	18	0	1.3	1.4	0.6
India[c]	3.0	27	47	19	6	0.8	1.4	0.6
Indonesia	3.7	62	27	9	2	2.3	1.0	0.3
Korea	3.4	57	34	9	0	1.9	1.1	0.3
Malaysia	6.0	36	34	26	4	2.2	2.1	1.5
Nepal	1.8	41	21	35	3	0.7	0.4	0.6
Papua New Guinea	6.9	45	18	28	10	3.1	1.2	1.9
Philippines	1.8	64	16	20	0	1.2	0.3	0.4
Sri Lanka	2.8	43	41	16	0	1.2	1.2	0.5
Thailand	3.6	58	24	12	6	2.1	0.8	0.4
Regional average	3.0	48	31	19	3	1.6	1.0	0.7

a. Figures may not add up to 100 percent because of rounding errors. See also footnote 2 in text.
b. Figure includes expenditure on universities, colleges, polytechnics, and technical institutes.
c. For India, the data on the distribution of spending refer to 1980.
Source: See appendix table B3.8.

tion makes it possible for the government to allocate a large share of its limited budget to primary education. This contrasts sharply with the pattern in Bangladesh where private institutions for secondary and higher education receive substantial government subsidies. As a result, public spending on primary education in the Philippines (expressed as a percentage of GNP) is more than 1.7 times as high as in Bangladesh.

Differences in the structure of enrollments, in the pattern of unit costs, and in financing arrangements are other relevant factors to consider. For instance, the share of spending for secondary education is significantly lower in Papua New Guinea than in Malaysia (countries with comparable levels of overall public spending on education) because the system's coverage at this level is much smaller in Papua New Guinea. But in such countries as Indonesia, Korea, and Thailand, the intrasectoral distribution of public spending on education is similar despite differences in enrollment structures. This result is partly because of differences in unit costs and cost recovery in the sector.

Variation in the unit costs of public education

To compare costliness across levels of education and across countries, the appropriate statistic is the operating costs of education, regardless of the source of finance.[2,3] Following common practice, unit costs are expressed as a percentage of per capita GNP.[4] To make the comparison among countries even more transparent, an additional cost index is defined: for each level of education, unit costs are expressed as a ratio to the regional average unit cost.[5] An index exceeding unity implies that unit costs in the country are above the regional average, and an index below unity implies the opposite. An overall cost index is also defined: the average of the cost index for the three levels of education. It is a measure of the global costliness of a country's education system in relation to its Asian neighbors.

Comparing countries by level of education

For all the Asian countries in the study (except Papua New Guinea), the unit costs of primary education are on average 10 percent of per capita GNP, comparable to the level in Latin America. (Unit costs in Papua New Guinea are exceptionally high at all levels of education, comparable to the costs of education in African countries (table 3.2). Because the country is an outlier in this respect, it is not taken into account in the comparisons discussed here.) The countries fall into three groups: Bangladesh, India, the Philippines, and Sri Lanka are low-cost countries, with average unit costs around 6 percent of per capita GNP; a second group consists of Indonesia, Korea, Malaysia, and Thailand, with unit costs that are 2 or 3 times as high as for the first group; China and Nepal form the in-between group, with moderate levels of costs.

Table 3.2 Unit operating costs of public education, selected Asian countries, mid-1980s

Country	Unit operating costs as a percentage of per capita GNP			Ratio of unit cost to regional average		
	Primary	Secondary	Higher[a]	Primary	Secondary	Higher
Bangladesh	6.4	30.0	284.6[b]	0.65	1.62	1.91
China	6.7	22.6	199.2	0.68	1.22	1.34
India	6.0	17.3	231.1	0.61	0.94	1.35
Indonesia	12.6	23.3	91.1	1.28	1.26	0.61
Korea	16.5	23.4	70.6	1.67	1.27	0.47
Malaysia	14.1	21.3	190.3	1.43	1.15	1.28
Nepal	9.0	13.5	249.0	0.91	0.73	1.67
Papua New Guinea	29.0	65.0	1050.0	2.94	3.52	7.05
Philippines	5.8	8.6	50.0	0.59	0.47	0.34
Sri Lanka	6.1	9.3	83.3	0.62	0.50	0.56
Thailand	15.5	15.3	39.9	1.57	0.83	0.27
Regional average[c]						
Without Papua New Guinea	9.9	18.5	148.9	..	..	..
With Papua New Guinea	11.6	22.7	230.8	..	..	..

a. In countries with distance systems, the unit costs of higher education is the average for public regular and distance education, weighted by their respective enrollment shares.

b. Figure refers to unit costs in universities.

c. The unit costs of education in Papua New Guinea (PNG) are exceptionally high, raising the average for Asia considerably. In comparing individual countries to an Asian average (last three columns of this table), the relevant denominator is the average that excludes data for PNG.

Source: See appendix table B4.1.

In secondary education, Asia's average unit costs are 19 percent of per capita GNP. This figure is somewhat less than the average of 26 percent for Latin America. The Philippines and Sri Lanka have the lowest costs, less than 0.5 times the regional average; Bangladesh and China have the highest costs, about 1.5 times the regional average. Among the remaining countries, India, Nepal, and Thailand have slightly less than average levels of unit costs, and Indonesia, Korea, and Malaysia have above average costs.

The unit costs of Asian higher education are, on average, 153 percent of per capita GNP, compared with an average of 88 percent in Latin America. The variance within the region is very wide: the Philippines and Thailand have unit costs that do not exceed 50 percent of per capita GNP, but Bangladesh and China have costs that are nearly 6 times as large. It is sometimes argued that poor countries tend to have higher costs when these are expressed in relation to per capita GNP: for instance, in higher education, some education inputs that are tradable goods command international prices, regardless of a country's domestic conditions. If this argument holds, it would be more valid to express costs in absolute terms, using a common currency.

Furthermore, if the international prices of inputs are of primary importance, there should be a rather flat relationship between absolute unit costs and per capita GNP. But this expectation is not entirely borne out in figure 3.1.

The international-prices argument is further weakened because countries with similar levels of per capita GNP have vastly different unit costs: US$900 in China compared with US$599 in India; US$453 in Bangladesh compared with US$354 in Nepal; US$2,132 in Korea compared with US$3,540 in Malaysia; and so on. These comparisons suggest that the costliness of a country's higher education is influenced at least as much by internal policies pursued in the sector, as by external factors.

For costs in higher education it is important to distinguish between regular and open universities,[6] because their cost structures are so different (table 3.3). On average, the unit costs of open universities are only 18 percent as large as those of regular public institutions. The gap between the two types of institutions is widest in Korea and Thailand: open universities cost no more than 10 percent as much as regular institutions.

Comparing the global costliness of education across countries

Expressing unit costs relative to the regional average yields indexes reflecting the costliness of education at the various levels (table 3.2). This information is used in chapter 5 to analyze equity in the structure of public spending across levels of education. For the discussion here, the data are consolidated for an assessment of the

Figure 3.1 Relationship between the unit costs of regular public higher education and per capita GNP, selected Asian countries, around 1985

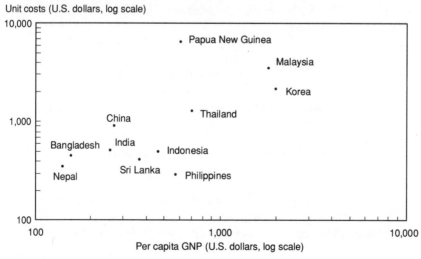

Unit costs (U.S. dollars, log scale)

Source: See appendix table C.3.

Table 3.3 Unit operating costs of public higher education, selected Asian countries, mid-1980s

| Country | Regular institutions | | Ratio of unit costs of open/distance education to those of regular institutions |
	Unit costs (US$)	Costs as percentage of per capita GNP	
Bangladesh	453	284.6	..
China	900	329.8	..
India	599	231.1	..
Indonesia	497	105.7	0.35
Korea	2,132	104.5	0.10
Malaysia	3,540	190.3	..
Nepal	354	249.0	..
Papua New Guinea	6,521	1,050.0	..
Philippines	291	50.0	..
Sri Lanka	416	111.2	0.20
Thailand	1,267	177.9	0.08
Regional average			
With Papua New Guinea	1,045	183.4	0.18
Without Papua New Guinea	1,543	262.2	..

Source: See appendix table B4.1. Unit costs are converted to U.S. dollars using exchange rates for 1985 reported in Unesco (1987).

Table 3.4 Index of overall costliness of public education, selected Asian countries, mid-1980s

Country	Index
Bangladesh	1.39
China	1.08
India	1.03
Indonesia	1.05
Korea	1.14
Malaysia	1.29
Nepal	1.11
Papua New Guinea	4.50
Philippines	0.46
Sri Lanka	0.56
Thailand	0.89

Source: Data reflect the arithmetic mean of the last three columns of table 3.2.

overall costliness of education in the various countries. This is done simply by taking the arithmetic average of the cost indexes at the three levels (table 3.4). The result gives a single measure for comparisons across countries.

Papua New Guinea's astoundingly large index of 4.38 means that its system is nearly 4.5 times as costly as that of its Asian neighbors. Among the remaining countries three groups can be distinguished: Bangladesh, China, Korea, and Malaysia have high to moderately high unit costs; India, Indonesia, Nepal, and Thailand have costs that are close to the average for the sample; the Philippines and Sri Lanka are well below the average. In the last two countries, unit costs have risen sharply since 1985 because of substantial increases in teacher salaries; even so, they remain below the Asian average.[7]

What relationship is there, if any, between the costliness of education and a country's level of development? A priori, education may cost more in poorer settings because inputs are more expensive, either because they must be imported, or because qualified manpower is scarce. But this expectation is not entirely supported by the data (figure 3.2). For example, Indonesia's overall unit cost index is 85 percent higher than Sri Lanka's, even though the countries have comparable levels of per capita GNP. The wide disparities suggest that there is substantial room for choosing policies with vastly different cost implications. However, when a country's education costs differ from the regional mean, it does not necessarily imply that costs should be raised or reduced. The regional mean facilitates comparative analysis, but is clearly not a normative target in policymaking, because the costs of education have to be balanced against education outcomes. High costs nonetheless flag a strong need to examine the efficiency of the system, focusing, in particular, on the policies that have resulted in high costs.

Figure 3.2 Relationship between overall costliness of public education and per capita GNP, selected Asian countries, around 1985

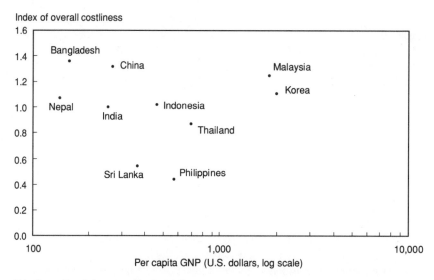

Note: Papua New Guinea, an outlier, is not shown.
Source: See appendix table C.3.

Sources of variation in unit costs

Most of the variation in unit costs stems from differences in the way education is provided. Education characteristics that affect costs include: teacher pay scales and workloads, the pre- and in-service training of teachers, the grouping of students into schools and classes, the use of pedagogical methods and materials, the evaluation and supervision of teachers and students, the criteria used in student selection between levels of education, and so on.[8] Because teachers are typically the most costly education input and because of data constraints, we focus here mainly on teacher salaries and pupil-teacher ratios (a rough indicator of the intensity in the use of teachers' time). In higher education, an added dimension is the distribution of enrollments in selective and open universities, two types of institutions with vastly different cost structures. For ease of presentation, the data for primary and secondary education are discussed separately from the data for higher education.

Primary and secondary education

Comparisons of teachers' pay are problematic because countries use different currencies[9] and because the absolute size of salaries tends to rise with a country's level of economic development. To overcome these difficulties, a common approach is to express salaries relative to per capita GNP because it avoids the need for currency conversion while controlling for countries' different levels of economic development.[10]

In primary education, salaries in Asia in the mid-1980s averaged about 2.9 times per capita GNP (table 3.5), comparable to the mean of 2.4 in Latin America (Mingat and Psacharopoulos 1985).[11] Ratios ranged from a high of 6.8 in Papua New Guinea to a low of 1.6 in the Philippines and Sri Lanka. As a result of recent policy changes, teachers' salaries in the Philippines and Sri Lanka have risen (respectively) to 2.2 and 2.0 times the per capita GNP by 1988, bringing them nearer the norm in Asia. Excluding the sample's outliers (Korea and Papua New Guinea), the average salaries of primary school teachers are concentrated in a narrow band, between 2 and 3 times the per capita GNP. In all countries, secondary school teachers earn higher salaries than their primary school colleagues, averaging 4 times the per capita GNP. Still in some countries the gap in pay is quite small. Again Korea and Papua New Guinea are outliers with secondary school teachers earning exceptionally high salaries compared with their counterparts in other Asian countries.

For the pattern of pupil-teacher ratios, the regional average is 33 in primary education and 23 in secondary education. These averages contrast with the corresponding figures of 29 and 18 in Latin America and 19 and 14 in developed countries. Overall, Asian teachers are used more intensively as an education input than teachers elsewhere.[12] However, the variation among Asian countries is pronounced. In primary education the ratio ranges from 58 in India to 19 in Thailand; in secondary

Table 3.5 Annual teacher remuneration and pupil-teacher ratios in public primary and secondary schools, selected Asian countries, mid-1980s

Country	Teacher remuneration as ratio to per capita GNP[a]		Number of pupils per teacher	
	Primary	*Secondary*	*Primary*	*Secondary*
Bangladesh	2.2	..	47.0	26.2
Bhutan	..	..	38.5	10.1
China	1.6	2.8	24.9	17.2
Hong Kong	..	..	27.3	25.1
India[b]	2.9	3.1	57.6	20.2
Indonesia	2.5	3.2	25.3	15.3
Korea[b]	5.0	5.5	38.3	34.3
Lao PDR	..	..	24.9	11.2
Malaysia	2.4	3.1	24.1	22.1
Myanmar	..	..	46.4	28.5
Nepal	2.8	5.0	35.5	27.5
Papua New Guinea	6.8	10.0	31.0	25.4
Philippines	1.6	1.7	30.9	32.2
Singapore	..	..	27.1	20.4
Sri Lanka	1.6	2.1	31.7	26.1
Thailand	2.5	2.9	19.3	19.6
Regional average				
With Papua New Guinea	2.5	3.3	..	..
Without Papua New Guinea	2.9	3.9	33.1	22.6

a. Teacher remuneration includes basic pay and allowances.
b. Data on remuneration are estimates based on unit costs and pupil-teacher ratios.
Source: See appendix tables B2.4, B2.5, and B4.2.

education, from 34 in Korea to 10 in Bhutan.

The reasons for unit cost differences vary among Asian countries. For example, in Bangladesh and Sri Lanka the unit costs of primary education are only about 60 percent of the regional average; but in Bangladesh the cost level is due mostly to very high pupil-teacher ratios, and in Sri Lanka it stems largely from relatively low teacher salaries. In India and Thailand primary school teachers' salaries are comparable, but because of vast differences in pupil-teacher ratios, the result is a wide gap in unit costs: 6 percent of per capita GNP for India compared with 15.5 percent for Thailand.

Because of their effect on costs, teacher salaries and pupil-teacher ratios are possible targets for policy intervention. The diversity among countries in these characteristics, coupled with the observation that neither characteristic is strongly linked to levels of economic development (as proxied by per capita GNP; figures 3.3 to 3.6), suggests that there is room for policy maneuver: levels of teacher salaries can be affected by public wage policies and regulations on teacher qualification; and pupil-teacher ratios can be affected by student grouping, multigrade teaching, the use of specialized teachers and other academic staff, and so on.

Figure 3.3 Relationship between average teacher pay in primary education and per capita GNP, selected Asian countries, around 1985

Average teacher pay (ratio to per capita GNP)

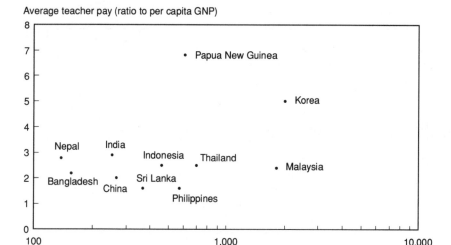

Source: See appendix table C.3.

Figure 3.4 Relationship between pupil-teacher ratio in primary education and per capita GNP, selected Asian countries, around 1985

Pupil-teacher ratio

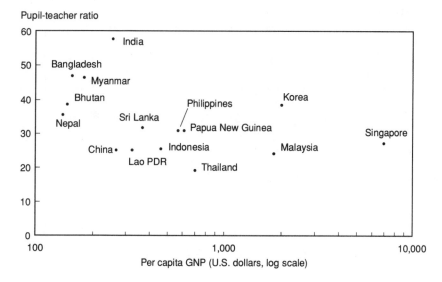

Source: See appendix table C.3.

Figure 3.5 Relationship between average teacher pay in secondary education and per capita GNP, selected Asian countries, around 1985

Average teacher pay (ratio to per capita GNP)

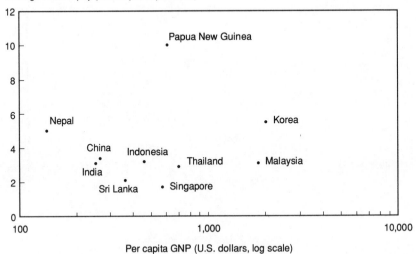

Source: See appendix table C.3.

Figure 3.6 Relationship between pupil-teacher ratio in secondary education and per capita GNP, selected Asian countries, around 1985

Pupil-teacher ratio

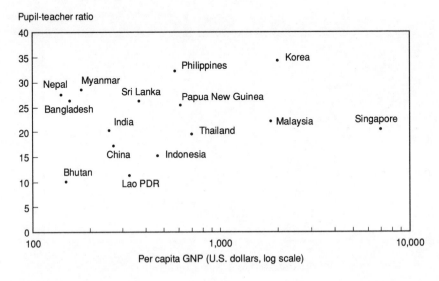

Source: See appendix table C.3.

Higher education

For public higher education data are available on student-faculty ratios but not on the salaries of teaching staff (table 3.6). On average, the student-faculty ratio is 14 for regular institutions in the public sector, comparable to the average for Latin America (13.5) and that for developed countries (12). Again, there is great diversity among countries in the region: the ratio is relatively low in China, Papua New Guinea, and Thailand (less than 9 in each country), and remarkably high in Korea (nearly 40); the remaining countries have ratios in the 10 to 20 band. In distance education, the variation in student-faculty ratio is even wider, stretching from a low of 36 in China to a high of over 770 in India. These differences illustrate the tremendous range of choices in student-faculty ratios, both in regular institutions and in the open universities. Given the absence of a systematic link between student-faculty ratios and per capita GNP (figure 3.7), these choices appear, a priori, to be feasible in all country settings.

In three countries—Indonesia, Korea, and the Philippines—data are also available for private higher education. Only in Korea is the student-faculty ratio comparable between the public and private sectors. The gap is very wide in the other two countries: the ratio in private higher institutions is 2 to 3 times as high as in the public

Table 3.6 Student-faculty ratios in higher education, selected Asian countries, 1985

| Country | Regular institutions | | Open/ distance education |
	Public	Private	
Bangladesh	15.9	..	..
Bhutan	10.9	..	..
China	5.2	..	36.0
India	15.7	..	776.5[a]
Indonesia	14.0	46.1	689.7
Korea	42.2	41.1	414.7
Lao PDR	10.1	..	..
Malaysia	11.4	..	..
Myanmar[b]	30.3	..	..
Nepal	13.2	..	..
Papua New Guinea	7.7	..	..
Philippines	16.0	48.0	..
Sri Lanka	10.7	..	84.9
Thailand	8.3	17.6	618.8
Regional average[c]	13.9	..	..

a. Refers only to Andhra Pradesh Open University.
b. Data includes pupils in correspondence courses.
c. Data for Myanmar excluded in calculating the average for the reason given in footnote a above.
Source: See appendix table B2.6.

Figure 3.7 Relationship between student-faculty ratio in conventional public higher education and per capita GNP, selected Asian countries, around 1985

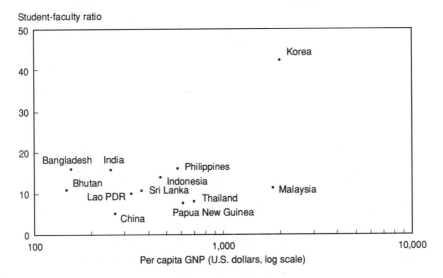

Source: See appendix table B2.6.

sector.[13] A possible reason for Korea's uniqueness is that public higher education is subsidized to a lesser extent in Korea than in Indonesia and the Philippines; so from a financing perspective, public institutions are like private ones and face similar pressures to use teacher time efficiently.[14]

The distribution of enrollments among types of institutions also affects the overall costliness of public higher education (table 3.7). Except in Indonesia, Korea, and the Philippines, the public sector is clearly the predominant sector in higher education in Asian countries. This is even true for Bangladesh and India—despite their large share of private enrollments—because most private institutions are heavily subsidized by the government. A distinction should be made, however, between countries that rely heavily on relatively cheap distance education or open universities (China, India, Myanmar, Sri Lanka, and Thailand) and those that rely on the more costly regular institutions.

In Indonesia, Korea, and the Philippines the public sector's share of enrollments for higher education is less than 50 percent. To meet excess demand in Indonesia and Korea, governments have relied on private institutions and open universities—cheaper alternatives to regular public institutions. But in Indonesia private institutions are subsidized, with close to 30 percent of their staff seconded from government service. In the Philippines distance education does not really exist, so the demand for higher education is satisfied almost entirely by the private sector.

Table 3.7 Distribution of higher education enrollments by type of institution, selected Asian countries, mid-1980s

Country	Total enrollments (thousands)	Enrollments in local institutions (as percentage of total enrollments)			Enrollment in overseas institutions (as percentage of total enrollments)
		Public	*Distance*	*Private*[a]	
Bangladesh	811.4	40.5	0.6	58.4[b]	0.5
Bhutan	1.1	95.8	0.0	0.0	4.2
China	3,470.6	68.6	30.2	0.0	1.2
India	3,314.5	37.4	4.8	57.3[a]	0.5
Indonesia	1,295.6	32.5	8.8	57.7	1.0
Korea	1,478.2	21.4	12.0	65.1	1.5
Malaysia	131.2	60.5	1.0	7.6	30.9
Myanmar	185.1	54.4	45.4	0.0	0.2
Nepal	74.3	73.3	1.3	23.4	2.0
Papua New Guinea	11.4	82.6	8.8	6.1	2.5
Philippines	1,549.6	16.7	0.0	83.0	0.3
Sri Lanka	34.5	62.0	28.5	0.0	9.5
Thailand	724.0	14.5	77.9	6.3	1.3

a. Data in this column differ slightly from those in the last column of table 2.9 since overseas enrollments are included in the denominator in this table, but not in table 2.9. The discrepancy in wide only for Malaysia because of the large number of Malaysian students abroad.
b. Data include enrollments in privately managed institutions.
Source: See appendix table B1.6.

Among Asian countries, overseas enrollments are substantial only for Malaysia where more than 30 percent of higher education students are abroad, most of them self-financing. Sri Lanka has the next highest share of enrollments abroad, but at 9.5 percent the outflow is hardly comparable to that of Malaysia. In a sense, Malaysia's large overseas student population represents the country's private sector.[15] Thailand faced a similar situation in the 1960s (Watson 1981). At that time, the government embarked on a two-pronged strategy to stem the outflow: it lifted the ban on private education and it invested heavily in open universities. Judging from the institutional makeup of higher education in Thailand today, those policies seem to have succeeded.

Private financing of education

Just as countries vary in the costs of education, they also differ in the way those costs are financed. For public education there are two main sources of financing: government appropriations, and private contributions in the form of tuition and other fees.[16] In some countries, additional resources are generated from income-earning activities (such as consultancies, school production, and fund-raising events) and through endowments and other donations from philanthropists, local communities, parents' associations, and so on. But in aggregate these sources yield relatively little income for public education and are not as amenable to policy intervention as direct charges to students. For these reasons, the data in table 3.8 simply show the share of unit costs financed through school fees; its complement is assumed to be the share of government funding.

On average, fees finance a larger proportion of the costs of public education in Asia than they do in other developing regions: 3.2, 17.8, and 10.0 percent respectively in primary, secondary, and higher education, compared with the corresponding figures in Latin America of 0.9, 1.7, and 6.6 percent (World Bank 1986). There is, however, substantial deviation from the mean: some Asian countries rely to a significant extent on private financing (Indonesia and Korea), while others rely on it little, if at all (Bangladesh, China, Malaysia, and Sri Lanka). Moreover, countries differ in the structure of cost recovery across levels of education. In Korea and the Philippines the share of costs recovered through fees shows a definite and consistent rise with the level of education. The opposite trend is present in Bangladesh and China. And there is a third pattern, in which the rate of cost recovery rises steeply from primary to secondary education and then drops, sometimes very sharply, at the level of higher education (Indonesia, Nepal, Papua New Guinea, and Thailand).

Data on the financing of private education are scanty and have been pieced together to provide rough estimates for higher education (table 3.9). Three models of financing appear to exist among Asian countries. In the first model the private sector is largely self-financing, depending on nongovernment funding (usually student fees) for the bulk of operating incomes (Korea, Malaysia, Nepal, the Philippines, and Thailand). In the second model, the private sector receives the major share of its

Table 3.8 Fees for public education as a percentage of unit operating costs, selected Asian countries, mid-1980s

Country	Primary	Secondary	Higher education Regular	Open
Bangladesh	7.4	4.0	0.1	..
China	4.8	3.2	0.3	..
India	0	11.6	4.5	59.0[a]
Indonesia	7.1	27.4	18.9	..
Korea	0	34.2	45.9	32.0
Malaysia	3.7	4.0	5.8	..
Nepal	0	40.7	10.4	..
Papua New Guinea	8.7	39.8	0.0	..
Philippines	0	9.3	15.3	..
Sri Lanka	3.1	3.1	3.4	57.7
Thailand	0.1	18.3	5.0	27.5
Regional average	3.2	17.8	10.0	..

a. Refers only to Andhra Pradesh Open University.
Source: See appendix table B4.3.

funds through government subventions (Bangladesh and India). In the third model, private institutions receive a moderately high level of public subsidies, covering about 30 percent of their costs. (Indonesia alone among Asian countries fits this model.)

The overall extent of private financing in higher education can be summarized by constructing an index based on the rate of cost recovery across types of institutions, weighted by the corresponding shares of total enrollments (table 3.9). According to this indicator, four groups of countries emerge. China, India, and Papua New Guinea form one group, where private financing is extremely limited. Indonesia, Korea, and the Philippines form a second group with extensive private financing. In Nepal, Sri Lanka, and Thailand—the third group—the extent of private financing is moderately high. The fourth group consists of Bangladesh and Malaysia, with a somewhat below average rate of private financing. Although Malaysia's index would have been significantly higher had overseas education been included, for comparison across countries the lower figure is relevant because it reflects the extent to which private resources are mobilized to finance the development of local higher education.

To what extent does the level of private financing depend on the wealth of a country? A priori, a positive link might be expected for at least two reasons. First the demand for education is probably stronger because job prospects are better in wealthy

Table 3.9 Estimated rate of private financing in higher education, selected Asian countries, around 1985

Country	Cost recovery in private sector	Index of overall private financing[a]
Bangladesh	28	16.5
Bhutan	..	..
China	..	0.3
India	5	7.1
Indonesia	70	48.7
Korea	95	76.6
Malaysia	90	15.1 (35.1)
Myanmar	..	..
Nepal	100	31.8
Papua New Guinea	100	6.3
Philippines	100	85.8
Sri Lanka	..	20.5
Thailand	100	26.9

a. Reflects the rate of cost recovery across institution types, weighted by their share of total enrollments. Figure in parentheses for Malaysia denotes the rate of private financing if privately financed overseas education were included.
Source: Authors' estimates based on table 3.8 and on appendix tables B1.6 and B4.3 and on data, discussion, and estimates in King (1988) for Bangladesh; ACU (1988) for India; World Bank-Indonesia (1988b); Korea (1987); Malaysia (1988); Timilsina (1988) for Nepal; World Bank-Papua New Guinea (1987); and Mingat and Tan (1988) and James (1988) for the Philippines.

countries; thus, people are more willing and able to pay for their education. Second, the institutional infrastructure in wealthy countries is better developed to support cost recovery policies. Although the index of private financing is positively correlated with per capita GNP, the link is quite weak (figure 3.8). Countries with comparable per capita GNP, such as Indonesia, Papua New Guinea, the Philippines, and Sri Lanka, vary widely in their level of private financing, ranging from 6 percent in Papua New Guinea to 86 percent in the Philippines. And countries with comparable rates of private financing, Nepal and Malaysia, differ significantly in per capita GNP.

Figure 3.8 Relationship between degree of private financing in higher education and per capita GNP, selected Asian countries, around the mid-1980s

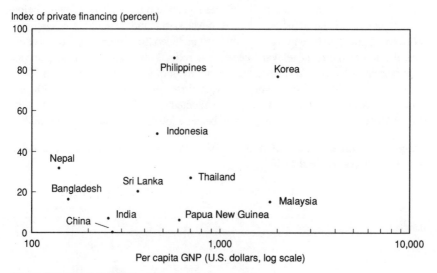

Index of private financing (percent)

Source: See appendix table C.3.

The pattern of variation suggests that although a country's level of economic development affects the administrative and social feasibility of tapping private resources for higher education, there is nonetheless scope for this policy in all country settings. Options for implementation include charging fees for public education and allowing a largely self-financing private sector to develop.

Notes

1. Table 3.1 shows the distribution of spending across all three levels of education. In some countries the classification of enrollments and expenditures at secondary and higher levels is not always made on a consistent basis. So care is needed when interpreting the data for indications of the relative emphasis on secondary and higher education. But in most countries the definition of primary education is unambiguous, so its share of total spending

provides a good idea of the overall emphasis it receives in government spending on education.

2. The focus here is on public education, partly because there is little data on private education.

3. In deriving unit operating costs from basic statistics, fees are added to the public unit cost if the cost reflects only what the government spends from general revenue. This adjustment is required where fees are retained by the school (normally when such collections are small), as in Malaysia.

4. This treatment avoids problems associated with currency conversion, and helps control for differences in the price of education inputs. It is especially relevant in primary and secondary education where most inputs are nontradables. In higher education, the case is stronger for conversion to a single currency, because some inputs—books, equipment, and even some categories of teachers—are tradable, and input prices tend to concentrate in a narrower band, regardless of the conditions within a single country. If the costs of inputs primarily reflect the outcome of international market forces, then expressing the unit costs of education in terms of a country's per capita GNP would distort comparisons: unit costs would always tend to be high in a poor country and low in a rich country, largely because of the size of the denominator. However, analysis in chapter 4 shows that there is little relationship between unit costs expressed as a percentage of per capita GNP and per capita GNP itself. So standardizing costs in relation to per capita GNP remains a valid basis for comparison.

5. Papua New Guinea is not included in reckoning the regional average unit cost, because the costs of education in this country are exceptionally high. Its inclusion would have caused most countries' cost index to fall below the average.

6. For this paper, education by correspondence and other similar arrangements are included whenever open universities are referred to.

7. For the data on unit costs in 1988, see appendix table B4.1.

8. Apart from their impact on costs, these aspects in the organization of schooling are, to some extent, also likely to affect student achievement. This issue will be touched on in chapter 4, but the treatment is necessarily brief due to the scarcity of data and resource materials.

9. The first problem can be overcome by conversion to a common currency, but cross-country comparisons remain hampered because official exchange rates often fail to reflect true purchasing power.

10. This procedure rests on the implicit assumption that teacher pay in absolute terms bears, on average, a strictly proportional relationship to per capita GNP. The assumption may not be completely valid because absolute costs tend to be larger in lower-income settings because of the relative scarcity of qualified manpower. As a result, salaries expressed relative to per capita GNP should decline as per capita GNP rises. However, this expectation is not borne out by the data for Asia, as figures 3.3 and 3.5 show.

11. The salaries of other comparable professionals might have been a better numeraire than per capita GNP for comparing teachers' salaries; unfortunately, this alternative could not be implemented for lack of data.

12. A high pupil-teacher ratio means a high number of classes per teacher or large class sizes or both. Both arrangements mean that teachers are used intensively.

13. In most countries the private sector tends to concentrate more on nonscience courses. Probably because there are fewer logistical constraints to large classes for such courses, pupil-teacher ratios tend to be higher.

14. The effect of private financing on unit costs will be explored in more detail in chapter 4 in this report.

15. The outflow of students abroad is a familiar phenomenon wherever the demand for education outstrips the capacity of local institutions. In Greece, for example, a government ban on private universities, coupled with limited provision of heavily subsidized public higher education, has led to a large outflow of students to institutions abroad. Psacharopoulos (1988) described this outflow as the country's de facto private sector.

16. Private contributions also include school-related private expenses other than fees, such as expenses for books, materials, and transport. In some countries these items are provided by the school; in this case the amount of fees paid relative to schools' operating costs would, by and large, capture the private share in the total direct costs of education. In other countries such items are not provided by the school, but are purchased separately by students; in this case fees alone would understate the share of private contributions. Although some micro-level data are available on the amount of private spending on education other than for fees (for example, the 1982 Household and School Matching Survey in the Philippines), the data are patchy and usually dated; they are therefore not considered here.

4

Efficiency in Education

The data in chapters 2 and 3 give a regional perspective on the costs and financing of education in individual Asian countries. But the data are inadequate for assessing alternative policies because policy choice depends not so much on a country's ranking in relation to its neighbors (at least in the aspects considered so far), as on its educational and social objectives. In general, these objectives include increasing efficiency and equity in the use of education resources.[1] Efficiency in the sector is discussed in this chapter, equity in the next.

The term efficiency describes the relationship between inputs and outputs. When output refers to broad societal goals—such as better health, lower fertility rates, and the production of educated manpower for the labor market—the analysis focuses on the external efficiency of education: the economic returns to investing in education in general, the allocation of spending across levels and types of education, and so on. When output refers to goals internal to the education system—such as drop-out and retention rates, students' achievement of curriculum objectives, and so on—the focus is on the system's internal efficiency. These aspects complement each other in determining the global efficiency of the education system.[2]

External efficiency

Data on the effect of education on economic growth and social welfare reveal that countries with a better educated population have higher economic growth rates and more equitable distributions of income; and at the micro level, that individuals with more education tend to enjoy higher incomes, better health, more geographical mobility, and so on (Psacharopoulos 1984). Weighing such evidence against the recent attacks on the role of education in productivity growth and in income distribution,[3] Psacharopoulos concluded that the argument for investing in schools and training remains unassailable, particularly in developing countries where human capital tends to be relatively scarce.

The benefits of education investments derive largely from skill formation. In considering such investments, two points are salient. First, investments should produce skills that have economic value beyond their intrinsic merit. Thus, although English and Serbo-Croatian have the same absolute value as languages, English is probably more highly sought for jobs in international business and should therefore attract heavier investment. Second, the usefulness of a skill is only one dimension to consider: the quantity in which it is produced is also relevant. To illustrate, although computers skills are valuable, if too many computer specialists are produced, demand for them will weaken. And the demand for workers with apparently lesser skills, such as plumbers, could strengthen because of their scarcity in the labor market.

So it is important that investments in education respond to the economy's demand for workers by level and type of education. Because socioeconomic conditions vary, the issue is an empirical one, requiring an assessment of the costs and benefits of producing workers with different endowments of education and training. To do this rates of return are often used.[4] These rates are derived by comparing the productivity of educated people, usually proxied by their wage profile, to the productivity of people with less education or training, and weighing the difference against the costs of their extra schooling or training. This permits comparison not only within the education sector, but also between education and other sectors. For example, the fact that investments in education in developing countries fetch, on average, an economic return exceeding 12 percent a year is often taken to imply that such investments are at least as profitable as investment in physical capital.[5]

The value of investments in education differs according to whether the viewpoint is that of society or the individual. Not all the costs of education are borne by individuals—the gap is made up by society through public subsidies.[6] Policy choices for education investments require an assessment of societal priorities—by measuring the social rates of return; and an understanding of individuals' priorities—by measuring the private rates of return.

Investing in education

Because education is publicly subsidized to some extent almost everywhere in the world, private returns to education investment invariably exceed social returns (table 4.1).[7] The heavier the subsidies are, the larger the gap between social and private returns. For Asia, the gap is relatively small compared with other regions (and it is negligible at the secondary level), a result consistent with the greater involvement of private financing in post-primary education in the region.

For social profitability of the various levels of education in the typical developing country, the social returns to education show two characteristics: they are high at all levels and they decline with ascending levels of education. A further finding is that

Table 4.1 International patterns of social returns to education, world regions
(percent)

Region/country type	Social			Private		
	Primary	Secondary	Higher	Primary	Secondary	Higher
Africa	26	17	13	45	26	32
Asia	27	15	13	31	15	18
Latin America	26	18	16	32	23	23
Developing countries	27	16	13	29	19	24
Intermediate countries	16	14	10	17	13	13
Advanced countries	..	10	9	..	14	12

Note: Table reflects data for about 16 countries in Africa, 10 in Asia, and 10 in Latin America. Thirty-six are developing countries, 7 are at intermediate stages of development, and 15 are developed countries. Dates range from 1960s to 1980s.
Source: Psacharopoulos (1981) and (1985).

returns drop with rising levels of economic development. But the decline is gradual when compared with the vast expansion of education as countries develop, a pattern revealed by cross-section and time-series data (Psacharopoulos 1981).

These international patterns have two direct implications for Asian countries: in the less developed countries in the region, primary education deserves top priority in the intrasectoral allocation of education resources; in the more developed countries where education is better developed, the lower levels of education continue to warrant the highest priority. This bias in the allocation of public spending on education is reinforced when externalities and equity are taken into account.

How do these general conclusions fit with the data on individual Asian countries? Recent estimates of rates of return to education exist for only seven Asian countries (table 4.2). India, Indonesia, and Papua New Guinea have the classic pattern of returns across levels of education: highest in primary education and lowest in higher education. In Papua New Guinea, however, the returns to higher education, at an estimated 2.8 percent, are so low as to render investments at this level "wasteful" (Gannicott 1987). One reason for this result is the country's astronomical unit costs at this level of education. The somewhat below-average returns to higher education in Malaysia also are partly attributable to higher-than-average unit costs.

In the Philippines the returns to education at all levels are still moderately high, despite the rapid expansion of education during the last two to three decades. (The time-series data for higher education in Thailand show the same result.) Furthermore, the returns are comparable among the three levels of education. Both outcomes stem in part from the country's relatively low unit costs, particularly in higher education. The low costs result from the system's relatively heavy reliance on private financing.[8] At all levels of education, returns to complete cycles of education exceed returns to incomplete cycles. The gap in returns emphasizes the social profitability of

Table 4.2 Rates of return to education, selected Asian countries, selected years, 1975-85

(percent)

Country	Year	Social			Private		
		Primary	Secondary	Higher	Primary	Secondary	Higher
India	1978	29.3	13.7	10.8	33.4	19.8	13.2
Indonesia	1982	18.0	15.0	10.0	..	..	..
		(14.5)	..	..	..	..	..
Korea	1982	..	10.9	13.0	..	..	..
Malaysia	1983	..	..	7.6	..	..	12.2
Papua New Guinea	1982	19.9	12.0	2.8	29.4	14.7	8.1
Philippines	1985	11.9	12.9	13.3	18.2	13.8	14.0
		(4.4)	(9.3)	(11.6)	(7.2)	(10.2)	(12.5)
Thailand	1975	12	24	12.8	..	..	..
	1985	..	..	13.3	..	..	17.4

Note: The figures in parentheses denote the rates of return for incomplete education.
Source: Psacharopoulos (1985) for India; USAID (1986) for Indonesia, KEDI (1983) for Korea; Mehmet and Yip (1986) for Malaysia; Gannicott (1987) for Papua New Guinea; Tan and Paqueo (1989) for Philippines; and Thailand (1987a) and Suppachai (1976) for Thailand.

reducing drop-out rate, particularly in primary education where that gap is widest. The data for primary education in Indonesia point to a similar conclusion. In Thailand, which enjoys moderately high returns to education at all levels, the highest returns are for secondary education, in contrast to the pattern in other developing countries. Although the data are somewhat old, they support the current perception that secondary education is relatively underdeveloped compared with the other levels in Thailand (World Bank-Thailand 1988).

Distinguishing between returns to different types of education investments is particularly relevant in secondary and higher education, where there is wide variation in unit costs between general and vocational programs, and among alternative specializations (table 4.3). Expensive programs tend to have lower returns than cheaper ones. But this generalization should be interpreted cautiously because the same program labels may describe quite different curricula across countries, with correspondingly different unit costs. Moreover, labor market conditions are likely to change from country to country, affecting the pattern of earnings across specializations. In Thailand, for example, courses in agriculture currently yield a respectable 15 percent in economic returns to society, compared with only 10.4 percent for medicine (appendix table B5.3). In science, engineering programs fetch a higher return than courses in the pure sciences. And in the arts, law courses earn much better social returns than courses in education. So the data make clear that specific conclusions about investment priorities in the sector depend on each country's unique conditions. But worldwide evidence does support placing priority on the lower levels of education. (This ranking also is supported by considerations of social equity.)

Investing in literacy

Literacy is a main reason for high rates of return to investments in primary education (see Hartley and Swanson 1984 for a survey of the literature on literacy). What factors account for the variance in literacy rates across nations? A priori, expectations are that the most important factors include (1) past investments in primary education, (2) the length of the primary cycle, and (3) the proportion of pupils surviving to the end of the cycle. To test the relationship of these factors to literacy rates, a regression equation was estimated, using as the dependent variable adult literacy rates in 1985 (table 4.4). The independent variables (reflecting primary schooling conditions in 1975) include the enrollment ratio, the cohort survival rate, and the length of the cycle.

The model explains a remarkably high proportion (70 percent) of the variance in literacy rates across countries.[9] All the independent variables have the expected sign and are statistically significant at the 5 percent level of confidence. An increase of one standard deviation in the primary enrollment ratio (from the sample mean of 79.7 percent to 107 percent) lifts the adult literacy rate by 19.1 percentage points (from the sample mean of 59.3 percent to 78.4 percent). A comparable one-standard-deviation increase in the cohort survival rate or in the length of the primary school cycle would raise the corresponding adult literacy rates by 6.2 and 7.5 percentage points.

Results confirm that simply expanding coverage does not maximize the achievement of literacy in a population. It is also important for pupils to persist through the

Table 4.3 International evidence on the social returns to selected secondary and university programs
(percent)

Program	Rate of return
Secondary[a]	
General, academic	16
Vocational, technical	12
University[b]	
Economics	13
Law	12
Social sciences	11
Medicine	12
Engineering	12
Sciences, math, physics	8
Agriculture	8

a. For secondary programs, countries include Colombia, Cyprus, France, Indonesia, Liberia, Taiwan, and Tanzania. No dates are given in Psacharopoulos 1985.
b. For university programs, countries include Belgium, Brazil, Canada, Colombia, Denmark, France, Great Britain, Greece, India, Iran, Malaysia, Norway, the Philippines, and Sweden. Dates range from 1960s to 1970s.
Source: Psacharopoulos (1985).

Table 4.4 Ordinary least squares regression of the determinants of adult literacy rates, world regions, 1985

Determinants of literacy rates	Regression		Sample mean	Standard deviation
	Coefficient	t-statistic		
Primary enrollment ratio, 1975	0.70[a]	8.90	79.7	27.3
Percent surviving to end of primary education, 1975	0.30[a]	2.74	68.3	20.6
Length of primary cycle, 1975	9.43[a]	3.19	6.2	0.8
Constant	-75.64[a]	3.37	..	..
Dependent variable: adult literacy rate, 1985	59.3	25.5	..	..
Number of observations	46			
R^2	0.7			

a. The coefficient is statistically significant at the 5 percent level of confidence.
Source: Data on literacy rates are from UNICEF (1987); data on primary enrollment ratios in 1975 and length of primary cycle in 1975 are from Unesco (1987); data on per capita GNP in 1985 are from World Bank (1986); and data on percent surviving to end of primary cycle in 1975 are from World Bank (1986).

system once they are enrolled.[10] Most Asian countries have achieved, or are close to achieving, universal coverage in primary education. Improving persistence through the system is important if literacy rates among future adults are to rise. To this end, two types of policy options exist: increasing cohort survival rates, while keeping unchanged the length of the primary cycle; or lengthening the cycle, on the assumption that current rates of cohort survival remain constant. Both strategies raise the average years of schooling in the population, but the first is probably less elitist. Another argument in its favor is that primary schooling in all Asian countries already exceeds the minimum four years generally considered necessary for achieving permanent literacy (appendix table B1.1).

Internal efficiency

An education system is judged internally efficient if it produces the desired output at minimum cost, or if for a given input of resources, the system maximizes the desired output. The output is often measured by such indicators as cohort retention rates (the proportion of pupils persisting to the end of the cycle), scientific know-how, cognitive and technical skills, conformity to social norms of behavior, and so on. For this reason, issues of educational quality are normally discussed in the light of an education system's internal efficiency.[11] Many interventions may be used to increase efficiency in education; the following discussion will touch on some of them.[12]

Efficiency of selection processes in primary and secondary education

Selection in an education system occurs through various mechanisms and is reflected in the pattern of cohort survival.[13] Distinguishing between selection within cycles of education and selection between cycles is helpful in gauging the system's internal efficiency. A high rate of survival (or retention) within cycles of education, particularly in primary and secondary education, is a necessary, although insufficient, mark of an efficient system; conversely, a system that exhibits low intracycle retention rates is invariably inefficient. The reason is that the curriculum for a cycle of study is designed to impart and reinforce certain cognitive skills; students who exit before the end of the cycle will acquire these skills only partially, and probably temporarily. As much as this outcome holds, the resources invested in these students' education would be wasted, leading to inefficiency in the system.

Patterns of cohort survival, particularly within the primary cycle, also offer clues about an education system's quality. If students fail to progress in learning, the chances of premature exit probably increase, reinforcing the effect of such other factors as household poverty, social customs, distance to school, and so on. In other words, low survival rates likely reflect problems of educational quality and relevance on the one hand, and demand factors on the other. (The relative importance of these factors is difficult to evaluate in the absence of individual survey data.)

Patterns of cohort survival in Asia. Access to primary schooling is universal in all but 5 of the 14 Asian countries in the sample (table 4.5).[14] China and India are only a short way from that goal; Nepal and Papua New Guinea are somewhat further away; but Bhutan is very far away from it.

Perhaps more dramatic are the differences across countries in the pattern of cohort survival through the education system. In the primary cycle, for example, the incidence of drop-out is negligible in four countries: Korea, Malaysia, Papua New Guinea, and Singapore. But in such countries as Bangladesh and Bhutan, dropping out occurs so frequently that only 24 and 17 percent, respectively, of all grade 1 entrants reach the last grade of primary schooling. It is probably reasonable to infer that the education systems of these countries, as well as those of India and Nepal, suffer from serious quality problems.

The patterns of cohort survival are somewhat puzzling in light of the common finding of high private returns to primary education (tables 4.1 and 4.2).[15] One explanation is that the traditional estimates of rates of return neglect differences in education quality (Behrman and Birdsall 1983). Another is that rate of return is a reduced-form statistic, calculated without incorporating the noneconomic costs and benefits of schooling that affect households' decisions. So the statistic's link to actual behavior is not a direct one, particularly among rural populations.

To elaborate, the literature shows that investments in education have three distinct effects on agriculture: (1) they can boost technical efficiency by increasing farmers' ability to correctly apply agricultural inputs and techniques; (2) they can improve farmers' managerial capability, particularly in the choice of effective input and output mixes; and (3) they can facilitate greater mobility to more lucrative nonagricultural occupations. These benefits may not be fully perceived by decisionmakers in rural families. Improvements in managerial capability, for ex-

Table 4.5 Patterns of cohort survival in primary and secondary education, selected Asian countries, mid-1980s

Country	Primary gross enrollment ratio, 1985	Percentage of population entering grade 1	Percentage of entrants surviving to end of primary	Lower secondary 1st year	Lower secondary Last year	Upper secondary 1st year	Upper secondary Last year
Bangladesh	60	100	24	22	11	5	4
Bhutan	25	54	17	8	7	3	3
China	118	90	68	41	31	7	6
India	92	83	37	31	22	17	11[a]
Indonesia	118	100	60	37	34	18	18
Korea	96	100	97	95	93	46	44
Lao PDR	94	100	40	30	20	11	7
Malaysia	99	100	97	78	70	42	40
Nepal	79	75	33	32	28	25	21
Papua New Guinea	69	74	67	25	16	2	2
Philippines	106	100	66	56	41	..	..
Singapore	115	100	100	75	75	20	20
Sri Lanka	103	100	85	76	57	19	19
Thailand	97	100	80	32	29	15	13
Regional average	91	91	62	46	38	18	16

a. Some enrollments in tertiary education in fact correspond to the last two years of the four-year upper secondary cycle. For this reason, data from schools show a much smaller number reaching the end of upper secondary. The data from Unesco have been adjusted accordingly.
Source: See appendix table B2.2.

ample, tend to occur across generations rather than within a generation. And rural families are often ambivalent about the benefit of increased mobility, for it also implies a weakening of familial ties and relationships. These perceptions, which clearly enter into households' decisions, are generally not captured by the rate-of-return statistic. They explain why high rates of return may sometimes be juxtaposed against low attendance or completion rates, particularly in primary education and among rural populations.

Returning to the data in table 4.5, countries with comparable gross enrollment ratios can have very different student flow patterns. Examples are Bangladesh and Papua New Guinea, whose gross enrollment ratios are, respectively, 60 and 69 percent. Bangladesh's ratio reflects a high entry rate, combined with a high drop-out rate; Papua New Guinea's ratio reflects a somewhat lower entry rate, combined with a much smaller drop-out rate. These differences mean that different strategies must be used to expand coverage: in Bangladesh the main focus should be on improving the system's ability to retain pupils; but in Papua New Guinea the emphasis should be on attracting more school-age children to enter the system.

Noteworthy too is that a high gross enrollment ratio does not necessarily imply universal or close-to-universal coverage. India's ratio, for example, is probably inflated by the presence of overage pupils[16]: the entry and survival rates in primary education suggest that a much smaller proportion of primary-school-age pupils are in fact enrolled.[17] Similar caution is advisable in reading the data for such countries as China, Indonesia, Lao PDR, and the Philippines.

A look at the pattern of survival for the system as a whole reveals big differences in the proportion of grade 1 entrants who reach the end of secondary schooling. Korea and Malaysia belong in one group, with a survival rate of about 40 percent; Indonesia, Nepal, the Philippines,[18] Singapore, and Sri Lanka comprise another group with a moderately high survival rate of about 20 percent; India and Thailand form a third group with a survival rate around 12 percent; the remaining five countries have very low rates of survival, averaging no more than 5 percent.

Comparing intra- and intercycle selection. The profile of cohort survival through the education system shows differences across countries between selection within and selection between cycles of education (figure 4.1). In Malaysia a high proportion of selection takes place between cycles; but in Bangladesh most selection occurs within cycles (as a result of student drop-out). In Papua New Guinea, the drop-out problem appears to be less severe, and a moderately high proportion of selection takes place at the official selection points.

Figure 4.1 Cohort survival profiles in three Asian countries, mid-1980s

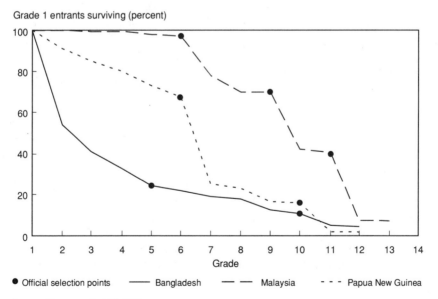

Grade 1 entrants surviving (percent)

● Official selection points   —— Bangladesh   — — Malaysia   - - - Papua New Guinea

Source: See appendix table B2.2.

Data across Asian countries support an expected selection pattern, with the proportion dropping out within each cycle or subcycle diminishing with rising levels of education (table 4.6).[19] The exception is Papua New Guinea, where the survival rate is slightly smaller in lower secondary education than in primary education. Across countries the survival rate in lower secondary education is low only in Bangladesh

Table 4.6 Intra- and intercycle selection in primary and secondary education, selected Asian countries, mid-1980s

Country	Percentage of first year entrants surviving to last year in cycle[a]			Index of intercycle selection[b]
	Primary	Lower secondary	Upper secondary	
Bangladesh	24	48	80	8
Bhutan	17	83	88	13
China	68	76	81	54
India	37	72	65	15
Indonesia	60	92	96	46
Korea	97	98	95	87
Lao PDR	40	65	68	21
Malaysia	97	90	96	79
Nepal	33	89	81	5
Papua New Guinea	67	63	95	57
Philippines	66	74	..	18
Singapore	100	100	97	99
Sri Lanka	85	75	100	58
Thailand	80	91	87	72
Regional average	62	80	87	45

a. The denominator for each column is the number of entrants to the corresponding cycle.
b. The index is defined as the ratio between the proportion of grade 1 entrants eliminated at the transition between cycles of education to the total proportion eliminated from the system by the end of secondary schooling. It ranges from 0 to 100; the larger it is, the more efficient the selection process in the education system.
Source: See appendix table B2.2.

(less than 50 percent); at the upper secondary level, India's survival rate lags significantly behind that of other countries.

For comparison, an index of intercycle selection is calculated showing the proportion of students eliminated from the system at official selection points (regardless of process) relative to the number eliminated from the system by the end of secondary schooling. In systems with little drop-out within cycles, this index would be close to 100; in systems where dropping out is the main form of selection, the index would be close to 0. The higher the index, the more efficient a system's selection process. But the value of the index depends partly on the size of the group that drops out between grade 1 and the end of secondary schooling. So comparison is probably valid largely among countries that are similar in this respect.

Of the countries with the lowest rates of survival to the end of secondary education, China and Papua New Guinea have the best results (even though dropping out is
still high in the primary and lower secondary levels), while Bangladesh lags furthest
behind. In the second group of countries with comparable survival ratios, India lags
considerably behind Thailand. In the third group, Nepal's index (and to some extent
that of the Philippines) is noticeably worse than that of the other countries. Finally,
both countries in the fourth group (Korea and Malaysia) appear comparably efficient
in the selection process.

Links between cohort survival patterns and country characteristics. To what
extent are the cohort survival patterns discussed above linked to different economic
conditions across countries? And to what extent are the patterns linked to differences
in policy choices?

Consider the pattern of cohort survival in primary education. In general, the
poorer the country, the lower the proportion of grade 1 entrants reaching the end of
the primary cycle (figure 4.2). But there remains considerable variation in this overall pattern; for example, China and India share similar levels of per capita GNP, but
the cohort survival rate in the former is 68 percent, compared with only 37 percent in
the latter. This suggests that low cohort survival rates are not inevitable outcomes in
poor countries, and that policy choices within primary education probably also play a
role. Countries in which cohort survival rates are currently below the level suggested

**Figure 4.2 Relationship between survival rates in primary education and per capita GNP,
selected Asian countries, around 1985**

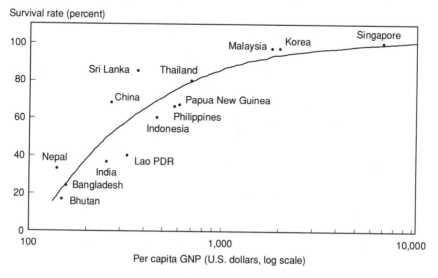

Source: See appendix table C.3.

by the per capita GNP include Bhutan, India, Indonesia, Lao PDR, Papua New Guinea, and the Philippines.

The design of effective interventions to increase retention rates in primary education depends on country conditions and is beyond the scope of this study to examine in detail. But note that cohort survival rates are low in poor countries partly because of inadequate resources per pupil in primary education (measured as a percentage of per capita GNP).[20] Figure 4.3 illustrates an overall pattern of rising cohort survival rates with rising levels of per pupil spending.[21]) The argument for more resources should not be pushed too far, however, because wide variation exists around the average pattern. For example, Bangladesh and Sri Lanka share the same level of unit operating costs (as a percentage of per capita GNP), but the retention rate in primary schooling is 85 percent in Sri Lanka compared with only 24 percent in Bangladesh. Survival rates can probably be improved through better use of existing resources in Bangladesh, Indonesia, Nepal, Papua New Guinea, and Thailand. Some increase in the level of per pupil spending is probably also called for in Bangladesh, India, and Nepal.

It is nonetheless noteworthy that survival rates show only a weakly negative link with pupil-teacher ratios (figure 4.4). It appears that raising per pupil spending in the form of reduced class sizes is probably relevant mainly in such countries as Bangladesh and India, where retention rates are extremely low and pupil-teacher ratios excep-

Figure 4.3 Relationship between cohort survival rates and unit operating costs in primary education, selected Asian countries, around 1985

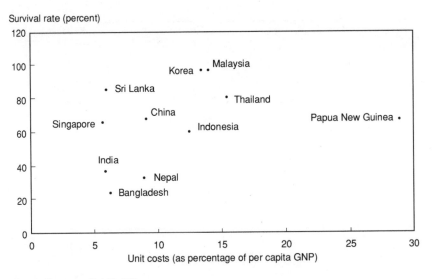

Source: See appendix table C.3.

Figure 4.4 Relationship between cohort survival rates and pupil-teacher ratios in primary schooling, selected Asian countries, around 1985

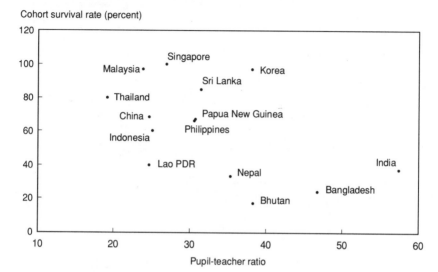

Cohort survival rate (percent)

Source: See appendix table C.3.

tionally high. But in countries where the average pupil-teacher ratio is not high, say not more than 40, the indications are that such a strategy may not be the best one. These conclusions require further confirmation in light of country-specific conditions, particularly because the data reflect averages that may conceal highly skewed distributions across localities.

Consider next patterns of inter- and intracycle selection in education systems (up to the end of secondary schooling) suggest that the poorer a country, the more selection takes place within cycles of education (figure 4.5).[22] But again, wide variations among countries contradict the average pattern. Although the Philippines and Thailand are at similar levels of economic development (as indicated by per capita GNP), the gap between them in the efficiency of the selection process is very wide: in Thailand, 80 percent of the selection in the system takes place between cycles of education, whereas in the Philippines, only 18 percent does. Similar comparisons can be made between China and India and between Sri Lanka and Lao PDR. So the efficiency of the selection process depends not only on a country's level of economic development, but also on its policy choices in the education sector.

Student achievement in basic education

The formation of cognitive skills, a main goal of the education process, results from the interaction between students and their learning environment. An individual's

Figure 4.5 Relationship between the relative importance of intercycle selection in primary and secondary education and per capita GNP, selected Asian countries, around 1985

Index of intercycle selection

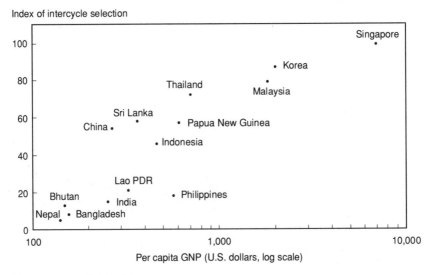

Source: See appendix table C.3.

progress in skill acquisition depends on his personal characteristics (motivation, innate ability, family background, and so on) and education environment (possession of books, materials, and so on) and on the characteristics of his school, classroom, teachers, and peers. Since different combinations of these factors produce different results in achievement, the challenge to education planning is discovering the best or most efficient mix—one which maximizes learning outcomes for a given budget.[23]

The debate about education planning centers on lower levels of education because learning outcomes are less easily measured in higher education. Moreover, because the scope for policy intervention resides mostly, although not exclusively, in the way schooling is organized, attention is focused on the effect of schooling inputs (class size, teacher qualification, supply of textbooks and other pedagogical materials, and so on) on student achievement. Comparing input costs with their effectiveness in boosting learning outcomes offers a basis for choosing an efficient mix.

This aspect of internal efficiency is not easily assessed in aggregate-level studies where countries, rather than individual students or schools, are the basic unit of observation. One problem is that internationally comparable data on achievement are scanty, particularly for developing countries. But even if abundant, such data offer a limited basis for identifying inefficient systems. For example, not all low-scoring countries have education systems that are internally inefficient; poor performance can result from inadequate levels of funding, not from inefficient operations. A further limitation is that clearcut conclusions about efficient mixes of school inputs are hard to reach: countries differ widely in initial conditions (including current provision of different school inputs at different prices); so even if an input were shown to be generally effective in lifting achievement scores, it does not follow that increasing its provision would be the most efficient intervention in all settings.[24] For these reasons, the following discussion will only present the latest available and internationally comparable achievement data.

In a study conducted by the International Association for the Evaluation of Achievement (IEA), separate science tests were administered to 10- and 14-year-old students in a number of countries (table 4.7).[25] China and Papua New Guinea participated in the study, but their data are not yet available. Among the five developing Asian countries in the study, only Korea's achievement scores exceed the sample mean for both the 10- and 14-year-old populations. The performance of Philippine students lies well below the average.

The Roh statistic (table 4.7) offers interesting insights into the operation of each country's education system. A value of 0.16, for example, indicates that the variance

Table 4.7 Science achievement in Asia and other countries, mid-1980s

Country	10-year-old population			14-year-old population		
	Score	Roh[a]	Normalized deviation from mean[b]	Score	Roh[a]	Normalized deviation from mean[b]
Asian countries						
Hong Kong	11.2	..	-1.1	16.4	0.29	-0.6
Korea	15.4	0.16	1.4	18.1	0.15	0.2
Philippines	9.5	0.56	-2.1	11.5	0.48	-2.9
Singapore	11.2	0.39	-1.1	16.5	0.56	-0.5
Thailand	..	..	..	16.5	0.24	-0.5
Selected developed countries						
Japan	15.4	0.04	1.4	20.2	0.04	1.2
Finland	15.3	0.07	1.3	18.5	0.05	0.4
Sweden	14.7	0.03	0.9	18.4	0.08	0.4
United States	13.2	0.14	0.1	16.5	0.29	-0.5
Mean score for all countries in the study[c]	13.1	..	..	17.6	..	..
Standard deviation of mean score	1.7	..	..	2.1	..	..
Maximum score	24.0	..	..	30.0	..	..

a. The Roh statistic indicates the proportion of the total variance in achievement score that is accounted for by between school differences in achievement.

b. The normalized deviation from mean is calculated by dividing by the sample standard deviation, the difference between a country's mean score and the mean score for all countries in the sample.

c. In addition to the above countries, the others were Australia, Canada, England, Hungary, Italy, Netherlands, Norway, and Poland; for the 10-year-old population, data for 15 countries (excluding Netherlands and Thailand) were available; for the 14-year-old population, data for 17 countries were available.

Source: IEA (1988).

in achievement between schools is 16 percent of the total variance in achievement in the population. The larger this statistic is, the more schools in the country differ in the academic performance of their students. This result may reflect a "deliberate [government] policy of differentiation among schools in terms of resources and curriculum" (IEA 1988, p.8), as is probably the case in Singapore. In the absence of such policy, a high Roh statistic suggests that there may be inefficiencies in the allocation of resources across schools and in the use of resources within schools. This situation probably exists in the Philippines.

Although differences in achievement across schools beg further explanation, most analyses in the literature focus on differences within, rather than across, countries. And much of the work relates to developed countries (Hanushek 1986). Empirical work on developing countries is largely constrained by the scarcity of data,[26] but some commonalities do emerge from the available results, as summarized by Lockheed and others (1990). They identify several promising avenues for enhancing school effectiveness, including greater attention to the implementation of a coherent and appropriately paced and sequenced curriculum; and improvement in supplying good textbooks and teacher guides and in setting and maintaining standards for instruction. In contrast, several options are thought to be blind alleys, including adjusting the curriculum, lowering class size, and supplying computers in the classroom.

As an input to the schooling process, teachers warrant special mention, particularly at the lower levels of education where they typically absorb the largest share of the education budget. High costs have meant that much research has focused on improving the performance of teachers. Teacher motivation and subject knowledge are thought to be critically important. Deficiencies in these areas often lead to scrutiny of such factors as teacher pay, conditions of employment, and teacher preparation and in-service training programs (Lockheed and others 1990). The competitiveness of teacher pay, for example, is thought to affect morale and self-respect, which in turn can influence teacher motivation. At the micro level, merit pay—a system in which a significant portion of a teacher's pay is based on performance—is sometimes advocated to encourage performance. In practice, this arrangement has had mixed results (Murnane and Cohen 1986), so policymakers continue to search for other alternatives.

Analyses of efficient ways to promote student achievement and education quality are still at an early stage, particularly in developing countries. Available data document substantial cross-country differences—both in learning outcomes and in the retentive capability of school systems—but give only limited guidance on efficient ways to narrow these gaps in different country settings. Further research would be worthwhile, particularly to help guide policymakers in choosing among alternative allocations of resources among school inputs, and to identify promising incentives for mobilizing student and teacher inputs of effort into the schooling process.

Private financing as an incentive mechanism

The internal efficiency of a school or education system depends not only on its administrative characteristics, but also on the incentives that motivate the behavior of students, teachers, and school administrators. These incentives may exist in several forms. Achievement testing and evaluation constitutes an incentive mechanism, because it can stimulate students and teachers to better performance by clarifying expectations and by giving a basis for comparisons.[27] Merit pay is another arrangement that is sometimes thought to promote effective teaching by tying teacher pay to student academic achievement.

At the institutional level financing arrangements are another incentive mechanism. The expectation is that the more a school depends on private financing, through fees collected from students or contributions from the local community, or both, the more the school is likely to use resources efficiently (that is, to provide services in demand at least cost). When people share directly in the cost of a service, they are likely to monitor costs more closely and to guard against waste.[28] Such vigilance by students and families promotes greater efficiency by sharpening cost-consciousness among school managers and by creating pressures for greater accountability from them.

Even when public institutions charge no fees, the incentive for greater efficiency can be generated by allowing fee-charging private institutions to emerge and survive. Such institutions promote competition in the system and generate information (on such things as costs and student achievement) for judging the performance of public institutions. Even if no explicit comparison is made, outright wastefulness and inefficiency in public institutions are less easily concealed from public scrutiny. The argument for private financing is strongest in higher education where efficiency considerations are reinforced by concerns about equity.

Beyond theoretical expectations, the effect of private financing would need to be judged on the basis of empirical evidence. But such evidence is scanty because data are lacking and because researchers have neglected the subject. An exception is Jimenez, Paqueo, and de Vera (1987b) who used data for the Philippines to analyze the effect of funding source on the efficiency of schools. Results indicate that unit costs across schools varied inversely with the degree of dependence on local sources of funds, a finding that persists when differences in quality are taken into account. In the authors' view, the funding suggests that administrators in schools financed by local funds face greater incentives to minimize costs while maintaining quality.

Evidence on the effect of private financing on efficiency can also be mobilized by comparing whole systems of education. Asian countries differ widely in the way higher education is financed. Differences are reflected in the relative importance of private higher education, as well as the extent of public subsidization of private institutions and the degree of cost recovery, ranging from nearly full public financing in China and India to about 80 percent private financing in Korea and the Philippines (table 3.9). The cost side is shown in table 3.2. This diversity among Asian countries permits testing of the hypothesis that the more a country relies on private financing, the less costly its public institutions are likely to be.

The postulated relationship can be explored using regression analysis, which allows assessment of the statistical significance and magnitude of private financing's effect on costs and permits control for differences in economic development across countries. The estimated relationship is (t-statistics in parentheses):

$$UC = 2.22 - 0.028 \times PF + 0.0096 \times PCGNP$$
$$(3.01) \quad (1.59)^* \quad (0.13)$$

$$R^2 = 0.27; N = 11$$

* statistically significant at 15 percent level of confidence.

UC shows the unit costs of public higher education, regardless of source of finance. It refers to overall costs, rather than just the part financed by the government. It is expressed relative to a country's per capita GNP, and then divided by the average figure for the sample. Measured this way, UC yields the costliness of a country's public higher education relative to that of its neighbors. PF is an index of the extent of private financing in the system. It is a composite variable derived by weighting the distribution of enrollments between public and private institutions by the corresponding rate of cost recovery in each sector. Thus, it takes into account not only the existence and level of fees in public institutions, but also the extent of public subsidization of private institutions. PCGNP is the country's per capita GNP in 1985, expressed in units of US$1,000.

The coefficient of the index of private financing (PF) is negative and statistically significant at the 15 percent level of confidence. That of the per capita GNP variable is statistically insignificant, even though it has the expected positive sign. Although the results are tentative (given the small sample size), they imply that one cannot rule out the possibility that the more a system of education relies on private financing, the lower the overall unit operating cost of its public institutions.[29]

Because the regression results suggest the costliness of higher education is independent of a country's per capita GNP, a plot of the index of private financing against the costliness of higher education reveals a pattern that can be interpreted directly (figure 4.6). The curve flattens out as the rate of private financing approaches about 40 percent.[30] The marginal gain in efficiency diminishes significantly beyond this point. This result has an important policy implication: although it argues in favor of a moderately high rate of cost recovery, it also cautions against extremely high rates because the trade-off between efficiency and adverse social selectivity in the system tends to deteriorate with rising levels of private financing.[31]

Figure 4.6 Relationship between the costliness of public higher education and the overall extent of private financing in the subsector, selected Asian countries, around 1985

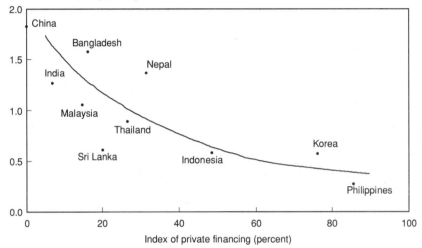

Index of costliness of public higher education

Index of private financing (percent)

Note: See chapters 3 and 4 for details on construction of indexes on both axes.
Source: See appendix table C.3.

Efficiency in the physical organization of schooling

Organizing students into discrete groups in schools and in classrooms[32] affects efficiency (and operating unit costs) through its effect on staff utilization.[33] All schools employ some nonteaching staff whose time is more fully occupied in large schools. If the curriculum calls for specialized teachers (in secondary and higher education) teachers also tend to be more fully utilized. So costs per student are often lower in large institutions than in small ones.[34]

But the economic benefits of large schools differ from place to place. In rugged terrain with sparse population and weak transportation networks, the consolidation of small schools into (a few) large ones greatly increases the average distance between pupils' homes and their school. Transportation costs rise (perhaps sharply), reducing the net economic benefit of larger schools and perhaps forcing some students to quit. In such settings it is desirable, for equity reasons, to continue with small schools. But the argument for siting schools close to pupils' homes is probably strongest for primary schooling. In secondary and higher education, the argument is weaker because older students can travel longer distances from home and because the difference in unit costs between large and small institutions tends to be much wider.[35]

Because local conditions are an important determinant of education costs, no one optimal school size can be specified for all types of institutions in all countries, nor even for all regions within one country. The following discussion is intended only to illustrate the existence of economies of scale and the possible benefit from improving the size distribution of institutions. (Data are for secondary schools in the Philippines and higher education in China.)

Economies of scale in Philippine secondary schools. Evidence from a sample of 497 national secondary schools suggests that unit costs drop with rising enrollments.[36] But the decline tapers off when enrollments exceed about 1,200 students (figure 4.7). This pattern exists in both comprehensive and vocational secondary schools, although unit costs are higher in the latter type of institution at all enrollment levels.

The scope for exploiting economies of scale is substantial because of the current predominance of small schools in the system (table 4.8). Nearly 30 percent of the national schools enroll fewer than 500 students. Among the newly nationalized local schools, the corresponding figure is nearly 85 percent for schools outside the national capital area (which comprise the major share of all local schools). As local schools acquire the staffing standards of national schools and as the use of specialized

Figure 4.7 Relationship between unit operating costs and school size, secondary education in the Philippines, 1986

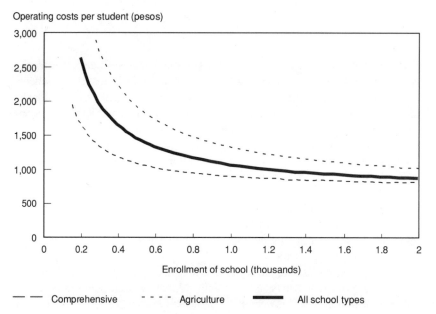

Operating costs per student (pesos)

Enrollment of school (thousands)

— — Comprehensive   - - - - Agriculture   ▬▬▬ All school types

Source: Mingat and Tan (1988).

Table 4.8 Size distribution of Philippine public secondary schools, 1986
(percent)

Individual school size	National schools	National capital area	Other regions
< 100	0.2	0.0	4.9
100–200	3.6	1.1	26.8
200–300	9.8	3.3	27.2
300–500	16.1	8.8	24.0
500–1,000	32.7	13.2	12.4
1,000–2,500	23.9	33.0	3.1
2,500–5,000	11.4	34.1	1.2
> 5,000	2.4	6.7	0.4
All schools	100	100	100
Total enrollments (thousands)	716	196	946
Average school size	1,145	2,150	373

Source: Mingat and Tan 1988.

teachers becomes more widespread, unit costs are likely to rise sharply, by as much as 72 percent in the long run (Mingat and Tan 1988). The indications are that it would be increasingly inefficient to maintain small secondary schools.

Economies of scale in Chinese higher education. A World Bank (1986) study of 136 institutions of higher education shows that unit costs in all types of institutions fall sharply with rising enrollments (table 4.9). Among those offering science-based courses, institutions with 4,000 students have unit costs that are only 59 percent of costs at institutions with 1,000 students. The decline in unit costs is most dramatic in colleges that specialize in the social sciences.

In 1987 less than 10 percent of China's 1,063 institutions enroll more than 4,000 students each, while nearly 60 percent enroll fewer than 1,500 students (table 4.10). So there appears to be substantial scope for rationalizing their size distribution. But

Table 4.9 Economies of scale in Chinese higher education, 1980s

Type of institution	Reference unit cost[a] (yuan)	Predicted unit cost per institution (percentage of reference unit cost)			
		Enrollment of 1,000	Enrollment of 2,000	Enrollment of 4,000	Enrollment of 6,000
Agriculture	1,789	100	73	59	55
Science and technology	1,751	100	72	59	54
Social sciences	1,321	100	63	45	39
Comprehensive	1,490	100	68	51	46
Teacher education	1,498	100	68	52	46

a. Data refer to the unit cost predicted from regression analysis for institutions with 1,000 students.
Source: Table 3.3, World Bank-China (1986b).

shifting toward larger institutions would probably require moving away from excessive institutional specialization by subject area. Only among the comprehensive universities are large institutions common. Few of the more specialized institutions enroll more than 3,000 students. Converting such institutions into comprehensive universities, likely a necessary condition for improving the internal efficiency of the system, is an important policy issue because more than 95 percent of all institutions currently belong to the specialized group.

The efficiency of alternative types of higher education

Beyond economies of scale, a more radical cost-saving intervention is distance education. In some countries, distance education consists of correspondence courses offered by regular universities, and in others it involves open universities. In all settings distance education is dramatically cheaper than conventional higher education.

But lower unit costs do not necessarily imply greater efficiency in open universities, because completion rates often are also lower. One reason is that open universities tend to attract weaker students because entry is usually noncompetitive. Another reason is that, with only a tenuous link to an institution, teachers, and fellow students, a student's motivation and discipline to complete a course is poorly reinforced.

Adjusting for differences in completion rates between open universities and regular institutions, would open universities still produce graduates more cheaply? Data from Thailand illustrate the comparison (table 4.11). Thailand's system of

Table 4.10 Size distribution of tertiary institutions in China by type, 1987
(percent)

Size of institution	All types	Agriculture and forestry	Science and technology[a]	Teacher education	Social sciences	Compre- hensive	Others[b]
< 300	7.2	1.4	3.3	1.5	8.8	2.1	27.0
301– 500	8.1	5.6	3.8	4.2	12.4	0.0	23.6
501–1000	23.6	21.1	18.5	26.5	30.1	6.4	32.0
1001–1500	19.7	22.5	20.3	29.2	19.5	2.1	7.9
1501–2000	13.7	11.3	16.5	18.1	12.4	6.4	5.1
2001–3000	12.6	28.2	18.0	7.3	10.6	12.8	3.4
3001–4000	5.6	9.9	8.4	2.7	4.4	10.6	1.1
4001– 5000	3.2	0.0	3.8	4.6	1.8	10.6	0.0
> 5000	6.3	0.0	7.4	5.8	0.0	48.9	0.0
All institutions	100	100	100	100	100	100	100
Number of institutions	1,063	71	394	260	113	47	178

a. Includes medical colleges.
b. Includes colleges of physical education and fine art.
Source: China (1987a).

higher education comprises three main types of institutions: selective regular institutions, open universities in the public sector, and private colleges. Unit costs are lowest in the open universities because of high pupil-teacher ratios: the average is 745 compared with 8 in selective public institutions and 18 in the private sector. The selective public universities achieve the best graduation rates. On average, graduates per year in selective public institutions represent 26 percent of the enrolled population, compared with only 5 percent in open universities and 17 percent in private institutions. The lower rates in open and private institutions reflect students taking longer to complete their course or dropping out. But despite low completion rates, open universities still produce more graduates per teacher than regular institutions, because of high pupil-teacher ratios. Conventional universities produce far fewer graduates per teacher, but the performance of public selective institutions is particularly weak in this respect.

Graduates per teacher relates to only one aspect of internal efficiency, because it reflects the aggregate production of graduates without differentiating by field of study. A more general shortcoming is that the comparison does not deal with issues

Table 4.11 Graduate output from various types of higher education in Thailand, 1980s

	Public institutions		Private institutions
Graduate ratios	Selective	Open	
Student-staff ratio	8.1	744.5	17.6
Ratio of graduates to enrolled population	0.258	0.050	0.172
Graduates-staff ratio	2.1	37.3	3.0

Source: Thailand (1985b).

of external efficiency. Even though open universities produce graduates efficiently, the output is wasted unless graduates are productive in the labor market. A more global comparison would require assessment of the labor market performance of people who have followed different university careers. This type of analysis is beyond the scope of this study because it requires survey data.

Notes

1. Political objectives clearly also affect policy choices, but they are beyond the scope of this paper. Such objectives depend strongly on country-specific political conditions, and are difficult to analyze in the economic framework adopted here.

2. Because efficiency in education is so broad a topic, it is not possible to cover all facets of it here. Topics considered important and for which relevant data are available will be discussed, but issues already covered in the extant literature will receive only brief mention.

The length of discussion on a topic does not indicate our judgment of its relative importance as a policy issue. Its significance depends on the circumstances of individual countries, and because those circumstances vary widely, there is no basis for establishing a general ranking of issues by their importance for policy purposes.

3. These attacks attempt to cast doubt on the social role of schooling by offering other explanations for the observed earnings advantage of the more educated: social class, job competition, youth unemployment, nonclearing wages, screening for ability, and so on (Psacharopoulos 1984).

4. The manpower approach is a different method of assessing the rationale for future investments in education. It suffers, however, from serious flaws and is generally discredited as a planning methodology (Hinchcliffe and Youdi 1985). Its application is mostly limited to projections of manpower needs in occupations that have relatively narrow and stable manpower-to-population ratios (such as teachers and health personnel). The rate-of-return methodology is admittedly not perfect either. But it may offer the most concise basis for comparison because the calculations reflect both the costs and benefits of an investment. Although externalities and other unquantifiable aspects are neglected, the resulting statistics give a first indication of the value of different investments in society (see Mingat and Tan 1986 for further elaboration).

5. This result, which refers to the profitability of an extra year of schooling at the mean in the reference populations, is derived from Mincerian regressions. In such regressions, the dependent variable is the logarithm of income, and the independent variables are schooling and experience, measured in years. The coefficient on the schooling variable is the estimated (private) rate of return.

6. Some of the benefits of education, although good for society as a whole, may not be totally captured or perceived by individuals; nonetheless, rates of return are often calculated without taking explicit account of such externalities because it is difficult to quantify them.

7. The rate-of-return data may be biased if the estimates do not make allowance for quality as an output. But few studies on the returns to investment in quality in education exist (an exception is Behrman and Birdsall 1983).

8. There appears to be an inverse relationship between the costliness of a system and its degree of dependence on private financing.

9. The regression results, however, are only suggestive because of questions about the source and reliability of data on literacy rates.

10. Persistence through the system is important because (1) literacy may not be attained if education is interrupted too early and (2) an interruption in education may cause a lapse into illiteracy (Lestage 1981).

11. But what is accepted as a high quality system often simply means a system whose output compares favorably with that of other systems. To judge its internal efficiency would require assessing its value-added—that is, output adjusted for inputs (including resources, student characteristics, and so on). It is possible for a high quality system to be internally inefficient: its performance could be due to the quality of its students and the volume of resources used, rather than to the way these resources are put to use.

12. Interventions include such choices as the selection processes that affect students' progress through the system; the mix of school inputs and the use of alternative pedagogical methods to maximize student achievement; curriculum design; incentives to encourage students, teachers, and other actors in the system to perform their best; the spatial distribution of schools; the grouping of students in classes; and so on.

13. The cohort survival rate (CSR) (or the cohort retention rate) is defined as the proportion

of grade 1 entrants who survive to a given grade, say, the end of the primary cycle. The complement of CSR is the cohort drop-out rate (CDR), in this case defined as the proportion of grade 1 entrants who drop-out before reaching the end of the primary cycle. By definition, CSR = 1 - CDR. Thus, the two indicators can be used interchangeably. A common mistake is to confuse the CDR with the rate obtained by dividing the number of pupils who drop out in a year by the enrolled population. This calculation yields the period drop-out rate (PDR) because it refers to the incidence of dropping out at a specific calendar time. The PDR is often much smaller than the CDR because its denominator includes people from several cohorts (the number of cohorts depending on the length of the cycle of education in question). The two statistics have different uses: the CDR is relevant for assessing a system's internal efficiency and its pedagogical performance; the PDR is more relevant for space-planning purposes.

14. These profiles were derived from aggregate time-series enrollment data for the mid-1980s and were adjusted for the incidence of repetition. So they reveal patterns of survival, not in years of schooling, but in grade attained. For more information on the year-to-year survival pattern, see appendix table B2.2 (on which table 4.5 is based), which also retains information on the length of primary and secondary education in each country.

15. We owe this observation to Andrew Rogerson, a reviewer of this study.

16. The presence of underage pupils can also inflate the gross enrollment ratio, but the number of such students is probably limited.

17. If dropping out occurs uniformly throughout the system, the net enrollment ratio (defined as the ratio between the number of pupils in the school-age range to the total population in that age range) can roughly be estimated by taking the average of the entry and survival rates. Note, however, that in some countries (such as Bangladesh, Bhutan, and Nepal), dropping out occurs much more frequently in the early years of the primary cycle, so this method of estimation would be invalid. The relative size of the overage population is indirectly revealed by the difference between the gross and net enrollment ratios.

18. Although the Philippines does not have a formal system of upper secondary education, many students in fact enroll in the equivalent of such education in nondegree courses at the tertiary level. The proportion entering such courses is probably between 15 and 25 percent of the cohort.

19. This pattern is to be expected because those who have reached higher levels are precisely those with a lower propensity to drop out.

20. The level of per pupil spending in primary education (measured as a percentage of per capita GNP) is more a reflection of priorities in public policies than a reflection of inevitable links between the level of spending and per capita GNP (see chapter 5).

21. A simple straight-line regression linking the cohort survival rate to the unit operating cost shows an R-squared statistic of 0.141 if the data for Papua New Guinea (an outlier) is included; and 0.399 if it is excluded. The corresponding regression coefficients on the unit cost variable are +0.375 and +0.632.

22. Pedagogical and economic considerations suggest that intracycle selection is probably less desirable than intercycle selection.

23. This result is valid when resources are allocated such that additional spending on each input produces equal increments of learning.

24. It is generally known, for example, that textbooks have an important effect on student achievement. However, Paderanga (1987) and Jimenez, Paqueo, and de Vera (1987a) found in separate studies that their effect is limited in the Philippines. One explanation is that the provision of textbooks has already reached more or less adequate levels in most Philippine

schools. As a result, this input has a smaller marginal effect on student achievement than other inputs, such as the subject knowledge of teachers.

25. The test for each population was identical for all 24 countries in the study. Data are currently available for only 17 of these countries. In some countries, only one of the two populations was tested.

26. See Harbison and Hanushek 1990 for a rare example of empirical work in a developing country context.

27. The IEA study is an example of how testing can provide a useful incentive for low-scoring countries to examine the operation of their education systems more closely.

28. When part of the cost of education is borne by a student and his family, the student is also more likely to avoid waste in his own behavior. For example, in education systems with no tuition charges and generous stipends (not tied to academic achievement), students tend to take longer than the normal time to complete their course. Students who pay for their education are more likely to complete their course on time, sometimes even before the normal time.

29. This result implies that in systems that rely on private financing, the government bears a lighter fiscal burden because it finances a smaller share of a lower overall unit cost.

30. Even though this pattern is based only on data from Asian countries, the results nonetheless give a benchmark for judging whether or not the extent of private financing in a system is high enough to exploit its potential effect on efficiency in public higher education.

31. Increased private financing in higher education can be accomplished in at least two ways: imposing or raising user charges in public institutions, or promoting expansion of largely self-financing private institutions, or both.

32. In some situations classrooms are subdivided, as in the case of multigrade teaching (one teacher in a classroom of pupils at different grade levels).

33. Student grouping also affects efficiency in the utilization of physical facilities, but the costs affected are capital, not recurrent, costs.

34. The issue of economies of scope (that is, having more than one level of education under a single administration) is not addressed here. See Jimenez 1986 for a discussion.

35. At these levels of education, boarding can increase access to education for students from remote areas.

36. Until 1986 the public sector comprised national schools (funded by the central government) and local schools (funded by local governments and through fees paid by students). In 1986, the government nationalized local schools, and in the following year it abolished fees for public secondary education.

5

Equity in Education

In the broadest sense, equity refers to the distribution of income, wealth, position, and power in society. Public policies are an important determinant of that distribution because they define the conditions and rules of interpersonal competition. Policies in the education sector are particularly relevant for equity because they affect access to schooling and, subsequently, to jobs and income.

In the literature, three complementary types of analyses for assessing equity in education are those that (1) evaluate differences in access to specific levels or types of education[1]; (2) compare the distribution of benefits among people with different education[2]; and (3) assess who pays for and who benefits from education. Although the third approach is the most comprehensive, it usually requires survey data and thus is unfeasible for this study. The data and analysis presented below fall largely under the rubric of the first two approaches.

Global aspects

Two features of education systems with important implications for equity are the degree of emphasis on higher education and the distribution of cumulative public spending (implied by the structure of enrollments and government subsidies across levels of education). These two features describe different but complementary aspects that affect equity in an education system: one focuses mainly on relative emphasis within the education system; the other views the education system as a whole and incorporates the extent of nonenrollment as part of the assessment. Private financing is a third area that can affect equity in the sector.

Bias toward higher education

In some countries primary education is accorded the highest priority in the sector; in others, the stress may be on higher education. Three complementary pieces of data are used to compare these priorities in systems of education: resource-intensity (measured by unit costs), coverage, and the extent of government subsidization.

Resource-intensity in public education. Resource-intensity reveals the relative concentration of resources per pupil by level of education. Data on the total operating costs per pupil, regardless of funding source (table 3.2), are used here to assess the implicit priority in resource-intensity attached to the various levels of education.[3]

Consider first how unit costs deviate from the regional mean at each level of education (table 5.1 and figure 5.1).[4] In India, for example, unit costs in primary education are 41 percent below the corresponding regional mean, but unit costs in higher education are 51 percent above the regional mean. In contrast, the parallel figures for Malaysia are 39 percent and 24 percent above the regional means. These patterns suggest that resources in India are more heavily concentrated in higher education relative to primary education compared with the situation in Malaysia.

To facilitate cross-country comparisons, data on deviations at the three levels of education are compressed into a single index. To assess the bias toward higher education relative to the lower levels, a simple method is used to calculate the steepness of the deviations as the level of education rises. Consider figures 5.2 and

Table 5.1 Unit operating costs of public education, deviation of unit costs from regional mean, and index of cost bias toward higher education, selected Asian countries, mid-1980s

Country	Unit operating costs (percentage of per capita GNP)			Deviation of unit costs from regional mean (percent)[a]			Index of cost bias toward higher education[b]
	Pri-mary	Secon-dary	Higher	Pri-mary	Secon-dary	Higher	
Bangladesh	6.4	30.0	284.6	-37	58	86	61
China	6.7	22.6	199.2	-32	22	34	33
India	6.0	17.3	231.1	41	-9	51	46
Indonesia	12.6	23.3	91.1	25	23	-41	-33
Korea	16.5	23.4	70.6	63	23	-54	-58
Malaysia	14.1	21.3	190.3	39	12	24	-8
Nepal	9.0	13.5	249.0	-11	-29	62	37
Papua New Guinea	29.0	65.0	1050.0	187	243	585	199
Philippines	5.8	8.6	50.0	43	-55	-67	-12
Sri Lanka	6.1	9.3	83.3	-40	-51	-46	-3
Thailand	15.5	15.3	39.9	53	-19	-74	-64
Regional average							
With Papua New Guinea	9.9	18.5	148.9	..	..	..	..
Without Papua New Guinea	11.6	22.7	230.8	..	..	..	..

a. Deviations are taken from the regional mean computed without data for Papua New Guinea.
b. See text on the computation of this index.
Source: See appendix table B4.1.

Figure 5.1 Deviation of the unit operating costs of public education from the regional average, selected Asian countries, around 1985

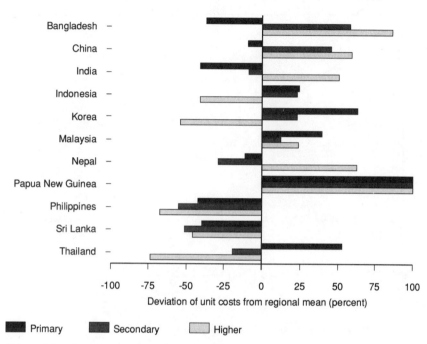

Primary   Secondary   Higher

Note: Deviations from mean are truncated at 100 percent.
Source: See table 5.1.

5.3, showing the pattern of deviations in Malaysia and India. For Malaysia, the overall pattern is one of declining deviations with rising levels of education, whereas for India it is one of rising deviations. An index of the rate of decline or rise in deviations is calculated by (1) establishing points A and B, the midpoints of the deviations between primary and secondary education and between secondary and higher education, and (2) taking the difference between these midpoints. For Malaysia the index is -8 (the result of $\{[28+15]/2 - [15+43]/2\}$); for India, it is +46 (the result of $\{[55+\{-6\}]/2 - [\{-6\}+\{-39\}]/2\}$).

Following the same procedure, the index of bias toward higher education is calculated for the other countries (table 5.1). In a group comprising Bangladesh, China, India, and Papua New Guinea, the deviations increase rapidly with rising levels of education, indicating a definite bias toward the higher levels. This pattern also exists in Nepal, but the bias is more moderate because secondary education is relatively less resource-intensive than primary education. In Sri Lanka the pattern is balanced across the three levels of education. In the Philippines and Malaysia there is

Figure 5.2 Deviation of unit costs from regional mean, Malaysia, around 1985

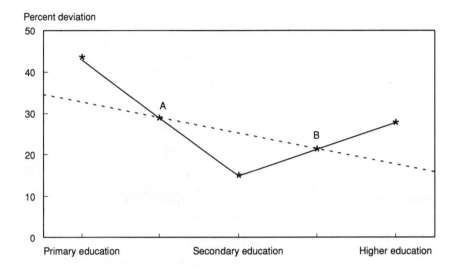

Source: Based on data in table 5.1.

Figure 5.3 Deviation of unit costs from regional mean, India, around 1985

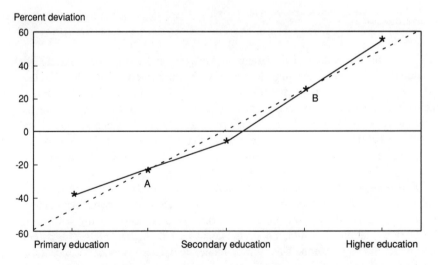

Source: Based on data in table 5.1.

a moderate bias in favor of the lower levels of education. In Indonesia, Korea, and Thailand, the bias toward the lower levels of education is stronger. In Thailand and Korea, for example, the relative unit cost in public primary and secondary education is 2 to 3 times that of public higher education, a pattern denoting a clear emphasis in resource-intensity on basic education.

Structure of coverage. A second source of bias toward higher education is the structure of coverage across levels of education, as reflected in enrollment ratios.[5] Because coverage tends to rise with income levels, a fair assessment would need to control for differences in countries' wealth. One approach is to compare actual enrollment ratios to those predicted on the basis of a country's per capita GNP.

The first step is to estimate the relationship between enrollment ratios and per capita GNP. (Appendix table C.1 shows the regression equations based on data for about 100 developing countries, and separately for 16 Asian countries. The regressions for Asia, which differ slightly from those based on world data (showing wider coverage at each level of income), are the ones used for the analysis here.[6] Each country's per capita GNP is plugged into the estimated regression equation to obtain the predicted enrollment ratio for the level of education concerned (table 5.2).

The predicted enrollment ratios should not be interpreted as normative targets for countries, but rather as a basis for judging the overall development of an education system in a comparative perspective.[7] Although not flawless, this approach is arguably better than direct comparisons among countries, or even comparisons based on regional averages.

Table 5.2 Actual and predicted enrollment ratios, selected Asian countries, mid-1980s

Country	Per capita GNP (US $)	Actual enrollment ratios (percent)			Predicted enrollment ratios (percent)		
		Primary	Secondary	Higher	Primary	Secondary	Higher
Bangladesh	159	60	18	5.2	82	24	5.0
China	273	118	39	1.7	83	27	6.1
India	259	92	35	9.0	83	27	5.9
Indonesia	503	118	42	6.5	86	35	8.2
Korea	2,040	99	74	31.6	103	72	18.8
Malaysia	1,860	99	53	6.0	101	69	17.9
Nepal	142	79	25	4.6	82	23	4.8
Papua New Guinea	621	64	14	1.7	88	38	9.2
Philippines	581	106	65	38.0	87	37	8.9
Sri Lanka	374	103	63	4.6	85	31	7.0
Thailand	712	97	30	19.6	89	41	10.0

Source: As in appendix table B1.2 for data on actual enrollment ratios and per capita GNP; predicted enrollment ratios are derived from the regressions for Asia in appendix table C.1.

Data for three levels of education make cross-country comparisons between actual and predicted enrollments cumbersome. A single index that reduces the data to one statistic per country would simplify the task, but such an index is hard to devise satisfactorily. One reason is that the enrollment ratio has, by definition, a limited range. So actual and predicted values converge as coverage expands, reducing variance in the gap between these values. This tendency is strongest at the primary level, because most countries in Asia either have reached universal coverage or are approaching it (according to official enrollment data). A second problem is that because coverage tends to rise with economic development, the gap between actual and predicted ratios will inevitably be smaller for richer countries than for poorer ones. But adjusting for these considerations would complicate construction of the desired index, and it is unclear that the result would have an intuitively clear meaning.

Because of this constraint, our assessment of the bias in coverage takes a qualitative approach, based on figure 5.4, which shows, for each Asian country in our sample, the deviation of actual from predicted enrollment ratios at the three levels of

Figure 5.4 **Deviation of actual enrollment ratios from those predicted on the basis of per capita GNP, selected Asian countries, around 1985**

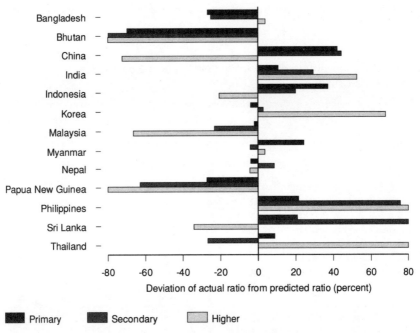

Deviation of actual ratio from predicted ratio (percent)

■ Primary   ■ Secondary   ☐ Higher

Note: Deviations from mean are truncated at plus and minus 80%.
Source: See table 5.2.

education. Consider, for example, Bangladesh and Malaysia. Bangladesh's gross enrollment ratio in primary education is 60 percent compared with a predicted value of 82 percent. In higher education the actual ratio is slightly larger than the predicted figure. These patterns imply a bias in coverage favoring higher education. In Malaysia the enrollment ratio for higher education is only 6 percent, compared with the predicted value of 18 percent. Since primary education is universal, this result suggests that the country places more emphasis on coverage at the primary level than at the higher education level.

Following this procedure for all countries in the sample, a comparison can be made of the bias in the structure of coverage. Bangladesh, India and, to a lesser extent, the Philippines are countries with a strong bias in coverage favoring higher education. In Thailand and Korea this bias is less pronounced because basic education is well developed and does not suffer from high drop-out rates. Coverage in Nepal is balanced across the three levels of education. In Indonesia, Malaysia, Papua New Guinea, and Sri Lanka, coverage is moderately skewed in favor of the lower levels of education. In China, the bias in favor of the lower levels of education is stronger.

Costliness of higher education to government. Higher education's costliness to government depends on how much countries rely on the following, not mutually exclusive, arrangements to minimize dependence on the public purse: low-cost distance education; (largely) self-financing private education; and user charges for public higher education. Korea, for example, exploits all three options; the Philippines and Thailand rely heavily on only one of them (self-financing private education in the Philippines and low-cost distance education in Thailand). In all three countries, the result is less government financing of higher education than in other countries. Countries like Bangladesh, India, Malaysia, and Papua New Guinea fall at the high end of the spectrum, because they rely little on the three instruments.[8]

The other Asian countries fall between these extremes. The extent of public subsidization in Indonesia is not as low as in, say, Korea, even though Indonesia has a large private sector and an open university. The reason is that Indonesia's private sector is heavily subsidized by the government through the secondment of civil servants to teaching posts in private institutions. China's ranking is moderately high, despite the presence of distance education, because the system fails to exploit the substantial economies of scale associated with it. Nepal ranks in the middle of the spectrum, because self-financing private education is moderately well developed. Sri Lanka is also in this position because the country has a reasonably large system of low-cost distance education.

Overall assessment of the bias toward higher education. Resource-intensity, coverage, and costliness to government give the basis for an overall assessment of bias toward higher education. For cross-country comparisons, we scored performance along each of these three aspects using plus and minus signs to indicate the direction and degree of bias (table 5.3). Positive signs signify a bias in favor of higher

Table 5.3 Relative degree of emphasis on higher education, selected Asian countries, mid-1980s

Country	Structure of public unit costs	Coverage	Costliness to the government	Overall degree of emphasis
Bangladesh	+ + +	+ +	+ +	+ 7
China	+	- -	+	+ 0
India	+ +	+ +	+ +	+ 6
Indonesia	-	-	-	- 3
Korea	- -	+	- -	- 3
Malaysia	-	-	+ +	0
Nepal	+	0	0	+ 1
Papua New Guinea	+ + + +	-	+ +	+ 5
Philippines	-	-+	- -	- 2
Sri Lanka	0	-	0	- 1
Thailand	-	+	- -	- 3

Source: Authors' assessment based on data on unit costs, coverage, and the extent of public subsidization of higher education. See discussion in text for additional information.

education, negative signs signify the opposite tendency, and zeros denote the absence of a bias in either direction. The number of positive or negative signs indicates the strength of the bias. Adding up these qualitative scores gives a consolidated index of bias toward higher education in each country.[9] The result is only a rough indicator of implicit priorities across the various levels of education, revealing broad rather than fine differences across countries. The index is nonetheless useful, because large gaps among countries can be interpreted as signifying differences in education priorities.

The Asian countries in the sample fall into three groups. The bias toward higher education is particularly strong in Bangladesh, India, and Papua New Guinea. In China, Malaysia, Nepal, and Sri Lanka, this bias is largely absent. In the remaining countries—Indonesia, Korea, the Philippines, and Thailand—the emphasis is on the lower levels of education. China's ranking reflects a strong trade-off between costs and coverage. This trade-off is missing in Bangladesh and India and only slightly present in Papua New Guinea.

To what extent is a country's emphasis on higher education linked to its level of economic development? A weak inverse relationship appears to exist, as indicated by figure 5.5 in which the index of overall bias is plotted against per capita GNP. This result implies that the poorer a country, the stronger the overall emphasis on higher education. But there is wide variation around this general pattern. Papua New Guinea and Thailand, for example, have similar levels of per capita GNP, but the bias toward higher education is much stronger in Papua New Guinea. Similarly, although levels of per capita GNP in China and India are comparable, India shows a stronger bias toward higher education. These comparisons imply that poor countries are not necessarily condemned to systems that are skewed toward higher education:

the degree of bias depends as much on policy choices as on conditions in the country.

Equity in distribution of cumulative public spending on education

Cumulative public spending on education refers to the total amount of public resources appropriated to a generation of people passing through the school system. The concept of benefits is therefore a longitudinal one: the focus is on the distribution of cumulative benefits among people with different schooling careers, rather than on the distribution of single period benefits at a given level of education.[10]

Equity in the distribution of cumulative benefits depends on enrollment and public subsidization structures across the three levels of education, that is, a system's structural equity. Achieving structural equity depends more on broad policy choices in education than on specific interventions aimed at altering the social composition of individuals in the system. If a government allocates most of its spending on education to the higher levels to benefit a few people, leaving few resources for primary school pupils, it achieves a lower level of structural equity in the education system than a government that pursues the opposite policies.

Measuring structural equity in an education system requires knowledge of (1) the amount of public subsidies an individual accumulates at various stops on the educa-

Figure 5.5 Relationship between emphasis on higher education and per capita GNP, selected Asian countries, around 1985

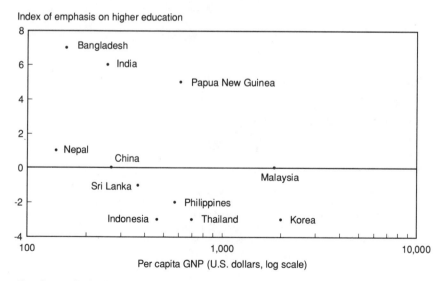

Index of emphasis on higher education

Note: See text for details on the index of emphasis on higher education.
Source: See text discussion.

tional ladder and (2) the distribution of individuals in a generation by education attainment upon exit from the system. These data yield a picture of the distribution of cumulative public subsidies among members of a generation.

Total public subsidies to an individual are derived from data on public spending per pupil by level of education (table 5.4). These data reflect the weighted average of subsidies in the public and private sectors.[11] The amount accumulated by a person exiting the system with primary education is the product of this average and the number of years in the cycle.[12] A person exiting with higher education accumulates the sum of subsidies in all three cycles of education.

Consider the computation for Bangladesh. Those who exit the education system with no schooling get no resources; those who exit with primary education get a public subsidy amounting to 5.3 percent of per capita GNP per year. Over five years in the primary cycle, each will accumulate resources equal to 27 percent of per capita GNP (that is, 5.3 times 5 years). Those exiting with secondary education accumulate resources amounting to 196 percent of per capita GNP (that is, 28 times 7 years) over this cycle. Adding this amount to what has been accumulated in the primary cycle gives a total of 223 percent of GNP for the schooling career of a secondary school graduate. The cumulative subsidies per higher education graduate amount to 1,223

Table 5.4 Average public subsidies per pupil, selected Asian countries, mid-1980s

Country	Subsidies by level of education[a]			Cumulative subsidies[b]		
	Primary	Secondary	Higher	Primary	Secondary	Higher
Bangladesh	5.3	28.0	250	27	223	1,223
China	6.3	21.9	199	38	169	964
India	5.2	15.0	180	26	116	836
Indonesia	10.8	16.3	30	65	163	283
Korea	16.6	8.3	12	100	149	197
Malaysia	13.6	20.5	170	82	225	905
Nepal	8.5	7.2	170	43	79	759
Papua New Guinea	26.4	39.0	978	158	392	4,304
Philippines	5.5	4.5	6	33	51	77
Sri Lanka	5.8	8.8	77	35	96	404
Thailand	11.6	13.3	30	70	149	269
Regional average	10.5	16.6	191	61	165	929

Note: Spending per pupil is expressed as a percentage of per capita GNP.
a. The data refer to the average for the public and private sectors at each level. They reflect overall operating costs per pupil minus the amount financed through fees, and are adjusted for the share of private education and the extent of government subsidization of that sector.
b. The data reflect the annual recurrent subsidies multiplied by the number of years in the cycle; the figures for secondary and higher education include the subsidies received in the previous cycles of education.
Source: Authors' estimates based on method discussed in text.

percent of per capita GNP (that is, 27 in the primary cycle, 196 in the secondary cycle, and 1,000 [=250x4] in higher education) (table 5.4).

The distribution of members of a generation by education attainment upon exit from the system is derived from data on enrollment ratios by level of education. Consider again the data for Bangladesh. The proportion of individuals with higher education is the same as the current enrollment ratio (5 percent)[13]; the percentage without schooling is the residual of the primary enrollment ratio (40 percent = 100 - 60). The proportion with primary education is the difference between the enrollment ratios in primary and secondary education (42 percent = 60 - 18); the share with secondary education is derived similarly (13 percent = 18 - 5).

In all but three Asian countries (Korea, the Philippines and, to a lesser extent, Thailand), the enrollment pyramid is steep, because no more than 10 percent of future adults will exit the education system with higher education. In Bangladesh, Nepal, and Papua New Guinea, it is particularly steep, because a sizable group in the cohort does not even enter the system.

Having calculated the subsidies per individual both by education attainment and by the distribution of members of a cohort by education attainment, it is possible to combine these results to obtain the distribution of total accumulated subsidies among cohort members. Continuing with Bangladesh, the 40 individuals in a cohort of 100 with no schooling get none of the accumulated public resources; the 42 individuals exiting the system with primary education get an aggregate total of 1,134 (=27 x 42); the 13 attaining secondary education obtain an aggregated total of 2,899 (=223 x 13); and the 5 attaining higher education get a total of 6,115 (= 1,223 x 5). As a whole, the cohort accumulates a grand total of 10,148 (0 + 1,134 + 2,988 + 6,115) in public subsidies. The share of the groups by education attainment is easily derived: zero in the case of those with no schooling; 11 percent (=1,134/10,148 x 100) for the group attaining primary education; and 28 percent and 61 percent respectively for those attaining secondary and higher education.

Results for the sample of Asian countries reveal wide differences across countries (table 5.5): compare the share of 61 percent of cumulative subsidies benefiting the 5 percent attaining higher education in Bangladesh, with the much smaller share of 23 percent benefiting the corresponding population in Sri Lanka. Clearly, graduates of higher education absorb a much larger share of public subsidies in Bangladesh than they do in Sri Lanka.

Two summary indexes. The comparison between Bangladesh and Sri Lanka is straightforward because the proportion of the cohort attaining higher education happens to be the same—5 percent. Because this is not usually the case, comparisons of equity in the distribution of public subsidies need to be standardized in some fashion. Two indexes can be used: (1) the Gini-coefficient, an index widely used in the economics literature to quantify the concentration of benefits in a population; and (2) the share of subsidies benefiting a predetermined privileged subset of the cohort.

Table 5.5 Projected distribution of education attainment and cumulative public subsidies among members of current school-age population, selected Asian countries, mid-1980s
(percent)

Country	Education attainment (percentage of school-age population)				Share of cumulative subsidies (percent)			
	No Schooling[a]	Primary	Secondary	Higher	No Schooling	Primary	Secondary	Higher
Bangladesh	40	42	13	5	0	11	28	61
China	0	61	37	2	0	22	60	18
India	8	51	32	9	0	11	30	60
Indonesia	0	58	36	7	0	33	50	12
Korea	4	21	43	32	0	14	43	43
Malaysia	1	46	47	6	0	19	54	27
Nepal	18	57	20	5	0	31	20	49
Papua New Guinea	30	57	11	2	0	41	20	39
Philippines	0	35	27	38	0	21	25	54
Sri Lanka	0	37	58	5	0	14	63	23
Thailand	3	67	10	20	0	40	13	47
Regional average	9	48	30	12	0	23	37	40

a. This population did not in fact enter the education system.
Source: Authors' estimates based on data on enrollment ratios from Unesco (1987a) and data on public subsidies per pupil presented in earlier chapters.

To derive the Gini-coefficient, consider again the data for Bangladesh. In figure 5.6 point A represents the 40 percent of the cohort without schooling, with no share of the cumulative subsidies; point B depicts the 82 percent with primary schooling or less, with a cumulative share of 11 percent of the subsidies; point C shows the 95 percent with secondary schooling or less, with a cumulative share of 39 percent of the resources; and point D corresponds to those with higher education or less (that is, the entire population, with all the cumulative subsidies). The Gini-coefficient is defined as the area of ABCDE relative to the area of triangle ED'D.[14] It has a range of 0 to 100; the closer it is to 100, the more resources are concentrated among those who reach the higher levels of education and the more inequitable the distribution of benefits.

The second summary statistic for comparison across countries is the share of cumulative subsidies accruing to the best-educated 10 percent in a generation. This cutoff group of 10 percent is an arbitrary choice, but it does offer a reasonably good idea of the concentration of public spending on education. To calculate the group's share of cumulative subsidies, the following procedure was used: where the proportion attaining higher education is less than 10 percent—as in Bangladesh—the shortfall is made up by adding population from the group attaining secondary education and augmenting the cumulative subsidies of the higher education group by the prorated subsidies of the make-up population from the secondary group. In Bangladesh, for example, 5 percent of the cohort attain higher education, accumulating 61 percent of the subsidies. To reach the 10 percent level in population, we add 5 percent of the secondary population; correspondingly, this group's prorated share of resources, 10.7 percent (= [5/13] x 28), is added on the subsidy side. Summing up, the 10 percent best-educated accumulates subsidies amounting to 71.7 percent (= 61 + 10.7) of the total for the cohort. For countries where those attaining higher education exceed 10 percent, the statistic is simply a prorated share of the subsidies accruing to this group. In Korea, for example, the share of the 10 percent best-educated is 13.3 percent (= [10/32] x 43).

Applying the two summary indexes, Asian countries fall into three groups (table 5.6). The first group comprises Korea and the Philippines, where education subsidies are equitably distributed, with the 10 percent best-educated obtaining no more than 15 percent of total subsidies. The second group includes China, Indonesia, Malaysia, Sri Lanka, and Thailand, with moderately equitable distributions. The share of cumulative subsidies benefiting the best-educated 10 percent ranges from 20 percent to a little more than 30 percent. In the third group—Bangladesh, India, Nepal, and Papua New Guinea—the distribution of subsidies is significantly less equitable than in the rest of Asia, with Bangladesh and India performing worst.

Figure 5.6 Cumulative distributions of cohort population by education attainment and of cumulative public subsidies for education, Bangladesh

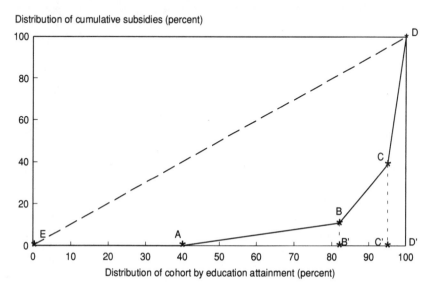

Source: See table 5.5.

Table 5.6 Distribution of public spending on education, selected Asian countries, mid-1980s

Country	Gini-coefficient[a]	Cumulative spending received by 10 percent best-educated (percentage of total cumulative spending)
Bangladesh	81.9	71.7
China	44.4	31.1
India	65.8	60.8
Indonesia	27.3	21.4
Korea	15.9	13.4
Malaysia	37.9	32.0
Nepal	57.9	53.5
Papua New Guinea	62.1	53.5
Philippines	18.6	14.1
Sri Lanka	32.6	28.1
Thailand	32.9	23.3
Regional average	43.4	36.3

a. This statistic has a range of 0 to 100. The closer it is to 100, the more unequal the distribution of public spending on education in a generation of school-age population.
Source: Authors' estimates based on data in tables 5.2 and 5.3; see text discussion on method of derivation.

Equity in the distribution of cumulative education subsidies and countries' economic wealth. Is there a systematic link between these variables? A priori, we expect that the richer a country, the less subsidies are likely to be concentrated among the privileged. This is because education opportunities tend to widen with economic development, spreading public subsidies for education more evenly. There is also greater scope for tapping private financing for higher education in wealthier countries, which makes it easier to channel larger shares of public spending to the lower levels of education.

Figure 5.7 plots the share of cumulative subsidies accruing to the best-educated 10 percent in the population against the country's per capita GNP. The overall pattern shows a negative link between these two indicators, but the relationship is quite weak, with wide variance around the average pattern. So although poorer countries tend to have more inequitable distributions of education subsidies, some countries perform much better than others at comparable income levels. The result suggests that policy choices can probably have a significant effect on equity in the distribution of public spending on education, regardless of economic context.

The potential for improvement is especially strong in countries where (1) cumulative public spending is highly skewed toward the best-educated, and (2) the best-educated's share of resources exceeds what might be expected on the basis of the country's per capita GNP. The vertical axis in figure 5.8 shows the share of cumulative resources received by the 10 percent best-educated in a cohort; the horizontal

Figure 5.7 Relationship between share of cumulative public spending on education received by the 10 percent best-educated and per capita GNP, selected Asian countries, 1985

Share of cumulative resources received by 10 percent best-educated (percent)

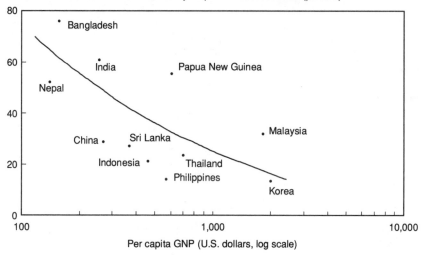

Per capita GNP (U.S. dollars, log scale)

Source: See table 5.6 and text.

Figure 5.8 Share of cumulative public spending on education received by the 10 percent best-educated, in absolute terms and relative to trend line in figure 5.7, selected Asian countries, 1985

Share of cumulative resources received by 10 percent best-educated (percent)

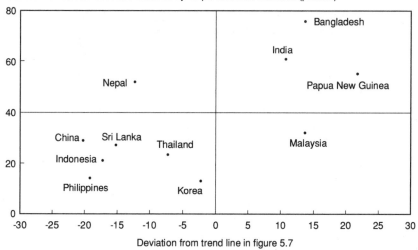

Deviation from trend line in figure 5.7

Source: See text discussion.

axis shows the deviation of this share from that associated with the country's per capita GNP (estimated roughly from figure 5.7). The figure is divided into four quadrants, using lines through the zero deviation point on the horizontal axis, and through an arbitrary cutoff level of 40 percent on the vertical axis. In countries in the top right quadrant, the current distribution of public spending is highly inequitable and the scope for improvement is large (Bangladesh, India, and Papua New Guinea). Although Malaysia falls in the bottom right quadrant, there is room for improving equity in the distribution of public spending on education, mainly by reducing the high cost and heavy public subsidization of higher education.

The effect of private financing on equity

The argument for increasing private financing is most persuasive when applied to higher education. Evidence from simple graphs and regressions demonstrates the likely effect of a policy on equity, both in the system as a whole and in higher education.

Effect on overall equity in the system. The share of cumulative public spending on education accruing to the 10 percent best-educated in a generation is a good measure of overall structural equity in an education system. How does this index vary with extent of private financing in higher education? Figure 5.9 suggests a negative relationship, implying that overall equity improves as private financing rises in higher education. This pattern arises partly because (1) cost recovery is more extensive in the wealthier countries in the sample, and (2) education systems in wealthy countries are generally better developed at all levels. But the link between per capita GNP and extent of private financing is weak, so the pattern in figure 5.9 is not only a reflection of countries' differences in per capita GNP.

Diminishing returns set in with rising rates of private financing, as shown by the dotted line's tendency to flatten out toward the right. This pattern has an important implication for the design of cost recovery policies in higher education: very high rates, say beyond 40 percent, are not necessary for maximum effect on global equity.

Another indicator of overall equity in the education system is the share of primary education in total public spending on education (Pshare). It is a simple measure of overall equity with an intuitively appealing meaning, because systems in which primary education has a large share of total public spending are likely to be more equitable than those with the opposite characteristic. The effect of private financing in higher education on Pshare is examined through the simple regression below, based on country-level data for around 1985:

Pshare = 36.2 + 0.47 x Eshare + 0.32 x PF
         (4.62)   (0.28)   (3.19)*

R-squared = 0.58; N = 11

* statistically significant at 5 percent level of confidence.

Figure 5.9 Share of cumulative public spending on education received by the 10 percent best-educated and extent of private financing in higher education, selected Asian countries, 1980

Share of cumulative resources received by 10 percent best-educated (percent)

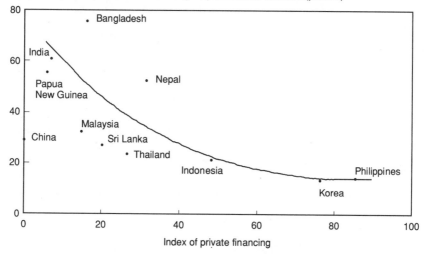

Index of private financing

Source: See appendix table C.3.

Eshare is the share of total public spending on education as a share of GNP[15]; and PF is the index of private financing in higher education (defined in chapter 4).[16]

The result of the regression, although tentative at this stage because of the limited sample size, is nonetheless suggestive. The PF variable has the predicted positive sign and is statistically significant at the 5 percent level. A 10 percent increase in its value (corresponding to a shift of 28 percent of its standard deviation from the sample mean of 32.7 percent) raises the share of primary education by 3.2 percentage points, from a sample mean of 47.6 percent, corresponding to an average rise of about 6.7 percent. The positive link revealed by the regression is due to two reinforcing effects: private financing in higher education reduces unit cost in public institutions and diminishes the government's share in the financing of that smaller unit cost. As a result, a larger share of government resources can be channeled to primary education.

Effect on equity in higher education. It is sometimes argued that private financing reduces access to education. The relationship depicted in figure 5.10—between the gross enrollment ratio in higher education and extent of private financing—gives preliminary support to a second argument—that private financing helps mobilize resources, thus augmenting public funds for expanding coverage.

Figure 5.10 Relationship between gross enrollment ratios in higher education and extent of private financing, selected Asian countries, around 1985

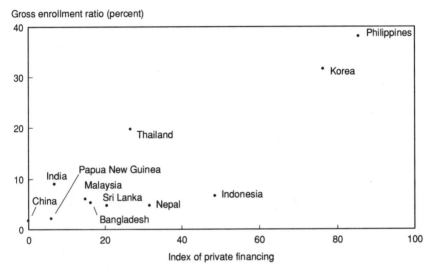

Gross enrollment ratio (percent)

Source: See appendix table C.3.

However, few countries in Asia have well-developed student loan schemes, and it is possible that the overall expansion of education opportunities resulting from an increase in private financing would also bring greater social selectivity in the system. In the absence of loan schemes, only students with access to private funds can enter the system, because most commercial banks do not accept future earnings as collateral for loans. Evidence on this possible adverse outcome is scarce, however, so an in-depth assessment of the problem is not made here.

Social selectivity

Equity in an education system is affected not only by the system's aggregate structure, but also by differences among population subgroups in access to education within that structure. Two systems might have identical distributions of cumulative public spending on education, but one is less equitable than the other if its best-educated graduates come largely from the more advantaged groups in society. In assessing social selectivity in the education system, subgroups in the population can be defined according to such criteria as sex, geographic origin, income and occupation of students' parents, and so on. Because each definition yields insights into different facets of selectivity, the analysis should ideally segregate the population in as many ways as feasible. But in practice the requisite data are often lacking. An added problem in this study is the scarcity of data that are comparable across countries.

Because of the data gaps, this discussion addresses only some aspects of social selectivity in Asian education. The study compares Asia to other world regions in distribution of cumulative public spending on education by socioeconomic group; it evaluates differences in females' access to schooling among Asian countries; and it assesses selectivity in the education systems of India, the Philippines, and Thailand, as reflected by differences in access among urban and rural populations, and among people of different social backgrounds.

Distribution of public spending on education by socioeconomic group

Distribution of benefits[17] among socioeconomic groups depends on differences in access to education. Although the aggregate data hide wide variation among countries in each region, they nonetheless give a broad picture of regional conditions (table 5.7). A bias exists in access to a level of education if a group's share in the school population exceeds its share in the reference population. This comparison is simplified by using an index of bias—the ratio between the school and reference population shares at each level of education. A value below 1 means a group is under-represented, and a value above 1, the opposite.

In Asia selectivity in access to education echoes the pattern for all developing countries: it is biased toward the children of white collar parents at all levels, but especially in higher education. There are some subtle regional similarities. In both Asia and Latin America access to secondary education improves substantially for children from blue and white collar backgrounds at the expense of farmers' children. The probability of entry to education for children of the blue and white collar groups is 3 and 7 times as high as that for the farmer group.[18] In higher education, the discrepancy remains around 3 to 4 times for the blue collar group, but it climbs to more than 10 times for the white collar group.[19]

Given the bias in access, farmers' children will clearly be less well educated than their peers from other social backgrounds. As a result, they benefit less from public spending on education. Their share of cumulative resources can be estimated using the same method discussed earlier in this chapter. The results appear in table 5.8 (first three columns). Comparing this distribution to that of the reference population reveals the extent of bias against farmers in the allocation of cumulative public spending on education (columns 4-6). In Asia, farmers' share of these resources is much less than their population share, while the opposite is true for the white collar group, the ratio between the resource and population shares being respectively 0.59 and 2.79 for the two groups. This pattern in fact is typical of most developing countries. However, if the outcome in developed countries is any guide, there is probably some scope for reducing the degree of social bias in the distribution of public spending on education.

Table 5.7 Composition of school and reference populations by socioeconomic groups, major world regions, 1980s

(percent)

Region	School population at each level (percentage of total)			Reference population[b]	School population as ratio of reference population[a]		
	Pri-mary	Secon-dary	Higher		Pri-mary	Secon-dary	Higher
Asia	100	100	100	100			
Farmers	53	25	19	58	0.91	0.43	0.33
Blue collar	34	43	38	32	1.06	1.34	1.19
White collar	13	32	43	10	1.30	3.20	4.30
Anglophone Africa	100	100	100	100			
Farmers	74	36	39	76	0.97	0.47	0.51
Blue collar	18	29	21	18	1.00	1.61	1.17
White collar	8	35	40	6	1.33	5.83	6.67
Francophone Africa	100	100	100	100			
Farmers	61	36	39	76	0.80	0.47	0.51
Blue collar	26	27	21	18	1.44	1.50	1.17
White collar	13	32	43	6	2.17	5.33	7.17
Latin America	100	100	100	100			
Farmers	31	12	10	36	0.86	0.33	0.28
Blue collar	52	54	45	49	1.06	1.10	0.92
White collar	17	34	45	15	1.13	2.27	3.00
Middle East and North Africa	100	100	100	100			
Farmers	33	15	22	42	0.79	0.36	0.52
Blue collar	43	57	31	48	0.90	1.19	0.65
White collar	12	28	47	10	1.20	2.80	4.70
OECD countries	100	100	100	100			
Farmers	12	11	11	12	1.00	0.92	0.92
Blue collar	53	45	32	53	1.00	0.85	0.60
White collar	35	44	57	35	1.00	1.26	1.63

Note: Socioeconomic groups in the school and reference populations are defined according to the occupation of students' fathers. For each region, the column figures add up to 100 percent.

a. Derived by dividing the first three columns respectively by the fourth column.

b. The reference population refers to the population of parents with school-age children.

Source: Mingat and Tan (1986).

Sex differences in access to education

In all Asian countries, the share of females in total enrollments at the three levels of education improved significantly from 1970-85 (table 5.9). For the most part, females' share in the education system seems positively linked to a country's level of economic development (figures 5.11 to 5.13). In primary education, this relationship levels off above a per capita GNP of US$500, signifying that the male-female gap in enrollment shares vanishes at about this point. In secondary education, the graph levels off as the per capita GNP rises to around US$700. In higher education, the female share in enrollment rises continuously over the range of per capita GNP represented in the sample.

Table 5.8 Distribution of cumulative public spending on education by socioeconomic group, major world regions, 1980s

Region	Farmers	Share of cumulative spending relative to share of population		Index of bias[a]	
		Blue collar	White collar	Blue collar	White collar
Asia	0.59	1.19	2.79	2.0	4.8
Anglophone Africa	0.74	1.19	3.78	1.6	5.2
Francophone Africa	0.58	1.15	5.93	2.0	10.3
Latin America	0.49	1.04	2.03	2.1	4.3
Middle East and North Africa	0.60	0.35	2.87	1.6	4.8
OECD countries	0.95	0.87	1.20	0.9	1.3

a. This index is calculated by dividing the figures in the preceding two columns by the corresponding figures for the farmer group. The larger this index public, the more public spending on education is concentrated in that group relative to the share by the farmer group.
Source: Mingat and Tan (1986).

Table 5.9 Female enrollment by level of education, selected Asian countries, selected years, 1970-85

(percent)

Country	Primary		Secondary		Higher	
	1970	1985	1970	1985	1970	1985
Bangladesh	32	40	..	28	10	19
Bhutan	5	34	3	18	..	17
China	..	45	..	40	..	30
India	37	40	28	34	22	29
Indonesia	46	48	34	43	25	32
Korea	48	49	38	47	24	30
Lao PDR	37	45	27	41	19	36
Malaysia	47	49	41	49	..	45
Myanmar	47	..	39	..	38	..
Nepal	15	29	17	23	..	20
Papua New Guinea	37	44	27	36	..	23
Philippines	..	49	..	50	56	54
Singapore	47	47	48	50	30	42
Sri Lanka	47	48	51	53	43	40
Thailand	47	48	42	48	42	46
Regional average	..	44	..	40	..	33

Source: See appendix table B1.3.

Figure 5.11 Relationship between female share of enrollment in primary education and per capita GNP, selected Asian countries, around 1985

Female share of enrollment in primary education (percent)

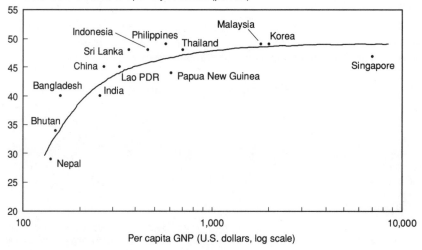

Per capita GNP (U.S. dollars, log scale)

Source: See appendix table C.3.

Figure 5.12 Relationship between female share of enrollment in secondary education and per capita GNP, selected Asian countries, around 1985

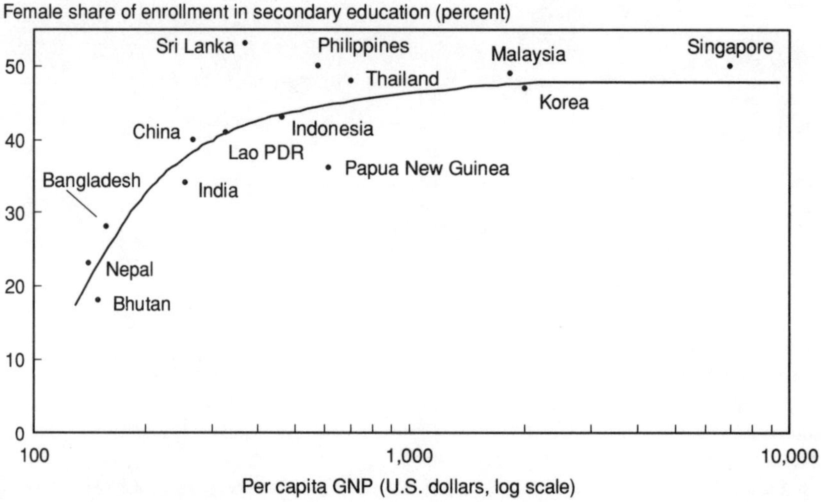

Female share of enrollment in secondary education (percent)

Per capita GNP (U.S. dollars, log scale)

Source: See appendix table C.3.

Figure 5.13 Relationship between female share of enrollment in higher education and per capita GNP, selected Asian countries, around 1985

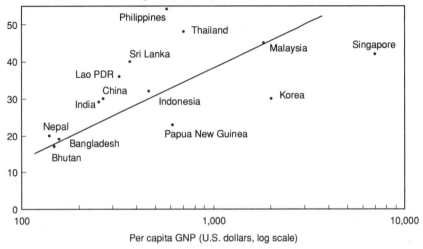

Female share of enrollment in higher education (percent)

Per capita GNP (U.S. dollars, log scale)

Source: See appendix table C.3.

Differences among countries nonetheless remain after controlling for the variation in per capita GNP, signifying that education policies can affect females' access to education. For example, the share of females in primary education is higher in Bangladesh (40 percent) than in Nepal (29 percent), even though the countries have comparable levels of per capita GNP. (A similar comparison can be made between China and India, and between Papua New Guinea and the Philippines.) At the secondary level, there is probably scope for improving females' access to schooling in Bhutan and Papua New Guinea, two countries that achieve much less than others at similar levels of economic development. The diversity among countries is especially wide in higher education. The below-average performers include Bhutan, Korea, Papua New Guinea, and Singapore. Korea's weakness in this respect (30 percent females) is striking compared with Malaysia (45 percent), a country with a somewhat lower per capita GNP. Surprisingly, Singapore also belongs to this group of poor performers.

What factors explain sex differences in access to schooling? Cultural and economic considerations account for part of the diversity among countries. But schooling conditions are probably also important. In primary education, the lower the cohort survival rates, the smaller the female share of enrollments (figure 5.14). This relationship levels off as survival rates rise above 50 percent. The implication is that when an education system's holding power is extremely weak (due, for example, to

Figure 5.14 Relationship between female share of enrollment in primary education and cohort survival rate in primary education, selected Asian countries, around 1985

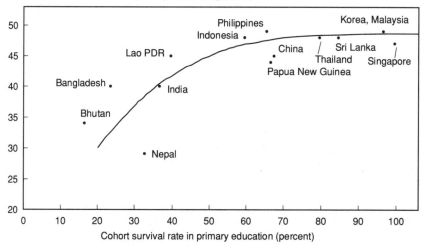

Female share of enrollment in primary education (percent)

Cohort survival rate in primary education (percent)

Note: Cohort survival rate refers to percentage of first year primary entrants surviving to end of the cycle.
Source: See appendix table C.3.

exceptionally poor quality), girls tend to suffer more than boys. Thus, aside from being a desirable pedagogical objective in itself, strengthening the retention capability of primary education is also a strategy for widening female participation at this level.[20]

In secondary education, the picture is more complicated. A plot of the cohort survival rate against the share of females reveals a random relationship (figure 5.15).[21] Selection at this level of education occurs mostly at the transition between subcycles of secondary education, usually on the basis of examination results (appendix table B2.2). One interpretation of the random pattern is that girls survive as well as boys in the competition for places within the secondary cycle. It is not a surprising result, because girls who reach secondary education represent a more select group of pupils than boys, the weakest of their cohort having exited the system at an earlier stage.

The bias against female enrollments in secondary education originates mainly in primary education. A plot of the cohort survival rate in primary education against the female share of enrollments in secondary education reveals an upward-sloping relationship that levels off as survival rates rise to about 70-80 percent (figure 5.16). This result is intuitively appealing because access to secondary education is contingent upon the completion of primary schooling. A further source of bias is that not all females who complete primary schooling continue to the next level. Data show that when the primary cohort survival rate is 30 percent, for example, the share of females is 38 percent in primary education, but only 26 percent in secondary education. The gap suggests that females have a lower rate of transition to secondary education. However, as the primary cohort survival rate rises, this gap diminishes, disappearing altogether as it reaches 80 percent.

The analysis suggests that an effective way to boost females' share of secondary enrollments is through a policy of increasing cohort survival rates in primary education. Direct interventions within secondary education are likely to be less effective, even though at first they may seem more focused and therefore more promising. Intervention at the primary level is more effective largely because it addresses the problem at its point of origin in the system.

Patterns of social selectivity in India, the Philippines, and Thailand

The following discussion illustrates the extent of bias against female enrollment in three countries at different levels of economic development.[22]

India. For this study, patterns of cohort survival rates in India by sex and urban-rural residence are based on the Fourth All-India Educational Survey[23] (table 5.10).

Figure 5.15 Relationship between female share of enrollment in secondary education and cohort survival rate in secondary education, selected Asian countries, around 1985

Female share of enrollment in secondary education (percent)

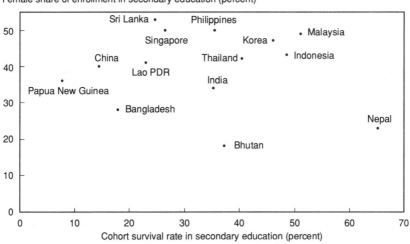

Cohort survival rate in secondary education (percent)

Note: Cohort survival rate refers to percentage of first year secondary entrants surviving to end of the cycle.
Source: See appendix table C.3.

Figure 5.16 Relationship between female share of enrollment in secondary education and cohort survival rate in primary education, selected Asian countries, around 1985

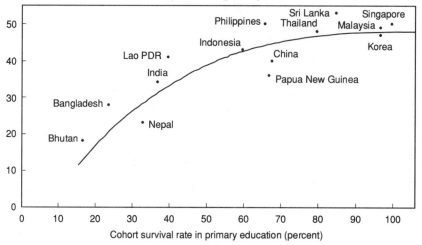

Female share of enrollment in secondary education (percent)

Note: Cohort survival rate refers to percentage of first year primary entrants surviving to end of the cycle.
Source: See appendix table C.3.

This source provides information up to grade 12, but because a significant share of students at this level are enrolled in colleges rather than in the school system, they are not captured in the survey. For this reason, this analysis concentrates on the first ten grades of the system.

On average, about a third of grade 1 entrants reach the end of the primary cycle (grade 5).[24] Girls lag slightly behind boys at this stage. By the end of middle school (grade 8), however, only 17 percent of the entering class of female first-graders remain, compared with 25 percent of males. This divergence arises because the transition rate to middle school is lower for girls than for boys, and the drop-out rate within this level of schooling is higher among girls. Beyond middle school, girls' survival rate is comparable to that of boys, so the male-female gap in survival rates remains stable up to grade 10. The bias against females is strongest in rural areas. Only 25 percent of female first-graders in rural areas reach grade 5, compared with 35 percent among rural males. By grade 10, the survival rate for rural girls is only half as high as the rate for rural males.

Further calculations based on the survey reveal the pattern of enrollment ratios by grade for boys and girls (figure 5.17).[25] To illustrate the dramatic gap between the most and least advantaged groups, only urban boys and rural girls are represented in the figure.

Table 5.10 Proportion of grade 1 entrants surviving first 10 grades of schooling, India, 1980

Population	*Percentage of grade 1 entrants surviving to various levels*		
	Grade 5	*Grade 8*	*Grade 10*
Overall population			
Boys	39.5	25.0	15.9
Girls	32.1	16.9	9.7
Both sexes	36.5	21.7	13.4
Urban population			
Boys	60.7	54.0	40.3
Girls	55.7	42.2	27.4
Both sexes	58.4	48.6	34.4
Rural population			
Boys	34.9	18.8	10.1
Girls	25.5	9.9	4.8
Both sexes	31.2	15.5	8.3

Source: Authors' estimates based on India (1985).

Figure 5.17 Net enrollment ratios by grade in overall population, and among urban boys and rural girls, India, around 1980

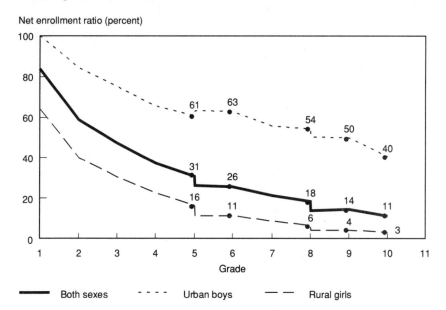

Net enrollment ratio (percent)

Both sexes — — — — Urban boys — — Rural girls

Note: Grades 1-5 form the primary cycle; 6-8, the middle cycle; and 9-10, part of the upper secondary cycle.
Source: See table 5.10.

Although this report does not analyze the reasons for the social differences in education, demand patterns reported by Caldwell and others (1985), based on a survey in south India (Karnataka), reveal that parents cite economic reasons for terminating a child's schooling 44 percent of the time, regardless of the child's sex. Weak academic performance has a weight of 55 percent among boys, but only 35 percent among girls. The onset of menarche is the other main reason for terminating a girl's education, with a weight of 20 percent. The importance of the last factor is an indication of the strength of cultural norms in affecting the demand for education. However, it is not as important as the other two factors—economic conditions and academic performance. This result suggests that policy interventions aimed at improving girls' academic performance and reducing the economic cost of schooling (including that of forgone child labor) would increase the representation of females in the education system.

The Philippines. The entry rate into primary schooling in the Philippines is nearly universal, but only 66.4 percent of entrants reach the end of the cycle (figure 5.18). Some fail to graduate and some do not enter the next cycle. So only 56.9 percent of the original cohort begin secondary education. Dropping out at the secondary level shrinks the proportion reaching the end of the cycle to 41.4 percent. Of secondary school graduates, half (corresponding to 20.7 percent of the original cohort from grade 1) enter college.[26] Those completing college education comprise 16.7 percent of the cohort of grade 1 entrants.

Figure 5.18 Cohort survival rates by grade in overall population, Philippines, around 1985

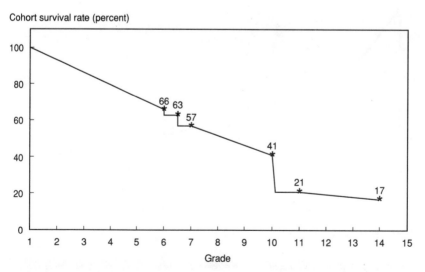

Cohort survival rate (percent)

Note: Grades 1-6 form the primary cycle; 7-10, the secondary cycle; and 11-14, the higher cycle.
Source: Mingat and Tan (1988).

To what extent does this pattern result from social selectivity in the education system? The relatively low rate of cohort survival in primary education suggests that social differentiation in the system originates at this level. And data indicate that wide disparities in cohort survival rates exist among children from different socio-economic backgrounds (table 5.11). For example, 43 percent of first-graders from families with income below P10,000 in 1982 drop out by the end of primary school-ing, compared with only 11 percent among children from families with an income exceeding P30,000. And figure 5.19 shows the differences in survival rates among groups defined according to the education attainment of pupils' fathers.

Table 5.11 Cohort survival rates in elementary education by socioeconomic groups, Philippines, 1982

Socioeconomic group	Survival rate (percent)[a]
Family income (pesos a year)	
< 10,000	57
> 30,000	89
Geographic origin	
Rural	57
Urban	80
Father's education	
No schooling	19
Elementary	51
Secondary	69
College	92
Father's occupation	
Farmer, fisherman	53
Manual worker	75
White collar worker	91

a. The cohort survival rate is defined as the proportion of entrants in grade 1 who survive to the end of a given cycle of education (here, elementary education).
Source: Mingat and Tan (1988).

The government recently implemented policies under which locally financed secondary schools were nationalized and fees for all public secondary education were abolished. These policies address widely perceived inequities in secondary education.[27] But the policies are likely to have only a limited effect on reducing overall social selectivity in the system: free secondary education benefits only those in the cohort who finish the primary cycle (63.2 percent), bypassing those who drop out in earlier grades, the majority of whom are from the poorer social classes. Increasing education opportunities for these groups calls for fresh policies aimed specifically at improving cohort survival rates in primary education.[28]

Figure 5.19 Cohort survival rates in primary education according to education attainment of pupils' fathers, Philippines, 1982

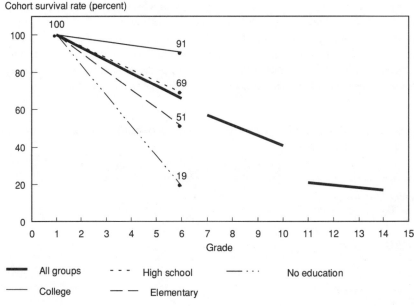

Source: Mingat and Tan (1988).

Thailand. The degree of social bias in the education system in Thailand can be assessed by comparing various socioeconomic groups' shares of enrollments to their shares in the population (table 5.12). In upper secondary education, for example, the professional group's share of enrollments is 25 percent compared with their population share of only 3 percent, for a ratio of 8.1. Farmers' share of enrollments is 20 percent compared with their population share of 69 percent, for a ratio of only 0.2. The other social groups' (business and laborer classes) access to upper secondary education also exceeds that of the farmer group, although by a smaller margin.

To render the comparison more transparent, an index of selectivity can be computed by dividing the ratio of the enrollment and population shares for each group by that for the farmer group. Results can be interpreted as the probability of entering upper secondary education for a child from a professional, business, or laborer background compared with a child from a farming background. In upper secondary education, children of professionals have a relative entry probability 27 times as high as that of farmers' children. The corresponding index for the children of businessmen and laborers is 7 and 6. For selective universities, the index for the children of professionals rises to almost 60.[29] The index for businessmen's children reaches nearly 16, while that for laborers' children remains the same as at the upper secondary level.

Because primary education is nearly universal in Thailand, differences among socioeconomic groups occur mostly in access to subsequent levels of education. It is at the transition between cycles of education that these differences arise, because intracycle selection is limited (table 4.5). Patterns in access (table 5.12) suggest that the professional and business groups continue to strengthen their advantage in the transition from upper secondary to higher education. The bias in favor of the laborer group occurs mainly at the transition from lower to upper secondary education and does not widen subsequently. Evidence suggests that some of the selectivity against farmers' children occurs as early as primary schooling—the overall cohort survival rate at this level is only 80 percent. But most of the bias against them is traceable to the transition from primary to lower secondary education—only 40 percent of primary school graduates systemwide are selected to continue.

These patterns of selection have important ramifications for policymaking to improve education opportunities for the disadvantaged. For instance, if laborers' children are the target, policy interventions should focus on widening their access to selective universities. But if the target group is farmers' children, policy interventions should occur much earlier in the system.

The foregoing data and patterns for India, the Philippines, and Thailand have significant implications for policymaking to ameliorate social selectivity in an education system. First, intra- and intercycle selection must be distinguished to locate the origin of adverse selectivity. Where the completion rate within a cycle is low, particularly at the primary level, reducing adverse social selectivity in the whole sector calls for interventions within primary education. But in systems where selection occurs mostly in between cycles of education, the issue of biases in the selection mechanism becomes much more prominent. And second, because the pattern of survival and transition can differ significantly among population groups, clarifying the intended target group is necessary for formulating appropriate interventions.

Table 5.12 Access to secondary and higher education in Thailand, 1980s

Socioeconomic group[a]	Population share (percent)	Enrollment share (percent)		Share of enrollments relative to share of population		Selectivity index (farmers = 1.0)[b]	
		Upper secondary	University	Upper secondary	University	Upper secondary	University
Professional	3.1	25.1	36.5	8.1	11.8	27.0	59.0
Business	9.0	19.1	28.0	2.1	3.1	7.0	15.5
Laborer	19.4	35.6	23.9	1.8	1.2	6.0	6.0
Farmer	68.5	20.2	11.6	0.3	0.2	1.0	1.0
All groups	100	100	100	..	..	..	..

Note: Data for open universities are not included under the "university" columns.
a. Defined according to the occupation of students' fathers.
b. Calculated from preceding two columns, dividing corresponding figure by figure for farmer group.
Source: Authors' estimates based on Thailand (1987b).

Notes

1. These studies assume that education is beneficial without specifying the nature or value of the benefits.

2. Benefits may materialize while a person is being educated or after graduation. In the first case, the benefits consist of the public resources that accrue to people who are enrolled in the system; in the second case, the benefits are higher earnings and upward social mobility.

3. Unit costs are expressed relative to per capita GNP. This statistic is valid for cross-country comparisons because it is not itself related to per capita GNP.

4. Another index for comparison is the ratio between a country's unit costs and the corresponding regional average at each level of education. But the resulting indexes would be asymmetric: for costs below the average, the indexes' possible range is zero to one; while for costs above the average, the range is one to infinity. This problem is avoided when using deviations from the mean as a basis for comparison. The regional mean excludes data for Papua New Guinea because it is an extreme outlier for cost levels.

5. The gross enrollment ratio—the most commonly available indicator of coverage—is the statistic used here. It is not a perfect measure, particularly at the primary level, because cohort survival rates vary widely, changing the meaning of the enrollment ratio in different settings. At the other two levels, cohort survival rates are high for most countries, so this problem is less applicable.

6. The results for secondary and higher education are more satisfactory than those for primary education. The t-ratios in the regressions for secondary and higher education are, on the whole, statistically significant despite the small sample size, and the substantial variation in enrollment ratios among the countries in the sample.

7. Predicted enrollment ratios are useful only as a starting point for assessing a country's future investment priorities in education. A thorough assessment would require analysis using such economic signals as wage trends, unemployment rates, rate-of-return estimates, and so on.

8. In Bangladesh and India the share of enrollments in the private sector is significant but private institutions are heavily subsidized by the government.

9. The implicit assumption in this approach is that each aspect of the bias toward higher education carries equal weight.

10. See Mingat and Tan 1985 for a fuller discussion of this approach and Mingat and Tan 1986a for its application to an analysis of the distribution of cumulative public spending by socioeconomic groups.

11. They differ from the data on overall operating unit costs in table 3.2. See footnote a of table 5.4 for details on the calculation of public subsidies per student in the system. The share of public subsidies received by people with the same exit level of education will differ according to the type of institutions they attended. But in the global analysis here, this distinction is not taken into account.

12. See appendix table B1.1 for data on the length of education cycles in Asian countries.

13. This and subsequent calculations implicitly assume that dropping out does not affect comparisons across countries, even though the actual profile of future adults' education attainment in each country will be influenced by it.

14. An easy way to compute the area of ABCDE is to subtract from the area of triangle ED'D, the areas of AB'B, BB'C'C, and CC'D'D. The mathematical formula for the area of a triangle is (0.5 x Base x Height); the area of a trapezoid is (0.5 x Sum of parallel sides x Distance between them).

15. It is important to control for this variable in the regressions to avoid a spurious link between the extent of private financing and the share of primary education in total public spending. With private financing in higher education, government spending on this level of education is likely to be smaller, leading to a lower level of overall spending on education. The spurious link arises because the relationship reflects mostly the impact of a smaller denominator.

16. The index is a composite variable derived by weighting the distribution of enrollments between public and private institutions by the corresponding rates of cost recovery in each sector.

17. As before, "benefits" refers to the cumulative public spending that is appropriated to a generation of people through publicly financed education.

18. In Asia, for example, the chance of entering secondary education for the blue collar group is 3.1 times (=1.34/.43) that for the farmer group.

19. These results have important implications for the design of policies to improve equity in the system. For instance, if the objective is to expand access to higher education for the farmer group (usually the most disadvantaged), intervention must begin at an earlier cycle of education. But if the target group is children from blue collar backgrounds, intervention can begin at the level of higher education.

20. In Nepal the share of females in primary enrollments is smaller than it is in countries with similar cohort survival rates (figure 5.8). One possible interpretation is that there is an especially strong cultural or economic bias against female education.

21. The survival rate in this figure is the proportion of first-year entrants to secondary education who reach the end of the entire secondary cycle. The data are based on appendix table B2.2.

22. The choice of these countries is determined largely by the availability of readily accessible data.

23. A fifth survey has been completed recently, but no published data are as yet available. It would be interesting to examine changes in survival rates between the two surveys. But because selectivity in an education system tends to evolve only slowly over time, it is unlikely that the more recent survey will reveal dramatic changes, particularly because the gross enrollment ratio in primary education rose only slightly between 1980 and 1985, from 81 to 92 percent.

24. The figures in table 5.11 differ slightly from those in table 4.5 because they come from different sources.

25. The grade 1 enrollment ratios for urban boys and rural girls are estimated on the basis of data on enrollments by sex and grade, assuming that all boys enter grade 1. The enrollment ratios at subsequent grades are derived simply by multiplying the result by the corresponding cohort survival rate.

26. The entrance to college is governed by the National College Entrance Examination. The passing mark is generally set at the 50th percentile of the distribution of scores.

27. See Mingat and Tan 1988 for a more detailed discussion of these inequities in secondary education.

28. This concern will be addressed partly through a World Bank loan now being prepared. However, designing interventions that are applicable on a countrywide scale would require using survey data to analyze the causes of dropping out.

29. Selective universities (which include both public and private institutions) differ from unselective open universities because they apply stricter entry criteria. The competition for places is usually very keen because they are more prestigious; in addition, the public selective universities are heavily subsidized by the government.

6

Synthesis of Findings and Conclusions

This chapter consolidates study findings about the strengths and weaknesses of education systems in Asian countries, and about the relationships between policy variables and education outcomes[1]; it summarizes the principal challenges facing the education sector across countries; and it identifies priorities for future analytical work.

Strengths and weaknesses of education systems

The status of education across countries can be compared by looking at systems' (1) overall development; (2) constraints on and prospects for evolution; (3) operational and student-flow characteristics; (4) structure of unit costs and relative costliness; and (5) financing and institutional arrangements.

Development of the education system

Data on adult literacy rates, a statistic that reflects the cumulative impact of past investments in education, show that countries vary widely around a regional mean of 65 percent (table 6.1).[2] In Korea, the Philippines, Singapore, Sri Lanka, and Thailand, most adults are literate. At the other extreme are such countries as Bangladesh, Bhutan, and Nepal, where only one-third or fewer of the current adult population is literate. The remaining countries have moderate rates of adult literacy, ranging from 43 percent in India to 84 percent in Lao PDR.

In countries where there is still room for improvement in literacy, progress depends on current investments in education, particularly at the primary level. Two factors are relevant: coverage in primary education and the ability to retain pupils long enough to impart permanent literacy.[3] Assessment based on these factors suggests that prospects for achieving universal adult literacy among the next generation of adults are particularly bleak in Bangladesh, Bhutan, and Nepal, and particularly good in Malaysia. In China, India, Indonesia, and Papua New Guinea, progress toward universal adult literacy is likely to be made, but will depend on the right choices in sectoral policies, particularly those affecting the development of primary education.

The current level of public spending on education is an indicator of a country's overall fiscal effort to invest in human capital and of intersectoral priorities in the allocation of public funds.[4] On average, government spending on education, expressed as a percentage of GNP, is somewhat lower in Asia than in other developing regions of the world: 3.3 percent compared with 4.0 percent in Africa, 3.5 percent in Latin America, and 5.3 percent in the Middle East (table 6.1). However, there is wide variation among countries: the size of spending is particularly low in Bangladesh (1.5 percent) and in Nepal and the Philippines (1.8 percent); it is particularly high in Malaysia (6.0 percent) and Papua New Guinea (6.9 percent).

Data for Asian countries reveal very different outcomes at comparable levels of fiscal effort, or, conversely, very similar outcomes with quite different levels of effort. For example, although public spending on education in Bangladesh is comparable to the spending level in the Philippines, coverage in Bangladesh is much smaller; in Korea and Malaysia coverage is comparable, but public spending is much smaller in the former country—3.4 percent of GNP compared with Malaysia's figure of 6.0 percent. These patterns support the finding that other considerations besides aggregate spending—for example, the efficiency with which the education system operates—also affect education outcomes.

Finally, consider the structure of coverage as indicated by the gross enrollment ratio. For most Asian countries, this statistic for primary education in 1985 exceeds, or approaches, 100 percent (table 6.1). The exceptions are Bangladesh, Bhutan, Nepal, and Papua New Guinea, where despite past growth, coverage still lags behind the rest of the region. Bhutan belongs in its own category, however, with a gross enrollment ratio of only 25 percent, compared with the range of 60-82 percent in the other three countries. The expansion of coverage in the fifteen years before 1985 was particularly remarkable at the post-primary levels; on average, the ratio for secondary education jumped from 26 percent in 1970 to 42 percent in 1985; and in higher education, it grew from 5 to 10 percent in the same period. The variance among countries widens with rising levels of education.

The structure of coverage in the education system can be summarized by the average grade attainment of the current school-age population. This statistic projects the education status of the next generation of adults based on current patterns of enrollment across the three levels of education and on cohort survival. This indicator ranges widely, from 1.4 years in Bhutan, to 11.4 years in Korea. Part of the variation reflects differences in level of economic development, because wealthier countries tend, on average, to have better developed systems of education. However, Sri Lanka has a per capita GNP comparable to that of Lao PDR, but its average grade attainment is nearly twice as high, 9.5 years compared with 4.8; similarly, the Philippines'

Table 6.1 Indicators of overall education development, selected Asian countries, mid-1980s

Country	Per capita GNP 1985 (US$)	Literate adults (percent)	Public spending on education[a]		Gross enrollment ratio (percent)			Average grade attainment[c]
			In budget (percent)	In GNP (percent)	Primary	Secondary	Higher[b]	
Bangladesh	159	33	10.3	1.5	60	18	5.2	3.9
Bhutan	151	15	7.3	3.8	25	4	0.1	1.4
China	273	69	7.8	3.3	118	39	1.7	5.1
India	259	43	13.7	3.0	92	41	9.0	4.8
Indonesia	470	74	15.0	3.7	118	42	6.5	7.3
Korea	2,040	92	16.6	3.4	96	75	31.6	11.4
Lao PDR	332	44	..	..	94	19	1.5	4.8
Malaysia	1,860	74	16.0	6.0	99	53	6.0 (9.0)	9.2
Myanmar	184	..	10.9	1.8	107	23	5.4	7.0
Nepal	142	26	9.6	1.8	82	25	4.6	3.6
Papua New Guinea	621	45	17.9	6.9	70	13	2.0	4.3
Philippines	581	86	11.5	1.8	106	65	38.0	10.2
Singapore	7,093	86	..	..	115	71	11.8	9.9
Sri Lanka	374	87	8.1	2.8	103	63	4.6 (5.1)	9.5
Thailand	712	91	19.4	3.6	97	30	19.6	7.0
Regional average	1,017	65	12.6	3.3	92	39	9.8	6.6

a. See appendix B for discussion of the coverage of this indicator.
b. Data in parentheses refer to the enrollment ratio if nationals studying abroad are included in the numerator.
c. Variable refers to the average educational status that the current school-age population is likely to attain given the current structure of the enrollment pyramid and the pattern of cohort survival in the system. The figure for Myanmar is not strictly comparable to those for other countries as it is based only on the enrollment structure. It is excluded in calculating the regional average.
Source: Data on per capita GNP are from World Bank (1988); other data are from sources cited in appendix B.

per capita GNP is comparable to Papua New Guinea's, but its grade attainment is significantly higher, 10.2 years compared with 4.3.

To standardize more systematically for differences in countries' wealth, a comparison is made of actual enrollment ratios with the ratios predicted on the basis of per capita GNP. (See chapter 5 for details of the analysis.) In Bhutan and Papua New Guinea, the education system's coverage is below expectations at all levels. Malaysia fits in this category to some extent, particularly in view of the pronounced gap between the predicted and actual rates in higher education.

In a second group, consisting of India and the Philippines, the actual ratios exceed those predicted at all levels of education. Korea also belongs in this category even though its primary enrollment ratio is smaller than the predicted value. This shortfall stems from the country's exceptionally high rate of retention in primary education. India's actual coverage in primary education is probably less widespread than this comparison indicates because the corresponding cohort survival rate is relatively low.

In a third group of countries, comprising Myanmar and Nepal, coverage at all three levels is more or less consistent with the country's per capita GNP. Finally, in the remaining countries, the actual ratio is greater than the predicted ratio at some levels, and smaller at others. However, the pattern and magnitude of imbalance differs among countries in this group. For example, Indonesia and Sri Lanka share China's pattern of imbalance, but the difference between their actual and predicted ratios is much smaller. Thailand's pattern is comparable to Sri Lanka's, but the bottleneck in coverage appears at the transition from primary to secondary education rather than from secondary to higher education.

Constraints and prospects

Overall constraints on education development are determined largely by two factors: demographic pressures and macroeconomic conditions (table 6.2). Other variables— such as the aggregate level of public spending on education, and the organization and financing arrangements of the education system—are also important, but they reflect policy choices in education rather than exogenous conditions, particularly in a longer term perspective.

An indicator of demographic pressures—the dependency ratio—looks at the ratio between the school-age population and the adult population. It reveals the fiscal obligation of adults (which they may or may not discharge) for the education of young people in the population. There are large differences across countries for this indicator: in 1985, it ranged from a low of 31 percent in Korea, to a high of 53 percent in Lao PDR. The difference is significant: if Korea had had Lao PDR's dependency ratio, other things being equal, Korea would have had to spend 70 percent more than it did in 1985 to achieve its education system's actual coverage in that year.

Table 6.2 Constraints and prospects for education development, selected Asian countries, 1970–2000

| Country | Projected rate of growth[a] | | | School-age population as percentage of adult population[b] | | | |
	Population age 5–14	GNP in real terms	Difference	1970	1985	2000	Percentage change 1985-2000
Bangladesh	2.0	4.9	2.9	55	49	42	-14
Bhutan	3.0	..	..	46	44	47	7
China	0.4	6.6	6.2	44	33	26	-21
India	1.3	4.8	3.5	49	44	35	-20
Indonesia	1.0	3.9	2.9	50	46	35	-24
Korea	0.3	6.8	6.5	52	31	24	-23
Lao PDR	..	..	..	45	53	49	-8
Malaysia	1.4	5.0	3.6	56	41	33	-20
Myanmar	1.0	3.5	2.5	44	47	35	-26
Nepal	3.1	3.8	0.7	46	49	51	4
Papua New Guinea	2.0	5.1	3.1	47	50	40	-20
Philippines	1.5	5.3	3.8	53	47	37	-21
Sri Lanka	1.1	4.8	3.7	49	36	31	-14
Thailand	0.5	6.0	5.5	56	41	29	-29
Regional average	1.4	5.0	3.6	49	44	37	-16

a. In percent a year for the periods 1985-2000 for population and 1990-2000 for GNP. Figures in the third column refer to the difference in growth rates between the GNP and the population age 5-14.
b. For the present purposes, the school-age population comprises children age 5-14; the adult population, people age 15-65.
Source: See appendix table B3.1.

The dependency ratio is projected to decline over time for most Asian countries, following a trend from the 1970s. On average, it is forecast to drop from 44 percent in 1985 to 37 percent by 2000. Assuming constancy in other variables, this decline implies a drop of 16 percent in each adult's fiscal obligation for public financing of education. However, the prospects are brighter in some countries than in others: the ratio is expected to drop by as much as 29 percent in Thailand and 26 percent in Myanmar, but it is projected to rise by 4 percent in Nepal and 7 percent in Bhutan.

A related indicator of demographic pressures on education development is the growth rate of the school-age population. It has the advantage of direct comparability with the rate of economic growth, and thus permits a contrast to be drawn between the future demand for education resources and the potential availability of those resources. For Asia as a whole, the school-age population is projected to grow slowly over the next decade, at about 1.4 percent a year. Because the GNP is expected to grow at roughly 5.0 percent a year, there is potentially a 3.6 percent a year growth in resources over the next decade for expanding or upgrading the education system, or both.[5] So for the region as a whole, the prospects for the sector are quite favorable. In

China, Korea, and Thailand the prospects are particularly bright because the difference between the population and economic growth rates is at least 5.5 percent a year. Bangladesh, Indonesia, and Myanmar are in a less favorable position, with a gap of less than 3 percent a year. In Nepal the prospects for expanding or upgrading education appear quite bleak because the economy is forecast to grow only marginally faster than the school-age population.

Operation of the education system

The formation of human capital through education depends, among other things, on entry rates into the system and on pupils' subsequent schooling careers. Differences in entry rates among Asian countries are relatively small. Most countries have achieved, or are close to achieving, universal entry in grade 1. There remains room for improvement in a few countries, however, notably in Bhutan, Papua New Guinea, Nepal and, to a lesser extent, in China and India (table 6.3).

For subsequent schooling careers of entrants to the education system, the variance among Asian countries is greater. This is reflected in the patterns of cohort survival within each cycle of education. For the region as a whole, with more than one-third of grade 1 entrants failing to reach the end of the primary cycle, low survival rates in primary education are an important issue. The wide variation around this average suggests three groupings of countries. In one group comprising Korea, Malaysia, Singapore, Sri Lanka, and Thailand, noncompletion is no longer a major problem. At the other extreme are such countries as Bangladesh, Bhutan, India, and Nepal, where two-thirds or more of all first graders drop out before the end of primary schooling. In these countries, reducing drop-out rates is a clear priority for public policy. In a third group of countries, including China, Indonesia, Lao PDR, Papua New Guinea, and the Philippines, cohort survival rates are higher, but are nonetheless still significantly below 100 percent. As with the previous group of countries, improving the system's retention capability deserves emphasis in sectoral policy.

In secondary education, cohort survival rates are generally higher than at the primary level. In the lower secondary cycle, however, the incidence of dropping out remains significant in Bangladesh, Lao PDR, Papua New Guinea and, to a lesser extent, in China, India, the Philippines, and Sri Lanka. In upper secondary education, the problem is largely absent in all Asian countries.

Assessment of the primary and secondary cycles together can point up the degree of intercycle selection relative to selection that takes place through dropping out within cycles of education. Intercycle selection is the more desirable and efficient process because it maximizes a student's exposure to the full curriculum in a particular cycle, improving the student's chances of acquiring the intended skills. This is particularly relevant in primary education where the pedagogical objectives have to do with the fundamental building blocks of learning—basic literacy and numeracy.

Table 6.3 Operational characteristics of education systems, selected Asian countries, early to mid-1980s

Country	Percentage of population entering grade 1[a]	Percentage of first year entrants surviving to last year in cycle[b]			Index of extent of intercycle selection[c]	Percentage of females in total enrollments		
		Primary	Lower secondary	Upper secondary		Primary	Secondary	Higher
Bangladesh	100	24	48	80	8	40	28	19
Bhutan	54	17	83	88	13	34	18	17
China	90	68	76	81	54	45	40	30
India	83	37	72	65	15	40	34	29
Indonesia	100	60	92	96	46	48	43	32
Korea	100	97	98	95	87	49	47	30
Lao PDR	100	40	65	68	21	45	41	36
Malaysia	100	97	90	96	79	49	49	45
Nepal	75	33	89	81	5	29	23	20
Papua New Guinea	74	67	63	95	57	44	36	23
Philippines	100	66	74	..	18	49	50	54
Singapore	100	100	100	97	99	47	50	42
Sri Lanka	100	85	75	100	58	48	53	40
Thailand	100	80	91	87	72	48	48	46
Regional average	91	62	80	87	45	44	40	33

a. Note possible overestimation of entry rate for Bangladesh discussed in appendix table B2.2.
b. The denominator in each column is the number of entrants to the corresponding cycle. See appendix table B1.1 for data on number of years in each cycle or subcycle. See appendix table B2.2 for note on possible recent rise in primary cohort survival rates in Indonesia.
c. See table 4.6 for the definition of this index. Note that the larger the index, the more efficient the selection process in the education system.
Source: See appendix B.

The index of intercycle selection—a measure of the relative importance of selection between cycles through the end of secondary education—ranges from zero, where all selection takes place through the process of dropping out, to 100, where all selection occurs between cycles of education (table 6.3). The larger the index is, the more efficient the selection process. For the region as a whole, the index has a value of only 45, confirming that dropping out is a significant regional issue. The problem is particularly serious in Bangladesh, Bhutan, India, Lao PDR, Nepal, and the Philippines, where dropping out is the principal instrument (although an implicit one) that regulates the flow of students in the education system.

In recent years attention has focused on the education system's ability to attract and retain females. In Asia the share of females in total enrollments declines with rising levels of education, from 44 percent in primary education, to 40 percent in secondary education, to 33 percent in higher education. The last figure suggests that, on average, an Asian male's chances of entering higher education are more than twice as high as those of a female.

Countries vary widely in the overall share of females in the system and in the pattern of access across levels of education. At all levels, females tend to fare badly in low-income countries, including Bangladesh, Bhutan, Nepal, Papua New Guinea and, to a lesser extent, India. In such countries as Indonesia, Korea, and Sri Lanka, females are relatively well represented at the primary and secondary levels, but their share of enrollments in higher education is significantly smaller than that of males. This pattern suggests the presence of a strong sex bias in access to higher education. In Malaysia, the Philippines, and Thailand, sex differences are limited or absent throughout the education system.

Education costs and their sources of differences

Expressed as a percentage of per capita GNP, the unit costs of public education in Asian countries are, on average, comparable to those in other world regions except Africa (table 6.4).[6] In primary education, unit costs are estimated at 10 percent of per capita GNP, compared with 12 percent for the Middle East and 9 percent for Latin America. In secondary education, unit costs are 19 percent for Asia, which compares favorably with the average of 28 percent for the Middle East and 26 percent for Latin America. In higher education, Asia's figure of 149 percent is comparable to the 150 percent for the Middle East, but is substantially larger than Latin America's average of 88 percent.

Within Asia, however, the range in unit costs is very wide (even if the extreme case of Papua New Guinea were disregarded)[7]:

• In primary education, unit costs are lowest in Bangladesh, India, the Philippines, and Sri Lanka, and highest in Korea, Malaysia, and Thailand. The difference between these two groups is substantial, with unit costs in the second group being, on average, more than twice those in the first group.

Table 6.4 Patterns of education costs and their sources of differences, selected Asian countries, mid-1980s

Country	Unit operating costs of public education (percentage of per capita GNP)[a]			Unit costs as a percentage of the regional average[b]				Average teachers' pay (ratio per capita GNP)		Pupils per teacher	
	Primary	Secondary	Higher	Primary	Secondary	Higher	Overall	Primary	Secondary	Primary	Secondary
Bangladesh	6	30	285	65	191	191	139	2.2	..	47	26
China	7	23	199	68	122	134	108	1.6	2.8	25	17
India	6	17	231	61	94	155	103	2.9	3.1	58	20
Indonesia	13	23	91	128	126	61	105	2.5	3.2	25	15
Korea	17	23	71	167	127	47	114	5.0	5.5	38	34
Malaysia	14	21	190	143	115	128	129	2.4	3.1	24	22
Nepal	9	14	249	91	73	167	111	2.8	5.0	36	28
Papua New Guinea	29	65	1,050	294	352	705	450	6.8	10.0	31	25
Philippines	6	9	50	59	47	34	46	1.6	1.7	31	32
Sri Lanka	6	9	83	62	50	56	56	1.6	2.1	32	26
Thailand	16	15	40	157	83	27	89	2.5	2.9	19	20
Regional average											
Without Papua New Guinea	10	19	149	100	100	100	100	2.5	3.3	33	24
With Papua New Guinea	12	23	231	..	..	..	..	2.9	3.9	33	24

a. The unit costs of higher education reflect the average for public regular institutions and distance education, weighted by their respective share of enrollments.
b. The figures under the "overall" column are the simple averages of the previous three columns.
Source: See appendix B.

112

• In secondary education, differences across countries are even wider. Unit costs remain relatively low in the Philippines and Sri Lanka, but the ranking among the remaining countries is quite different from that at the primary level. For example, Thailand's unit costs are 20 percent below the regional average, while those of Bangladesh exceed the regional average by more than 40 percent.

• In higher education, the overall level of unit costs depends on the distribution of enrollments across delivery systems, particularly between conventional and distance education. Since costs are dramatically lower for distance education, it follows that the greater its share of enrollments, the smaller the overall unit costs of public higher education.[8] The data indicate that costs are relatively high in Bangladesh, China, India, Nepal and, to a lesser extent, Malaysia, and relatively low—only one-third as high—in Indonesia, Korea, the Philippines, Sri Lanka, and Thailand.

To a large extent, variation in unit costs can be traced to differences in policy choices affecting the organization of the education system and the use of schooling inputs. In primary and secondary education, the main determinants of costs are teachers' pay and pupil-teacher ratios. In the Philippines and Sri Lanka, low costs are due mainly to the relatively low rate of teacher remuneration—the other variable, pupil-teacher ratio, is close to the regional average. In India, the main factor is the high pupil-teacher ratio (58 compared with the regional average of 33)—teachers' pay is comparable to the average for the region (2.9 times per capita GNP compared with 2.6 times).

A comparison between Korea and Thailand illustrates differences in choices in the use of schooling inputs. Both countries have relatively high unit costs in primary education, but for very different reasons. Thailand's education system is the more teacher-intensive, with an average pupil-teacher ratio only half as high as Korea's. But Korean teachers are paid at about twice the rate for Thai teachers (whose pay is close to the regional average). These factors balance each other, and the result is comparable unit costs in both countries. Thus, even within a similar resource constraint, there is a range of options for using those resources. The data for secondary education suggests a similar conclusion.[9]

An assessment of overall costliness of education across countries can be made using the average of the cost indexes at the three levels of education. Leaving aside Papua New Guinea (an extreme outlier), the index for the other countries varies markedly, from 45 percent of the regional average, to 136 percent. Public education is relatively low-cost in the Philippines, Sri Lanka, and Thailand, and relatively high-cost in Bangladesh, China, and Malaysia. In India, Indonesia, Korea, and Nepal, the index is close to the regional average.

Comparing patterns of costliness across levels of education reveals wide variation among countries. In one group—Bangladesh, China, India, and Papua New Guinea—deviations from the mean increase rapidly with rising levels of education, indicating a definite bias in costliness toward the higher levels. Nepal shares this pattern, although the bias is more moderate because secondary education is less resource-intensive than primary education. In Sri Lanka, there is balance in the structure of costliness across the three levels of education. In the Philippines and Malaysia, the pattern is one of moderate bias in favor of primary education; and in Indonesia, Korea, and Thailand, the bias in favor of primary education is even stronger.

Financing and institutional arrangements

In most Asian countries, both the provision and the financing of primary education is largely a public undertaking. For this reason, data on the private share of enrollments and the rate of cost recovery in primary education are not presented in table 6.5.

At the secondary level, private schools enroll, on average, 26 percent of all students, comparable to the share of 29 percent in Latin American countries. But variation among countries is very wide: countries such as Bhutan, China, Malaysia, Myanmar, Nepal, and Sri Lanka rely little on the private sector; others, such as Indonesia, Korea, and the Philippines, depend heavily on the private sector. The private share of enrollments in Bangladesh and India is exceptionally high, but most private schools are heavily subsidized by the government and are private mainly in their management.

The institutional composition is more diverse in higher education, with at least four alternatives: private institutions, conventional public institutions, distance education, and overseas studies. Conventional public colleges and universities enroll the largest share of students, but that share amounts, on average, to only 51 percent. Private institutions account for 28 percent of enrollments, distance education for 17 percent, and overseas studies for 4 percent. These averages mask significant differences among countries. In the group that relies mostly on public sector provision (China, Malaysia, Nepal, Papua New Guinea, and Sri Lanka), two have developed a sizable distance system (China and Sri Lanka) and the rest have adopted other strategies to satisfy excess demand for higher education—private institutions in Nepal and foreign institutions in Malaysia. And some countries place only limited reliance on regular public institutions, including Korea and the Philippines, which have a sizable private sector, and Thailand, which has a particularly large system of distance education consisting of two open universities.

Financing arrangements for education also vary significantly across countries. The rate of cost recovery (fees as a share of unit operating costs) for public higher education is minimal in Bangladesh, India, Malaysia, Papua New Guinea, Sri Lanka, and Thailand. In contrast, cost recovery is substantial in Korea, and moderately high in Indonesia and the Philippines. In many countries, the rate of cost recovery in secondary education exceeds the rate in higher education, a pattern that contradicts what might be expected on grounds of equity.

The extent of private financing in the sector as a whole depends on the rate of cost recovery across the various types of institutions. The required data are scanty, however, and have been pieced together only for higher education.[10] An index of private financing is constructed by weighting the rate of cost recovery in public higher education, private higher education, and distance education by the corresponding enrollment shares (table 6.5). The index of private financing distinguishes four groups of countries: China, India, and Papua New Guinea, with extremely limited private financing; Indonesia, Korea, and the Philippines, with a high level of private financing; Nepal, Sri Lanka, and Thailand with a moderate amount of private financing; and Bangladesh and Malaysia, with a somewhat below average rate of private financing.[11]

Finally, to assess the effect on equity of current financing arrangements, we start from the premise that people benefit from public spending as long as they remain in the education system; that those benefits accumulate over time; and that benefits are largest for people with the longest schooling careers. So the focus is on the distribution of cumulative benefits, rather than on single period benefits at a given level of education.

Two indexes—the Gini-coefficient and the share of cumulative spending received by the 10 percent best-educated people in a generation—were constructed using data on enrollment ratios, unit costs, and rate of private financing across the three levels of education. The ranking of countries is similar whichever index is used. For Asia as a whole, the top 10 percent (by education) in a cohort receive 36 percent of cumulative government spending on education. In Indonesia, Korea, the Philippines, and Thailand the distribution is much more equitable than is average for the region. In contrast, public spending on education in Bangladesh, India, Nepal, and Papua New Guinea is concentrated in the hands of the lucky few who survive longest in the system. In Bangladesh, for example, the top 10 percent receive an astonishing 72 percent of cumulative government spending on education.

Public spending appears to be more equitably distributed in countries with significant levels of private financing in higher education, such as Indonesia, Korea, and the Philippines. This finding casts some doubt on the commonly cited argument that private financing in education affects equity adversely, and suggests that private financing in higher education may increase equity.

Variables, outcomes, and policy implications

Beyond the simple statistical description summarized above, some lessons about education policies also emerge from the study, stemming from the relationships (or lack thereof) among indicators of education outcomes and policy regimes across countries.[12]

Correlates of overall education development

Regression analysis indicates that although demographic pressures have a negative effect on education development (as proxied by the average grade attainment of the current school-age population), a country's wealth and its overall level of public

Table 6.5 Indicators of financing and institutional arrangements in education, selected Asian countries, mid-1980s

Country	Secondary (percentage of private)	Percentage of enrollments by type of institution[a]				Fees in public education		Index of private financing in higher education[c]	Distribution of public spending on education[d]	
		Higher education								Share of 10 percent best-educated
		Private	Regular public	Distance	Overseas	Secondary	Higher regular		Gini-index	
Bangladesh	93	58	41	1	1	4	0	17	85	76
Bhutan	..	0	96	0	4	..	..	..	..	..
China	0	0	69	30	1	3	0	0	41	29
India	67[b]	57	37	5	1	12	5	7	66	61
Indonesia	50	58	33	9	1	27	19	49	27	21
Korea	40	65	21	12	2	34	46	77	16	13
Malaysia	2	8	61	1	31	4	6	15	38	32
Myanmar	..	0	54	45	0	..	..	..	..	..
Nepal	10	23	73	1	2	41	10	32	57	52
Papua New Guinea	..	6	83	9	3	40	0	6	62	55
Philippines	42	83	17	0	0	9	15	86	19	14
Sri Lanka	2	0	62	29	10	3	3	21	32	27
Thailand	20	6	15	78	1	18	5	27	33	23
Regional average										
With Bangladesh and India	26	28	51	17	4	18	10	31	37	31
Without Bangladesh and India	21	23	53	19	5	..	..	..	..	..

a. Data for primary education are not shown because most enrollments are in the public sector in all countries. The rate of cost recovery for public education is also very limited.

b. Figure refers to 1980 and is excluded from calculating the average in this column.

c. Index reflects the rate of cost recovery across all institutional types weighted by their share of enrollments. For Malaysia, it reflects the extent of cost recovery only for domestic higher education.

d. See chapter 5 for details on the calculation of these indexes.

Source: See appendix B.

spending on education exert only a weak influence (figure 2.2). Countries like Bhutan, China, India, Indonesia, Korea, Sri Lanka, and Thailand have comparable levels of spending but achieve dramatically different results of human capital formation. Conversely, countries such as Bangladesh, India, Nepal, and Papua New Guinea differ widely in aggregate spending on education but achieve comparable outcomes in average grade attainment.

The weak effect of wealth and aggregate spending appears counterintuitive but actually has a sensible explanation: countries organize and finance education services differently, with corresponding differences in the education system's efficiency.[13] Countries with higher per capita GNP and aggregate spending may succeed better—possibly because of a stronger administrative and institutional infrastructure—but their achievement can be matched by countries with a smaller per capita GNP and lower spending.[14] Favorable external conditions that facilitate human capital formation do not substitute for the right sectoral policies. Policies for the organization and financing of education affect efficiency, costliness and, ultimately, the volume of human capital formation achievable for given budgets and macroeconomic environments.

Correlates of education costs

The unit costs of public education at all levels vary widely across countries; when expressed in relation to per capita GNP, unit costs are only weakly linked to the per capita GNP itself. The overall costliness of education, reflecting the average of costs across the three levels, also show no systematic relationship to per capita GNP (figure 3.2).[15]

No relationship is observed because there is such diversity of choice in the components of education costs. In primary and secondary education, the main elements are teachers' salaries and pupil-teacher ratios. In absolute terms, teachers' salaries usually rise with per capita GNP—market forces cause it to move in step with the rising pay of other productive labor. But expressed as a share of per capita GNP, teachers' salaries are unrelated to per capita GNP, indicating that a range of options exists for the pay of teachers relative to the pay of other productive labor.[16] Similarly, no relationship is discernible between per capita GNP and pupil-teacher ratios, pointing to the variation among countries in the intensity with which teachers' time is used (figures 3.4 and 3.6).

In higher education costs depend on more factors, which include: the distribution of enrollments across types of institutions (particularly distance institutions versus conventional universities and colleges); the distribution of enrollments across fields of study; student-faculty ratios; and the relative pay of faculty. Available data have to do only with the indicators for enrollment distributions and faculty pay. As in the case of primary and secondary education, the link between these component variables of costs and per capita GNP is weak, suggesting that they reflect choices rather than inescapable outcomes arising from particular country conditions.

The above results suggest that at all levels of education, costs are determined to a significant extent by policy choices about the way education is organized. The lack of a strong relationship between the variables that determine costs, such as the relative pay of teachers and pupil-teacher ratios, implies that the full range of options in these variables is, a priori, available to all countries, regardless of their level of economic development. This finding calls for a greater willingness to explore and adopt—at least for long-term planning—shifts in policies that sometimes are not considered, because it is assumed that domestic conditions do not support those shifts.

The effect of private financing in higher education

Private financing in education is usually achieved by imposing user charges for public education or by permitting fee-charging private schools to exist, or both.[17] Several theoretical considerations suggest that such a policy is most relevant at the level of higher education because (1) it is probably more feasible to implement administratively, (2) its potentially adverse effect on equity within the subsector is blunted by the fact that most students at this level come from relatively advantaged social backgrounds, and (3) most of the benefits of higher education, particularly for undergraduate studies, are privately captured by students. Beyond these arguments, the practical usefulness of private financing depends on its actual effect and on the nature of the trade-offs, if any, between the policy's positive and negative effects.[18] Country-level data permit a partial assessment of these issues.

Although the degree of private financing tends to rise with per capita GNP, the correlation is quite weak (figure 3.8). Countries with comparable per capita GNPs, such as Indonesia, Papua New Guinea, the Philippines, and Sri Lanka, vary widely in level of private financing, ranging from 6 percent in Papua New Guinea to 86 percent in the Philippines. And countries with comparable rates of private financing— Bangladesh and Malaysia—differ significantly in per capita GNP. These differences suggest that although a country's level of economic development does affect the administrative and social feasibility of tapping private resources for education, there is nonetheless substantial scope in all country settings for such a policy.

An argument in favor of private financing in education is that such a policy creates incentives for cost containment by promoting competition with the private sector and by sharpening cost-consciousness among students and school managers. The data reveal a pattern of declining costliness of regular public higher education with rising rates of private financing in the subsector as a whole (figure 4.6). The relationship flattens out as the rate of private financing goes beyond 40 percent, suggesting that the gains in cost containment are minimal beyond this point. Thus, although private financing can promote efficiency, it is not essential to achieve full cost recovery, or even high rates of cost recovery, to maximize the benefits in efficiency.

On the issue of equity, the data show a positive correlation between private financing and coverage in higher education, and between private financing in higher education and the share of primary education in total government spending on the sector (controlling for the size of overall spending)(figure 5.7). By supplementing public funds, private financing in higher education enables an expansion of coverage if some of the resources mobilized are retained in the subsector, particularly when there is excess demand for education at this level as is the case in Asia. The availability of resources from private financing also permits a partial diversion of government spending to the lower levels of education.

The positive effect of private financing on equity in higher education is further supported by its negative link to the share of cumulative public spending received by the 10 percent best-educated people in a generation (figure 5.6). This pattern is due partly to the fact that (1) cost recovery is more extensive in the wealthier countries; and that (2) the education systems in the wealthier countries are generally more developed at all levels. However, the same pattern still exists even after these considerations are taken into account. Furthermore, diminishing returns set in with rising rates of private financing. So for policy design, it is again true that very high levels of cost recovery are not necessary to maximize the effect on global equity in the education system.

Cohort survival patterns in primary education

Low cohort survival rates in primary schooling is a major policy issue in many Asian countries. The rates tend to improve with rising per capita GNP, but beyond US$800 (in 1985 prices), the relationship levels off at a reasonably high rate of survival (figure 4.1). There is substantial variation around the average trend, however. Countries with similar per capita GNP achieve widely different rates of cohort survival: the survival rate is 85 percent in Sri Lanka compared with 40 percent in Lao PDR; 68 percent in China compared with 37 percent in India. These comparisons suggest that a country's wealth is not the sole factor responsible for low retention rates and that policies in primary education probably also make a difference.

Low retention rates are a concern because people who drop out prematurely are less likely to acquire permanent literacy. The implication is a low literacy rate among future adults, with adverse effects on economic development. Regression analysis suggests a statistically significant and negative relationship between adult literacy rates at one point in time and the rate of retention in primary education 10 to 15 years earlier. This relationship is fairly strong: a 25 percent increase in cohort survival rates (a magnitude of improvement that most countries in the region would probably need to consider) results in a 7.5 percentage point increase in literacy rates among future adults. Thus, if achieving universal adult literacy is envisioned, strengthening the holding power of primary education is an indispensable component of public policy.

Low cohort survival rates also raise concern because of their adverse effect on social selectivity.[19] Dropping out occurs more often among pupils from disadvantaged groups. For example, the data show that females' share of enrollments at both the primary and secondary levels is negatively related to survival rates in primary education (figure 5.11). The pattern indicates that when an education system's ability to retain students is weak, the toll is greater on females than on males. When survival rates are below 50 percent, the sex bias in participation rates is particularly pronounced.

These results are relevant in considering policies to promote females' participation in primary education. When should interventions to improve survival rates be targeted to females, and when should interventions be aimed at the system as a whole? Shaping policies to improve female retention rates is warranted mostly when the bias against females is substantial. But this situation occurs precisely when the entire system's retention rate is excessively low, say, less than 50 percent. At such levels, internal efficiency is so poor that it calls for intervention to improve overall survival rates. Females would benefit indirectly from such interventions—the pattern is one of rising female participation rates as the overall retention rate improves. Above the 50 percent threshold, and clearly when overall survival rates reach 75 or 80 percent, improving internal efficiency remains an important policy objective in primary education; but at these higher rates of retention, targeting interventions toward females is generally not warranted because their representation in the system is close to 50 percent.

For interventions to raise overall cohort survival rates, the question is whether or not more money would fetch better outcomes. The data for Asia suggest that countries with higher levels of spending per pupil achieve better cohort survival rates (figure 4.2). But there is wide variation around the average pattern, implying that although more resources per pupil is likely, on average, to improve a system's retentiveness, it does not insure against high drop-out rates.

Although studies show that the way resources are spent and the way a system is organized are also relevant to retention rates, the aggregate data do not permit specific interventions in these areas to be identified.[20] However, some conclusions may be drawn from a look at pupil-teacher ratios. On average, survival rates show only a weakly negative link with pupil-teacher ratios (figure 4.3). Raising per pupil spending in the form of reduced pupil-teacher ratios is probably relevant mainly in such countries as Bangladesh and India where retention rates are extremely low and pupil-teacher ratios exceptionally large.[21] But in countries where the average pupil-teacher ratio is not exceedingly large, say, not over 40, the indications are that such a strategy may not be the best one. These conclusions would require further refinement in light of country-specific conditions, particularly because the data reflect averages that may conceal highly skewed distributions across localities.

Policy challenges in Asian education

The prospects for education development look bright for most countries in Asia. Demographic constraints on the sector are projected to ease considerably in most countries as the dependency ratio (ratio of school-age population to working adults) drops from an average of around 0.42 in 1985 to 0.36 by the end of the century. The ratio nonetheless remains high in Bangladesh, Lao PDR, and Papua New Guinea, and is even expected to rise somewhat in Bhutan and Nepal.

The region's economies are expected to grow at moderate to high rates, averaging about 5 percent a year between 1990 and 2000, while the school-age population is forecast to grow much more slowly, by about 1.3 percent a year. Thus, if government spending on education as a share of GNP remains unchanged, public resources will be available not only to maintain current enrollment ratios but also to expand and upgrade education services. But prospects are less bright in such countries as Nepal and, to a lesser extent, Bangladesh and Papua New Guinea—in these countries the gap between the projected economic and population growth rates is relatively slim.

The amount of extra resources that actually materializes for expanding and upgrading education depends on future changes in education costs. Predictions are difficult because cross-sectional evidence shows no clear link between the costliness of education and a country's per capita GNP. At one extreme, it is possible that costs remain unchanged in real terms as the economy grows; at the other extreme, costs may grow at the same pace as the GNP. The outlook for costs is likely to lie somewhere between these extremes, depending on future government policies in the sector. If costs remain relatively unchanged in real terms, significant resources for expansion will become available beyond what is needed to maintain enrollment ratios at current levels; but if costs grow at, or close to, the same pace as the GNP, no scope for real expansion will exist because all the extra resources will be absorbed by rising costs.

Correct policy choices for the education sector are critical in the group of Asian countries where demographic and macroeconomic conditions will probably remain difficult (Bangladesh, Bhutan, Lao PDR, Nepal, and Papua New Guinea). Wrong choices are likely to worsen current inequities and may reverse past gains. For example, policies that perpetuate or raise high costs in higher education will reduce the effective amount of resources available for the lower levels—a particularly worrisome prospect in these countries because primary education still suffers from incomplete coverage, high drop-out rates, and inadequate resources.

In Asian countries where exogenous constraints on education are likely to ease considerably, the challenge is to avoid complacency. Consolidation and further strengthening of past progress must continue—the education sector in many of these countries still shows striking inequities and inefficiencies in the use and distribution of resources.

Education policies must respond to country-specific conditions and political realities. Three options warrant close consideration:

- Policy option 1: Increased public spending on education in selected countries. Because this option is quite limited as a policy lever, it must be applied selectively and cautiously. One limitation is keen intersectoral competition for resources. (This factor probably explains the relatively stable trend in most countries' spending on education as a share of the GNP.) A second limitation may be more important: regression analysis based on cross-sectional country-level data suggests that appreciable variation in education outcomes emerges only with relatively large differences in aggregate levels of public spending. So countries that spend more do not necessarily achieve better outcomes than countries that spend somewhat less.

Education services are produced in different organizational setups, with corresponding differences in efficiency. For most countries in Asia, the potential for improvement resides largely in the choice of policies within the education sector. In such countries as Bangladesh, Nepal, and Sri Lanka (and until recently the Philippines), where current levels of public spending are much below the Asian mean, the case for increased public funds for education is stronger, but even here policies within the sector remain important.

- Policy option 2: Improving primary education. Expanding coverage and minimizing drop-out rates in primary education yield significant external benefits by producing literate future adults, with implications for economic development, and by promoting equity, because the poor and such disadvantaged groups as females are the ones most adversely affected by incomplete coverage and low retention rates.

In a few Asian countries (Bhutan, China, India, Nepal, and Papua New Guinea), a two-pronged approach is required because not all school-age children enter grade 1 and many who enter drop out before the end of the cycle. In the remaining countries where entry into primary education is more or less universal, the main focus should be to reduce the incidence of noncompletion. Korea, Malaysia, and Singapore are the only countries in which problems of incomplete coverage and high drop-out rates in primary education have largely disappeared. (Hong Kong and Taiwan are probably also in this group, but no data for them were collected in this study.)

The analysis suggests that increased levels of spending per pupil in primary education may increase the attraction of schooling and strengthen its holding power by promoting the quality of education. However, throwing more money at schools is not the best of all strategies for improvement because countries with similar levels of resource-intensity per student achieve strikingly different results in entry and completion rates; and conversely, countries achieve comparable results under widely different schooling conditions. Thus, beyond a general policy of augmenting resources for primary education, a further and probably more important issue is to identify the most effective ways of spending those resources. This question is relevant not only in countries that currently spend little on primary education, but also in countries where seemingly adequate levels of spending still lead to poor results.

No specific conclusion can be drawn here about allocating the increased spending on primary education. Non-entry and high drop-out rates are caused by factors that vary across countries and probably also across regions within countries. So it is unlikely that a single approach or intervention will be effective in all situations. The scarcity of information on the conditions under which alternative policies are likely to succeed prevents the formulation of a strategy for effective intervention. If governments are to overcome the weak performance of primary education, further analysis of this topic must be given priority in future work.

• Policy option 3: Freeing up resources for primary education. The orientation of public policies in favor of primary education requires concomitant changes in other subsectors. Increasing efficiency, especially in secondary and higher education where operating costs are often much larger than in primary education, would increase the amount of resources effectively available for expansion. Options to increase efficiency include the mix of school inputs; arrangements for multigrade teaching; allocation of teaching duties and scheduling of classes; use of responsive management and teaching styles and use of evaluation instruments; administrative rules and regulations regarding teachers' qualifications, teachers' pay, and the criteria for teachers' promotion.

Data are lacking for most of these options, in part because of their diverse outcomes in different settings. There is evidence available only for the physical organization of providing education services, as reflected in the distribution of institutions by size. In some countries, the predominance of small establishments suggests that economies of scale—often possible in secondary and higher education—are probably not fully exploited. Although the potential savings in costs and the practical feasibility of consolidation are likely to vary across countries, this source of efficiency gain should probably not be neglected.

At the aggregate level, lessening the bias toward higher education in public policy is perhaps the most clearcut and important change called for. In all countries, government spending on education tends disproportionately to benefit the most advantaged group—here defined as the best-educated people in a generation. However, the bias is less strong in some countries than in others because of differences in policies. For example, the countries showing only a modest bias toward higher education have not relied on administrative regulation to ration places at this level; instead, they have sought ways to reduce the public cost of financing higher education.

Three strategies have been used successfully to reduce the spending bias toward higher education: increased private financing in public institutions; promotion of largely self-financing private institutions; and low-cost distance education. Some countries rely on all three strategies (Korea), while others choose only one or two of them (the Philippines with private education and Thailand with open universities and private institutions). Although the practicality of these options differs among countries, experience to date suggests that they lead to more equitable outcomes compared with systems where higher education consists largely of conventional institutions that are operated and financed by the government.

The positive outcome of increased private financing in higher education—whether it results from charging fees in public institutions or from encouraging the growth of private institutions—arises partly because it helps promote efficiency in public institutions. It permits the government to do two things at once: lower overall operating costs, and lower the government's share in financing those costs. The savings permit increased allocation of public spending toward the lower levels, a pattern revealed by the analysis of this study. And the cost advantage of distance education is well known and highly attractive. However, little is known about the fields of study for which distance education offers an effective alternative to conventional teaching. Evaluation of this promising option would require additional assessment, particularly a comparison of the labor market performance of people who have followed different careers in higher education.

The overall findings suggest that there is substantial scope for policy intervention to promote equitable and efficient outcomes in education, even though exogenous conditions will continue to hamper progress. The diversity in Asia, both in the strategies that governments have chosen and in the corresponding outcomes, gives a rich basis for identifying potential policy options. To the extent that poverty alleviation through education is a policy objective, the analysis indicates that an effective policy package would comprise increased focus on primary education and reduced public financing of higher education. The precise design of this policy package must respond to unique country conditions, but the general thrust is probably relevant in all settings.

Priorities for future research

Given the broad-brush nature of this study, inevitable gaps remain in our documentation of education conditions and policies. Additional research would be particularly appropriate in two areas: (1) the education system's generally weak ability to retain students, notably at the primary level, and (2) delivery systems for higher education that satisfy demand without diverting resources away from basic education and that achieve equitable and efficient patterns of investment within the subsector. Further research on both issues would strengthen the analytical basis for policy dialogue.

  • Study 1: Factors affecting retention rates in primary education

The rate of retention (or completion) in primary education varies widely among countries around a regional mean of about 60 percent. This pattern signifies that substantial scope for improvement exists, particularly to promote efficiency and equity in the education system. But knowledge about potentially effective interventions is limited. What is known from the available data is that low retention rates occur under very different conditions of schooling.

The objective of a regional study would be to discover the main factors, in school and out of school, that affect a pupil's probability of dropping out prematurely. Bearing in mind the design of policy interventions, it is important to distinguish between factors that can be manipulated and those that must be taken as exogenous. Among factors that can be manipulated, a further issue is to identify the most cost-effective interventions in different settings. This distinction is important because interventions that work well in rural schools, for example, may not be as cost-effective in suburban settings; and beyond urban-rural differences, regional differences are also likely to call for varied interventions attuned to local conditions.

Possible country settings for such a study include Bangladesh, India, Indonesia, Nepal, Papua New Guinea, and the Philippines.

• Study 2: Alternative ways of providing higher education

Higher education can be provided through conventional universities and colleges in the public and private sectors, correspondence courses (distance education), and open universities. Asian countries have followed markedly divergent strategies in providing higher education. For many, distance education is an important way of offering services, with the distinct advantage of affordability and wide accessibility. In other countries, the strategy is to rely on private education.

The various types of institutions for higher education differ in many ways, particularly in costs and entry criteria. Although there is some knowledge about their relative internal efficiency and about the social characteristics of their students, the information is tentative and incomplete. More serious is the lack of knowledge on the labor market performance of people who have followed different careers in higher education. Performance outcomes generally depend both on a student's academic and social background and on characteristics of the institutions attended. Sorting out the complex relationships between institutional characteristics, student characteristics, and labor market performance would (1) help clarify the role of the various types of institution, and (2) strengthen the factual basis for policy dialogue about the development of higher education.

Possible country settings for this study include China, Korea, Myanmar, Sri Lanka, Thailand, and possibly India and Indonesia.

Notes

1. The analysis relies largely on aggregated data and therefore sheds light mainly on broad policy issues affecting structural characteristics of the sector. Countries also face concerns in education that are unique to the local environment, but these are not addressed here because they belong to country-specific sector analysis.

2. Data in this and subsequent tables in this chapter pertain mostly to the latest available year, usually early to mid-1980s. Data for other years are given in later chapters and in the appendix tables.

3. Retention of pupils will be discussed in more detail later in this chapter.

4. Public spending usually refers to spending by the central government; however, in countries where lower levels of government also finance education to a significant extent (for example, India) their expenditure (net of transfers) is also included. For further remarks on this issue, see appendix B.

5. The scope for expansion depends on the evolution of education costs, which in turn depends importantly on how teachers' pay rises as the economy expands.

6. For a rationale for expressing costs relative to per capita GNP, see footnote 4 in chapter 3. Note that because Papua New Guinea is an outlier for costs, it is excluded in calculations of regional averages for cost and other related indicators, unless otherwise indicated.

7. Papua New Guinea's unit costs are three times as high as the regional average for primary and secondary education, and more than six times as high for higher education.

8. Other factors also influence unit costs, as will be discussed later. Here the discussion simply reflects the components that account for the differences.

9. A similar comparison for higher education is not presented for lack of data.

10. For efficiency and equity, the case for private financing is probably strongest at the higher education level.

11. For Malaysia, the index would have been significantly larger had overseas education been included in the computation: the outflow of students abroad is large, and most of the students overseas finance their studies privately. For the comparisons here, however, the lower figure is appropriate because it describes more accurately the extent to which private resources are tapped to finance domestic institutions.

12. Individual countries are treated as single units of observation in the analyses.

13. Differences in organization and financing are reflected by such indicators as the profile of teacher qualification and pay, pupil-teacher ratios, distribution of class sizes, use of distance education, extent of cost recovery and private financing, and so on.

14. The weak influence on aggregate spending in this cross-sectional analysis does not contradict the fact that in any single country the more the government spends, while keeping constant the education system's operational characteristics, the higher the grade attainment or volume of human capital formed.

15. The lack of a link between costs expressed in relation to per capita GNP to per capita GNP itself contradicts the popular belief that comparisons based on the indicator almost always identify low-income countries as high-cost countries, because of the effect of the denominator.

16. In view of the generally positive link between wages and a person's qualification, policies about teachers' pay are obviously related to decisions, implicit or otherwise, concerning the qualification of the teaching force.

17. Private schools may of course be partly subsidized by the government. As long as the extent of subsidization is limited, such schools help mobilize private resources for education.

18. On the positive side, private financing in higher education is likely to boost efficiency — therefore reducing costs — by encouraging greater accountability from school managers and by increasing cost-consciousness among the various actors involved — students, parents, teachers, school authorities, and so on. An added benefit is that it helps mobilize resources for education investments, thus easing constraints in the public budget and permitting the supply of school places to expand. On the negative side, such a policy may worsen biases against low-income groups, for by adding to the cost of forgone earnings or family production, fees could create an insurmountable barrier to higher education for such groups.

19. This adverse result tends to be perpetuated at subsequent levels of education, and it often worsens because drop-out rates tend to be higher among students from low-income

groups.

20. The cost-effectiveness of alternative interventions is likely to depend on local conditions. There is therefore no reason to expect that low cohort survival rates can be addressed by the same interventions across countries or even across different regions within a single country.

21. In Bangladesh a system of double shift teaching is in effect so that a teacher teaches two shifts of students. At the average student-staff ratio of 46 (a more recent estimate puts it as high as 59), the average class size is relatively low (and could arguably be raised). However, this arrangement also implies that students receive very few hours of actual teaching time, given that almost all schools operate a 10-period day (for about 5 hours) and that teachers teach a maximum of four hours daily (a workload advocated by the Primary Teachers' Association). Raising the pupil-teacher ratio would effectively mean increasing the contact teaching time that students receive. It would not mean a reduction in class size.

Appendix A

Country Profiles in a Regional Perspective

The comparative analysis in foregoing chapters gives a benchmark for evaluating the status of education development in individual Asian countries. This appendix comprises a summary assessment for 13 countries for which the relevant data exist. The data is for 1985 because data for this year are most complete for the largest number of countries. Where available, more recent data are reported in the appendix tables.

A standard format with five sections is adopted: overall assessment; development of the education system; constraints and prospects; the system's operational characteristics; and patterns of cost and financing. The indicators have been defined before, but some of the more specific ones are repeated here to facilitate the discussion:

• Grade attainment refers to the average grade that will be attained by the current school-age population given the present structure of the enrollment pyramid.

• Dependency ratio refers to the ratio of the school-age population (age 5-14) to the adult population (both sexes age 15-65).

• Completion rate (used interchangeably with survival rate and retention rate) refers to the percentage of first-year entrants in a cycle of education surviving to the end of the cycle.

• Pupil-teacher ratio refers to public institutions. In countries where distance education is sizable in higher education, the ratio refers only to regular conventional institutions, this being denoted by the word "regular" at the appropriate place in the table.

• Index of costliness refers to unit costs (expressed as a percentage of per capita GNP) relative to unit costs averaged across all Asian countries in the sample, except Papua New Guinea.

• Percentage of cost recovery refers to the share of operating unit costs financed privately. It usually refers to public institutions. However, where the word "global" appears, it is the weighted average rate of cost recovery across all institutional types. This statistic is presented in situations where the contribution of financing through private education (and overseas education in the case of Malaysia) is substantial.

• Distribution of resources refers to the distribution of cumulative public spending on education appropriated to an entire generation as it passes through its schooling years. A more detailed discussion of the longitudinal concept involved can be found in chapter 5. Note that the larger the Gini-coefficient, the more inequitable the distribution of those resources.

For quick reference, the data for all 13 countries are summarized in one table (table A.1) before presenting individual country profiles. The table contains additional data on the education system's operational characteristics and unit costs. A qualitative evaluation is given in table A.2: positive signs signify that a country's performance on the variable under consideration is better than is average among Asian countries; negative signs denote worse-than-average performance; a zero signifies that performance is about average. The larger the number of positive (negative) signs, the better (worse) a country's performance. For reasons discussed in chapter 5, the data on enrollment ratios are not compared with the Asian average in the qualitative evaluation, but with the average predicted on the basis of the country's per capita GNP. (In the appendix tables and country profiles, (..) indicates that data were not available.)

Table A.1 Summary of comparative data on education development, selected Asian countries, mid-1980s

	Bangladesh	Bhutan	China	India	Indonesia	Korea	Malaysia
Development of the education system							
Enrollment ratio (%)							
Primary	60	25	118	92	118	96	99
Secondary	18	4	39	41	42	75	53
Higher	5.2	0.1	1.7	9.0	6.5	31.6	6.0
Grade attainment	3.9	1.4	5.1	4.8	7.3	11.4	9.2
Adult literacy rate (%)	33	15	69	43	74	92	74
Constraints and prospects							
Growth rate (% p.a. to 2000)							
School-age population	2.0	3.0	0.4	1.3	1.0	0.3	1.4
Economy	4.9	..	6.6	4.8	3.9	6.8	5.0
Dependency ratio							
1985	49	44	33	44	46	31	41
2000	42	47	26	35	35	24	33
Operational characteristics							
Completion rate (%)							
Primary	24	17	68	37	60	97	97
Lower secondary	48	83	76	44	92	98	90
Upper secondary	84	88	81	77	96	95	96
Entry rate to grade 1 (%)	100	54	90	83	100	100	100
Percentage of grade 1 entrants reaching							
End of primary	24	9	61	31	60	97	97
End of lower secondary	11	4	28	18	34	93	70
End of upper secondary	4	2	5	9	18	44	40
Index of intercycle selection[a]	8	13	54	14	46	87	79
Institutional share of students							
Primary: % private	11	..	0	2	8	2	0
Secondary: % private	93	..	-0	4	50	40	2
Higher: % private	58	0	0	57	58	65	8
% regular public	41	96	69	37	33	21	61
% distance	0	0	30	5	9	12	1
% overseas	0	4	1	1	1	2	31
Pupil-teacher ratio							
Primary	47	39	25	58	25	38	24
Secondary	26	10	17	20	15	34	22
Higher (regular)	16	11	5	16	14	40	11

Myanmar	Nepal	PNG	Philippines	Sri Lanka	Thailand	Asia
107	82	70	106	103	97	90.2
23	25	13	65	63	30	37.8
5.4	4.6	2.0	28.0	4.6	19.6	9.6
..	3.6	4.3	10.2	9.5	7.0	6.5
..	26	45	86	87	91	61.3
1.0	3.1	2.0	1.5	1.1	0.5	1.4
3.5	3.8	5.1	5.3	4.8	6.0	5.0
47	49	50	47	36	41	42.9
35	51	40	37	31	29	35.8
..	33	67	66	85	80	60.9
..	89	63	74	75	91	76.9
..	81	95	..	99	87	89.0
..	75	74	100	100	100	89.7
..	25	50	66	85	80	57.1
..	21	12	41	57	29	34.3
..	15	1	..	19	13	14.8
..	5	57	18	58	72	42.6
..	5	1	6	1	9	4.1
..	10	..	42	2	20	26.0
0	23	6	83	0	6	28.0
54	73	83	17	62	15	50.9
45	1	9	0	29	78	16.9
0	2	3	0	10	1	4.4
46	36	31	31	32	19	33.1
29	28	25	32	26	20	22.6
..	13	8	16	12	8	13.9

Table A.1 (continued)

	Bangladesh	Bhutan	China	India	Indonesia	Korea	Malaysia
Share of females (%)							
Primary	40	34	45	40	48	49	49
Secondary	28	18	40	34	43	47	49
Higher	19	17	30	29	32	30	45
Patterns of cost and financing							
Public spending on education							
% in GNP	1.5	3.8	3.3	3.0	3.7	3.4	6.0
% in government budget	10.3	7.3	7.8	13.7	15	16.6	16
Unit operating costs (% of per capita GNP)[b]							
Primary	6.4	..	6.7	6.0	12.6	13.5	14.1
Secondary	30.0	..	22.6	17.3	23.3	23.4	21.3
Higher	284.6	..	199.2	199.0	91.1	70.6	190.3
Index of costliness							
Overall	139	..	108	103	105	114	129
Primary	65	..	68	61	128	167	143
Secondary	162	..	122	94	126	127	115
Higher	191	..	134	155	61	47	128
Teacher pay (% of per capita GNP)							
Primary	2.2	..	1.6	2.4	2.5	4.5	2.4
Secondary	..	..	2.8	3.1	3.2	5.4	3.1
Cost recovery (%)							
Primary	7.4	..	4.8	..	7.1	0.7	3.7
Secondary	4.0	..	3.2	..	27.4	34.2	4.0
Higher (public regular)[c]	0.1	..	0.3	4.9	18.9	45.9	5.8
Higher (global)[d]	16.5	..	0.3	7.1	48.7	76.6	15.1
Distribution of resources							
Gini-coefficient	82	..	44	66	27	16	38
Share of 10% best-educated	72	..	31	61	21	13	32

.. Not available.

a. Index refers to the extent of selection that takes place between cycles of education as opposed to within cycles. The larger the index, the more efficient the selection process.

b. In the column for Asia the figure refers to the average excluding data for Papua New Guinea; and the figure in parentheses refers to the average including data for Papua New Guinea.

c. Data refer to cost recovery in public regular institutions, that is, excluding distance education.

d. Data refer to the average across all institutional types, including private education; in the case of Malaysia, data include overseas education.

Source: Appendix B and text tables.

Myanmar	Nepal	PNG	Philippines	Sri Lanka	Thailand	Asia
..	29	44	49	48	48	43.6
..	23	36	50	53	48	39.0
..	20	23	54	40	46	32.0
1.8	1.8	6.9	1.8	2.8	3.6	3.3
10.9	9.6	17.9	11.5	8.1	19.4	12.6
..	9.0	29.0	5.8	6.1	15.5	9.9 (11.6)
..	13.5	65.0	8.6	9.3	15.3	18.5 (22.7)
..	249.0	1,050.0	50.0	83.3	39.9	149.0 (230.8)
..	111	450	46	56	89	100
..	91	294	59	62	157	100
..	73	352	47	50	83	100
..	167	705	34	56	27	100
..	2.8	6.8	1.6	1.6	2.5	2.5 (2.9)
..	5.0	10.0	1.7	2.1	2.9	3.3 (3.9)
..	0.0	8.7	0.0	3.1	0.1	3.6
..	40.7	39.8	9.3	3.1	18.3	18.4
..	10.4	0.0	15.3	3.4	5.0	10.0
..	31.8	6.3	85.8	20.5	26.9	30.5
..	57	62	19	33	33	43.4
..	54	54	14	28	23	36.3

Table A.2 Qualitative assessment of education development, selected Asian countries, mid-1980s

	Bangladesh	Bhutan	China	India	Indonesia	Korea	Malaysia
Development of the education system							
Enrollment ratio							
Primary	- -	- - - -	+	=	=	+	+
Secondary	-	- - - -	=	+	+	+++	++
Higher	0	- - - -	- - -	=	-	+++	-
Grade attainment	- -	- - -	-	-	+	+++	++
Adult literacy rate	- - -	- - - -	+	- -	++	++++	++
Constraints and prospects							
Growth rate							
School-age population	+	+++	- - -	0	-	- - -	0
Economy	0	..	++	0	-	++	0
Dependency ratio							
1985	+++	0	- - -	0	+	- - -	0
2000	++	+++	- - -	0	=	- - -	-
Operational characteristics							
Completion rate							
Primary	- - -	- - -	+	- -	=	+++	+++
Lower secondary	- -	+	0	- -	++	+++	++
Upper secondary	-	0	-	- -	++	++	++
Entry rate to grade 1	+	- - -	0	-	+	+	+
Percentage of grade 1 entrants reaching							
End of primary	- -	- - -	0	- -	=	+++	+++
End of lower secondary	- -	- - -	-	- -	=	+++	++
End of upper secondary	- - -	- - -	- - -	- - -	+	+++	+++
Index of intercycle selection	- - - -	- - -	+	- - -	=	+++	++
Institutional share of students							
Primary: % private	++	..	-	-	++	-	-
Secondary: % private	+++	..	- - -	- -	+++	++	- - -
Higher: % private	+	- - -	- - -	+	+++	+++	- -
% regular public	++	++++	++	++	- -	- -	++
% distance	- -	- -	++	-	-	0	- -
% overseas	-	0	-	-	-	0	++++
Number of teachers per pupil[a]							
Primary	- -	-	++	- - -	++	-	++
Secondary	-	++	+	0	+	- -	0
Higher (regular)	-	+	++	-	=	- - -	+

Myanmar	Nepal	PNG	Philippines	Sri Lanka	Thailand
+	-	- -	+	+	+
-	-	- - -	++	++	-
-	- -	- - -	+++	-	++
..	- -	-	+++	++	+
..	- - -	- -	+++	+++	+++
-	+++	+	0	-	- - -
-	-	0	+	0	+
+	++	++	+	- -	0
0	+++	+	0	-	- -
..	- -	+	+	++	++
..	++	-	0	0	++
..	-	++	..	+++	0
..	- -	- -	+	+	+
..	- -	-	+	++	++
..	-	- -	+	++	-
..	0	- - -	..	+	0
..	- - -	+	- -	++	+++
..	+	-	+	-	++
..	-	..	+++	- - -	-
- - -	0	- -	++++	- - -	- -
0	+++	+++	- - -	++	- -
+++	- -	-	- -	+	+++
-	0	0	-	++	-
- -	0	0	0	0	+++
-	-	-	- -	-	+
..	0	++	-	+	++

Table A.2 (continued)

	Bangladesh	Bhutan	China	India	Indonesia	Korea	Malaysia
Share of females							
Primary	-	- -	0	-	+	+	+
Secondary	- -	- - -	0	-	+	++	++
Higher	- -	- -	0	0	=	0	++
Patterns of cost financing							
Public spending on education							
% in GNP	- - -	+	0	-	+	0	+++
% in government budget	-	- - -	- - -	+	++	++	++
Index of costliness							
Overall	+++	..	+++	0	=	+	++
Primary	- -	..	0	- -	++	+++	++
Secondary	++	..	++	0	+	+	+
Higher	+++	..	++	++	- -	- -	+
Teacher pay							
Primary	-	..	-	0	=	+++	0
Secondary	..	..	0	0	=	++	0
Cost recovery (%)							
Primary	+	..	0	..	+	-	0
Secondary	- -	..	- -	..	++	+++	- -
Higher (public regular)	- -	..	- -	-	++	+++	-
Higher (global)	-	..	- - -	- - -	++	+++	0
Distribution of resources							
Gini-coefficient	- - -	..	0	- -	++	+++	+
Share of 10% best-educated	- - -	..	+	- -	++	+++	+

+ Better-than-average performance; number of signs increases with deviation from the average.

- Worse-than-average performance.

0 Average performance.

.. Not available.

Source: Authors' evaluation based on appendix table A.1.

Myanmar	Nepal	PNG	Philippines	Sri Lanka	Thailand
..	- - -	0	+	+	+
..	- -	0	++	+++	+
..	- -	-	+++	+	+
- -	- -	+++	- -	-	+
-	-	+++	-	- - -	+++
..	0	++++	- - -	- -	-
..	-	+++	- -	- -	++
..	- -	++++	- - -	- - -	-
..	++	++++	- - -	- -	- - -
..	+	++++	- - -	- - -	0
..	++	++++	- - -	- -	-
..	-	+	-	0	-
..	+++	+++	-	- -	0
..	0	- -	+	- -	-
..	0	- -	+++	0	0
..	- -	- -	+++	++	++
..	- -	- -	+++	++	++

Bangladesh

Overall assessment

There is substantial room for improvement. The education system currently suffers from a paucity of resources from both public and private sources. Although this constraint is likely to ease somewhat in the future-the economy is forecast to grow faster than the school-age population-it is unlikely that sufficient resources would be available for expanding coverage to all extent commensurate with the country's level of economic development. The current structure of enrollments and pattern of re-source allocation reflect an overemphasis on the higher levels. To promote efficiency and overall equity in the education system, priority should be shifted to strengthening primary education. This subsector's ability to retain students is extremely weak at present, due partly to inadequate levels of spending per pupil. Enhancing the quality of primary schooling may help to reduce drop-out rates, but the precise design of such an intervention requires more detailed analysis than has been possible in this study.

Development of the education system

Coverage of the education system is less extensive than is expected given the country's level of economic development. The gap widens with descending levels of education, and is thus most prominent at the primary level. The average grade attainment of the current school-age population is smaller than the Asian average, as is the rate of literacy among adults.

	Actual	*Predicted*
Enrollment ratio		
Primary	60	82
Secondary	18	24
Higher	5.2	5.0
	Bangladesh	*Asia*
Grade attainment	3.9	6.5
Adults literate (%)	33	61

Constraints and prospects

The dependency ratio is expected to drop over time, but will remain above the Asian average, as at present. The economy is likely to expand faster than the school-age population. Thus, if education costs in real terms and public spending on education as a share of the GNP remain unchanged, resources would become available not only to

	Bangladesh	*Asia*
Growth rate *		
School-age		
population	2.0	1.4
Economy	4.9	5.0
Dependency ratio		
1985	49	43
2000	42	36
* projected to 2000 in percent per year		

maintain current enrollment ratios, but also to expand coverage or increase inputs per pupil.

Operational characteristics

Completion rates are generally low at all levels, but especially in primary education. Private education appears to be relatively well developed. Note, however, that private schools in Bangladesh are heavily subsidized by the government, particularly at the post-primary levels. The shares of students in distance and overseas higher education are negligible. The pupil-teacher ratio for both secondary and higher education is close to the Asian average, but is substantially above the average for primary education. With rising levels of education, the share of females falls significantly below the average for Asia with rising levels of education.

	Bangladesh	Asia
Completion rate (%)		
Primary	24	61
Lower secondary	48	77
Upper secondary	84	89
Institutional share of students		
Primary: % private	11	4
Secondary: % private	93	26
Higher: % private	58	30
% distance	0	17
% overseas	0	4
Pupil-teacher ratio		
Primary	47	33
Secondary	26	23
Higher (regular)	16	14
Share of females		
Primary	40	44
Secondary	28	39
Higher	19	32

Patterns of cost and financing

Public spending on education is smaller than in other Asian countries, and remains relatively low despite its rise to 1.9 percent in 1988. In fact, as a share of GNP, the 1985 level of spending on education is the lowest in the region. The extent of private financing is relatively modest, particularly in secondary and higher education. Taken together, these features imply that the aggregate amount of resources for education is more limited in this country than elsewhere. The unit cost of primary education lies be-

	Bangladesh	Asia
Public spending on education		
% in GNP	1.5	3.3
% in government budget	10.3	12.6
Index of costliness		
Overall	139	100
Primary	65	100
Secondary	162	100
Higher	191	100
Teacher pay (% of per capita GNP)		
Primary	2.2	2.5
Secondary		3.3
Cost recovery (percent)		
Primary	7.4	3.6
Secondary	4.0	18.4
Higher (global)	16.5	33.7
Distribution of resouces		
Gini-coefficient	82	43
Share of 10% best-educated	72	36

low the regional mean, reflecting the combined effect of relatively low teachers' salaries and a relatively high pupil-teacher ratio. In contrast, the unit costs of secondary and higher education exceed the regional mean by substantial margins. As a result, average unit costs are higher than those in other Asian countries. The financing arrangements in the education system and the structure of enrollments result in highly inequitable distribution of public spending on education, with the 10 percent best-educated people in a generation receiving as much as 76 percent of the cumulative public spending appropriated to the entire generation through publicly financed education.

Bhutan

Overall assessment

Information about the education sector is scanty. The available data nonetheless highlight two issues that deserve further attention. First, although public spending on education appears to be reasonably high, the education system remains undeveloped. This suggests that unit costs are probably high, and that the contribution of private financing is limited. The second issue is the very low rate of completion in primary education. For reasons elaborated elsewhere in this report, improving the completion rate is probably a sectoral priority. Identifying effective interventions for improvement would require new data and further analysis.

Development of the education system

Coverage in the system is extremely limited at all levels, even after controlling for the country's level of economic development. The adult literacy rate is much below the Asian mean, as is the average grade attainment of the current school-age population.

	Actual	Predicted
Enrollment ratio		
Primary	25	82
Secondary	4	23
Higher	0.1	4.9
	Bhutan	*Asia*
Grade attainment	1.4	6.5
Adults literate (%)	15	61

Constraints and prospects

Because the school-age population is expected to grow at a brisk pace, the dependency ratio will remain high over the next decade. Thus, even if the economy grows at the average Asian rate-probably an optimistic assumption for Bhutan-the amount of public re-

	Bhutan	*Asia*
Growth rate*		
School-age population	3.0	1.4
Economy	..	5.0
Dependency ratio		
1985	44	43
2000	47	36
*projected to 2000 in percent per year		

sources available for expanding education will probably be limited.

Operational characteristics

The strikingly low rate of retention in
primary schooling suggests a need to
focus public policy on improving the
system's performance at this level. The
pupil-teacher ratio appears to be particularly low in secondary education,
pointing to the potential for efficiency
gains in this subsector. The same re-
mark also applies, although to a lesser
extent, to higher education. Access to
post-primary education is strongly biased against females. This problem
originates mainly in the transition from
primary to secondary education.

Patterns of cost and financing

Although public spending on education
is a relatively small share of the government budget, its share in GNP
slightly exceeds the average for Asian
countries. For other aspects of costs and
financing, there is no reliable information.

China

Overall assessment

The education system does not suffer
from extreme problems. Public spending on education is comparable to that

		Bhutan	Asia
Completion rate (%)			
Primary		17	61
Lower secondary		83	77
Upper secondary		88	89
Institutional share of students			
Primary:	% private	..	4
Secondary:	% private	..	26
Higher:	% private	0	30
	% distance	0	17
	% overseas	4	4
Pupil-teacher ratio			
Primary		39	33
Secondary		10	23
Higher (regular)		11	14
Share of females			
Primary		34	44
Secondary		18	39
Higher		17	32

	Bhutan	Asia
Public spending on education		
% in GNP	3.8	3.3
% in government budget	7.3	12.6
Index of costliness		
Overall	..	100
Primary	..	100
Secondary	..	100
Higher	..	100
Teacher pay (% of per capita GNP)		
Primary	..	2.5
Secondary	..	3.3
Cost recovery (%)		
Primary	..	3.6
Secondary	..	18.4
Higher	..	33.7
Distribution of resources		
Gini-coefficient	..	43
Share of 10% best-educated	..	36

in most Asian countries, and resources for expanding and/or upgrading education
services are likely to materialize in the future, given the favorable economic and
demographic conditions projected for the next decade. A few changes are nonetheless worth considering to improve the system's performance, particularly changes in
the way funds are allocated and the way education is organized. The rate of comple-

tion at the lower levels, although higher than that in other Asian countries, can still be improved. Expanding the coverage of higher education appears to be indicated, although the justification for it requires further confirmation. At all levels in the education system, but especially in higher education, there is scope for greater internal efficiency, mainly through improved use of teachers' time. In addition, the potential for exploiting economies of scale in higher education is also substantial.

Development of the education system

The enrollment pyramid reveals a distinct emphasis on coverage at the lower levels. In higher education, the gross enrollment ratio is clearly below what might be expected for a country at China's level of economic development. The average grade attainment of the current school-age population is slightly below the Asian mean, but adult literacy is more widespread.

	Actual	Predicted
Enrollment ratio		
Primary	118	82
Secondary	39	27
Higher	1.7	6.1
	China	Asia
Grade attainment	5.1	6.5
Adults literate (%)	69	61

Constraints and prospects

The economy is forecast to grow significantly faster than the school-age population. If public spending on education as a share of GNP and the pattern of unit costs remain unchanged, substantial resources would be available for expansion, beyond what is needed to maintain current enrollment ratios. The fiscal burden of financing education, already low by Asian standards, will continue to drop in the near future.

	China	Asia
Growth rate*		
School-age population	0.4	1.4
Economy	6.6	5.0
Dependency ratio		
1985	33	43
2000	26	36
*projected to 2000 in percent per year		

Operational characteristics

The system's ability to retain students, although comparable to the average in Asian countries, can still be improved, particularly in primary education. Two institutional characteristics are noteworthy: the minimal role of the private sector at all levels in the system; and the importance of distance education in higher education. Pupil-teacher ratios are low throughout the education system, but especially in higher education where the ratio is only 5. This feature also applies to distance education.

The female share of enrollments declines with rising levels of education, a pattern similar to that of other Asian countries.

Patterns of cost and financing

Despite a lower share in the government budget, overall public spending on education as a proportion of GNP is close to the average for Asia. On the whole, education costs in China are significantly higher than those elsewhere in the region. The structure of costs, however, reveals a definite bias against primary education. Low pupil-teacher ratios are responsible for the high unit costs of secondary and higher education. In primary education, the pupil-teacher ratio is also relatively low, but the effect on costs is diluted somewhat by the fact that teacher salaries are relatively low. It is interesting to note that primary school teachers are paid mostly by local communities, whereas teachers at the other levels are paid by higher levels of government. With regard to equity, the structure of enrollments and unit costs imply a fairly equitable distribution of public spending on education: the 10 percent best-educated in a generation receive 29 percent of public resources appropriated to the entire generation through government-financed education; this compares with a regional average of 36 percent.

	China	Asia
Completion rate (%)		
Primary	68	61
Lower secondary	76	77
Upper secondary	81	89
Institutional share of students		
Primary: % private	0	4
Secondary: % private	0	26
Higher: % private	0	30
% distance	30	17
% overseas	1	4
Pupil-teacher ratio		
Primary	25	33
Secondary	17	23
Higher (regular)	5	14
Share of females		
Primary	45	44
Secondary	40	39
Higher	30	32

	China	Asia
Public spending on education		
% in GNP	3.3	3.3
% in government budget	7.8	12.6
Index of costliness		
Overall	108	100
Primary	68	100
Secondary	122	100
Higher	134	100
Teacher pay (% of per capita GNP)		
Primary	1.6	2.5
Secondary	2.8	3.3
Cost recovery (%)		
Primary	4.8	3.6
Secondary	3.2	18.4
Higher	0.3	33.7
Distribution of resources		
Gini-coefficient	44	43
Share of 10% best-educated	31	36

India

Overall assessment

The aggregate level of public spending on education is probably adequate for the sector's development. But some changes are called for in the allocation of those resources. In particular, more spending should be allocated to primary education, mainly to improve its ability to retain students. Among other interventions, quality enhancement through a reduction in the pupil-teacher ratio should probably be considered. The shift in funding in favor of primary education can be achieved by increasing the contribution of private financing in higher education and by expanding distance education as a mode of delivery.

Development of the education system

The education system's coverage is reasonably extensive at all levels, particularly in secondary education and even more so in higher education. Nonetheless, the average grade attainment of the current school-age population is significantly lower than for Asia as a whole, as is the rate of adult literacy.

	Actual	Predicted
Enrollment ratio		
Primary	92	82
Secondary	41	25
Higher	9.0	5.9
	India	*Asia*
Grade attainment	4.8	6.5
Adults literate (%)	43	61

Constraints and prospects

The school-age population is expected to grow at a moderate pace, about the same as the average for Asia. As a result, the dependency ratio will decline quite sharply over the next decade or so. The economy is forecast to expand at a much faster rate than the school-age population, implying a probable easing of budgetary constraints on the sector's expansion.

	India	*Asia*
Growth rate*		
School-age		
population	1.3	1.4
Economy	4.8	5.0
Dependency ratio		
1985	44	43
2000	35	36
*projected to 2000 in percent per year		

Operational characteristics

A major problem of the education system is its weak ability to retain students, particularly in primary and lower secondary education. The bulk of selection takes place within cycles of education through dropping out. This characteristic partly explains why the country's adult literacy rate is relatively low despite the system's apparently extensive coverage. Intracycle selection also results in adverse social selectivity in the sector. The generally poor quality of primary education, as indicated by its exceptionally high average pupil-teacher ratio, is probably an important reason for the high drop-out rates. As for the institutional distribution of enrollments, the private sector's share is significant only in higher education. However, it should be noted that most all private institutions are heavily subsidized by the government, to nearly the same extent as the public institutions. At all levels of education, the share of female enrollment is slightly smaller than the regional average.

	India	Asia
Completion rate (%)		
Primary	37	61
Lower secondary	72	77
Upper secondary	65	89
Institutional share of students		
Primary: % private	2	4
Secondary: % private	4	26
Higher: % private	57	30
% distance	5	17
% overseas	1	4
Pupil-teacher ratio		
Primary	58	33
Secondary	20	23
Share of females		
Primary	40	44
Secondary	34	39
Higher	29	32

Patterns of cost and financing

Public spending on education as a share of GNP is close to the average for Asia. Unit costs, averaged across the three levels, are comparable to the regional mean, but their structure reveals a strong bias in favor of higher education at the expense of primary education. Because teacher pay is comparable to the Asian average, the relatively low unit cost of primary education is mainly attributable to the high pupil-teacher ratio in this subsector. The extent of private financing is extremely limited compared with that in other Asian countries. The structure of enrollments and financing arrangements result in a distribution of public spending that is skewed toward the privileged: the 10 percent best-educated members in a cohort receive as much as 61 percent of the cumulative public resources appropriated to the entire cohort through government-financed education.

	India	Asia
Public spending on education		
% in GNP	3.0	3.3
% in government budget	13.7	12.6
Index of costliness		
Overall	103	100
Primary	61	100
Secondary	94	100
Higher	155	100
Teacher pay (% of per capita GNP)		
Primary	2.4	2.5
Secondary	3.1	3.3
Cost recovery (%)		
Primary	..	3.6
Secondary	..	18.4
Higher (global)	7.1	33.7
Distribution of resources		
Gini-coefficient	66	43
Share of 10% best-educated	61	36

Indonesia

Overall assessment

The system does not suffer from major structural problems. However, the relatively low retention rate in primary schooling and the adverse social selectivity that it probably engenders signal a need for improvement. A second area that warrants attention is higher education: a moderate expansion of coverage-in a system that already has a reasonably good structural foundation with distance education and private financing-may be justified.

Development of the education system

The education system's overall development is generally well balanced in coverage and structure. A moderate expansion of higher education may be justified.

	Actual	Predicted
Enrollment ratio		
Primary	118	86
Secondary	42	35
Higher	6.5	8.2
	Indonesia	Asia
Grade attainment	7.3	6.5
Adults literate (%)	74	61

Constraints and prospects

The school-age population is projected to grow quite slowly in the next decade or so. Correspondingly, the dependency ratio is expected to drop significantly, in parallel to the pattern elsewhere in Asia. The country's economic prospects are not as bright as in the average Asian country, but with the easing of demographic pressures, resources would probably be available to finance a moderate expansion of education.

	Indonesia	Asia
Growth rate*		
School-age		
population	1.0	1.4
Economy	3.9	5.0
Dependency ratio		
1985	46	43
2000	35	36
*projected to 2000 in percent per year		

Operational characteristics

Although the completion rate in primary education is comparable to the average in Asia, it is still low at 60 percent. Improving the completion rate probably calls for interventions other than reducing the pupil-teacher ratio because the ratio is already relatively low by Asian standards; however, the precise design of interventions remains to be determined. Private education is well developed in the country, particularly at the post-primary levels. In higher education an open university was established recently and it enrolled about 9 percent of all students in 1985. Females are better represented in the system than in the average Asian country, particularly in primary and secondary education. The structure of their share across the three levels suggests a probable bias against females in the transition between secondary and higher education.

Patterns of cost and financing

Public spending on education as a share of GNP is at the Asian mean, as is the average costliness of education across the three levels. In structure, the pattern of costs reveals an emphasis on primary and secondary education rather than on higher education. Because teacher salaries are close to the average for Asia, the relaels are attributable mostly to the low pupil-teacher ratios. Unit costs in higher education are relatively low, partly because of the presence of private financing and distance education. The pattern of costs and financing arrangements results in a distribution of cumulative public spending on education that is much more equitable than that in the average Asian country.

Korea

Overall assessment

At the level of aggregation adopted in this study, no major problem is apparent in the country's overall education policies: the education system is well

	Indonesia	*Asia*
Completion rate (%)		
Primary	60	61
Lower secondary	92	77
Upper secondary	96	89
Institutional share of students		
Primary: % private	8	4
Secondary: % private	50	26
Higher: % private	58	30
% distance	9	17
% overseas	1	4
Pupil-teacher ratio		
Primary	25	33
Secondary	15	23
Higher (regular)	14	14
Share of females		
Primary	48	44
Secondary	43	39
Higher	32	32

	Indonesia	*Asia*
Public spending on education		
% in GNP	3.7	3.3
% in government budget	15.0	12.6
Index of costliness		
Overall	105	100
Primary	128	100
Secondary	126	100
Higher	61	100
Teacher pay (% of per capita GNP)		
Primary	2.5	2.5
Secondary	3.2	3.3
Cost recovery (%)		
Primary	7.1	3.6
Secondary	27.4	18.4
Higher (global)	48.7	33.7
Distribution of resources		
Gini-coefficient	27	43
Share of 10% best-educated	21	36

developed and has a balanced structure; and the financing arrangements promote efficient operations in schools and achieve a relatively high level of equity in the distribution of public spending on education. This favorable assessment does not imply the absence of more specific problems. However, identifying them would probably require more detailed analysis using disaggregated data.

Development of the education system

The education system is generally very well developed: coverage in primary education is almost universal, and in higher education it is nearly twice the coverage in the typical Asian country. Almost all adults are literate, and the average grade attainment of the current school-age population is well above the average for Asia.

	Actual	Predicted
Enrollment ratio		
Primary	96	103
Secondary	75	72
Higher	32	19
	Korea	*Asia*
Grade attainment	11.4	6.5
Adults literate (%)	92	61

Constraints and prospects

The school-age population is forecast to grow at a slow pace, well below the average rate in the region. As a result, an already low dependency ratio will decline further in the next decade, thus easing the tax burden of financing education. This outlook, together with the projected rapid expansion of the economy, suggests a strong likelihood that public resources would be available for expanding or upgrading the provision of education services.

	Korea	Asia
Growth rate*		
School-age		
population	0.3	1.4
Economy	6.8	5.0
Dependency ratio		
1985	31	43
2000	24	36
*projected to 2000 in percent per year		

Operational characteristics

The rate of retention is nearly 100 percent in the lower cycles of education. Thus, selection in the system takes place almost exclusively in the transition between cycles. Private education plays an important role in the sector, particularly at the post-primary levels. In higher education, a significant share of students, though not quite as large a share as the regional average, are enrolled in distance education. Throughout the system, pupil-teacher ratios exceed those in most Asian countries, the gap increasing with rising levels of education. In primary and secondary education, the relative pupil-teacher ratios do not seem to have an adverse effect on student achievement, as indicated by the results of international comparisons. Females are well represented at the lower levels of education, but their share in higher education is surprisingly low-slightly below the average for Asia.

Patterns of cost and financing

The wide coverage of the education system and the strong academic achievement of students are remarkable in view of the fact that the government spends no more on education than other countries in the region. The average costliness of education across the three levels slightly exceeds the Asian mean, but in structure the pattern of costs reveals a clear emphasis on primary education. At the first two levels the relatively high unit costs reflect a unique combination of high teacher salaries and high pupil-teacher ratios, with teacher salaries having a stronger effect. This combination does not appear to have an adverse effect on student achievement, given the high score of Korean students in the IEA study. In financing, the extent of cost recovery rises with levels of education, reaching 77 percent in higher education. As documented elsewhere, the presence of private financing is partly responsible for this level's relatively low unit costs. The distribution of public spending on education is highly equitable, with the 10 percent best-educated in a generation receiving close to their proportionate share of cumulative resources appropriated to the entire generation through government-financed education.

		Korea	Asia
Completion rate (%)			
Primary		97	61
Lower secondary		98	77
Upper secondary		95	89
Institutional share of students			
Primary:	% private	2	4
Secondary:	% private	40	26
Higher:	% private	65	30
	% distance	12	17
	% overseas	2	4
Pupil-teacher ratio			
Primary		38	33
Secondary		34	23
Higher (regular)		40	14
Share of females			
Primary		49	44
Secondary		47	39
Higher		30	32

	Korea	Asia
Public spending on education		
% in GNP	3.4	3.3
% in government budget	16.6	12.6
Index of costliness		
Overall	114	100
Primary	167	100
Secondary	127	100
Higher	47	100
Teacher pay (% of per capita GNP)		
Primary	4.5	2.5
Secondary	5.4	3.3
Cost recovery (%)		
Primary	1	3.6
Secondary	34	18.4
Higher (global)	76.6	33.7
Distribution of resources		
Gini-coefficient	16	43
Share of 10% best-educated	13	36

Malaysia

Overall assessment

Despite the substantial public spending on education, the country achieves less than similar Asian countries with lower levels of spending. This outcome results partly from the education system's limited reliance on private financing and from its generally high unit costs. At the lower levels, the system appears to be well developed, although there is scope for raising pupil-teacher ratios to reduce costs. An expansion of coverage at the post-primary levels, but particularly in higher education, appears to be warranted. Options to facilitate this expansion, without further increasing an already high level of public spending or diverting spending away from primary education, include increased private financing in higher education (by raising fees in public institutions and/or allowing private universities to operate) and establishment of a system of distance education.

Development of the education system

In enrollment ratios the education system is less well developed than is expected on the basis of the country's per capita GNP. The gap is particularly noticeable in higher education. The average grade attainment of the school-age population and the adult literacy rate exceed the average for Asia, reflecting the better internal efficiency of the Malaysian system.

	Actual	*Predicted*
Enrollment ratio		
Primary	99	101
Secondary	53	69
Higher	8	18
	Malaysia	*Asia*
Grade attainment	9.2	6.5
Adults literate (%)	74	61

Constraints and prospects

The school-age population is expected to grow at a moderate rate. In parallel to the trend in most other Asian countries, the tax burden of financing education is likely to drop significantly over the next decade as the dependency ratio declines. Because the economy is forecast to grow substantially faster than the school-age population, resources are likely to be available to expand or upgrade the provision of education services.

	Malaysia	*Asia*
Growth rate*		
School-age		
population	1.4	1.4
Economy	5.0	5.0
Dependency ratio		
1985	41	43
2000	33	36
*projected to 2000 in percent per year		

Operational characteristics

The rate of retention is nearly 100 percent at all the lower cycles of education. This achievement in primary education is particularly remarkable in view of most Asian countries' weak performance in this respect. The private sector does not play a significant role at all levels in the system. A unique feature, however, is that nearly one-third of the students in higher education are enrolled in overseas institutions, amounting to a sizable offshore private sector. Distance education is not well developed. Pupilteacher ratios are low, especially in primary education and to a lesser extent in higher education. Females are well represented throughout the system.

		Malaysia	*Asia*
Completion rate (%)			
Primary		97	61
Lower secondary		90	77
Upper secondary		96	89
Institutional share of students			
Primary:	% private	0	4
Secondary:	% private	2	26
Higher:	% private	8	30
	% distance	1	17
	% overseas	31	4
Pupil-teacher ratio			
Primary		24	33
Secondary		22	23
Higher (regular)		11	14
Share of females			
Primary		49	44
Secondary		49	39
Higher		45	32

Patterns of cost and financing

Aggregate spending on education exceeds the average for Asian countries by a wide margin, partly due to the system's relatively high unit costs and limited reliance on private financing. The structure of unit costs is quite even across the three levels. The contribution of private financing is comparable, on average, to the mean for Asia, but it reflects the combined result of limited cost recovery in local higher education (5.8 percent) and almost 100 percent private financing for the bulk of students enrolled abroad. Teacher salaries are slightly lower than the average for Asian countries. This pattern suggests that the high unit cost of primary edu-

	Malaysia	*Asia*
Public spending on education		
% in GNP	6.0	3.3
% in government budget	16.0	12.6
Index of costliness		
Overall	129	100
Primary	143	100
Secondary	115	100
Higher	128	100
Teacher pay (% of per capita GNP)		
Primary	2.4	2.5
Secondary	3.1	3.3
Cost recovery (%)		
Primary	4	3.6
Secondary	41	8.4
Higher (global)	15.1	33.7
Distribution of resources		
Gini-coefficient	38	43
Share of 10% best-educated	32	36

cation (in particular) is due mainly to the relatively low pupil-teacher ratio at this level. The overall characteristics of the system imply a distribution of public spending on education that is slightly more equitable than in the average Asian country.

Myanmar

Overall assessment

The data permit only the most superficial conclusions. The education system appears to be well developed in quantitative terms despite a modest level of public spending on education. This is probably due to the high share of enrollments in correspondence higher education and the relatively low unit costs of primary education. However, there is little information on other aspects of the system's characteristics and performance. Embarking on an overall sector study (with some emphasis on cost and financing issues) therefore appears to be a priority for future Bank work in this country.

Development of the education system

The education system's coverage is comparable to the coverage predicted on the basis of the country's per capita GNP. It is also balanced across the three levels of education.

	Actual	Predicted
Enrollment ratio		
Primary	107	82
Secondary	23	25
Higher	5.4	5.2

	Myanmar	Asia
Grade attainment	7.0	6.5
Adults literate (%)	..	61

Constraints and prospects

The school-age population is likely to grow only slowly. As a result, the dependency ratio is expected to drop quite sharply by 2000. The rate of economic growth is expected to be modest. But as the demographic constraint eases, resources beyond what is needed to maintain current enrollment ratios are likely to be available for expansion, assuming that the share of education in GNP remains unchanged.

	Myanmar	Asia
Growth rate*		
School-age population	1.0	1.4
Economy	3.5	5.0
Dependency ratio		
1985	47	43
2000	35	36
*projected to 2000 in percent per year		

Operational characteristics

The scantiness of data limits comment to two observations: the country has a sizable correspondence program in higher education; and the pupil-teacher ratio is somewhat high in primary education. It is not known whether the high pupil-teacher ratio has an adverse effect on the system's ability to retain students to the end of the primary cycle.

Patterns of cost and financing

Public spending on education as a share of GNP is low compared with that in most other Asian countries, even though as a share of the government budget it is comparable. There is no information on other aspects of the cost and financing of education in the country.

	Myanmar	Asia
Public spending on education		
% in GNP	1.8	3.3
% in government budget	10.9	12.6
Index of costliness		
Overall	..	100
Primary	..	100
Secondary	..	100
Higher	..	100
Teacher pay (% of per capita GNP)		
Primary	..	2.5
Secondary	..	3.3
Cost recovery (%)		
Primary	..	3.6
Secondary	..	18.4
Higher	..	33.7
Distribution of resources		
Gini-coefficient	..	43
Share of 10% best-educated	..	36

		Myanmar	Asia
Completion rate (%)			
Primary		..	61
Lower secondary		..	77
Upper secondary		..	89
Institutional share of students			
Primary:	% private	..	4
Secondary:	% private	..	26
Higher:	% private	0	30
	% distance	54	17
	% overseas	0	4
Pupil-teacher ratio			
Primary		46	33
Secondary		29	23
Higher		..	14
Share of females			
Primary		..	44
Secondary		..	39
Higher		..	32

Nepal

Overall assessment

The education system has at least two favorable features: its coverage is consistent with the country's level of per capita GNP, and the extent of private financing appears to be reasonably adequate. But there is room for improvement. One priority is to improve the low rate of completion in primary education. Although additional analysis is required to design specific interventions, improving the low completion rate most likely requires increasing resources for primary education. This increase likely calls for an overall rise in public spending on education because (1) the current level of spending is relatively low-1.8 percent of GNP compared with 3.3 percent on average in Asia-and (2) the projected demographic and economic conditions are such that over time at this level of aggregate spending, resources would be available only to maintain current levels of coverage, leaving little extra for upgrading the system. A second problem is the relatively high unit costs of higher education. The development of distance higher education is among the potential options for reducing those costs.

Development of the education system

The enrollment ratio at each level of education is comparable to that predicted on the basis of the country's per capita GNP. (Note that the figure for primary education is probably substantially overestimated.) However, the grade attainment of the school-age population and the adult literacy rate are very low and compare unfavorably with the averages for Asia.

Constraints and prospects

The rapid growth of the school-age population implies that the dependency ratio, already high in 1985, is unlikely to decline much over the next decade, in sharp contrast to the expectations elsewhere in Asia. A further constraint is that the economy is not expected to grow much faster than the school-age population. As a result, few extra resources would be available for expansion, if public spending on education remains at the current level.

Operational characteristics

The rate of completion in primary education is extremely low. Pupil-teacher ratios at all levels are comparable to the averages for the region. Private education appears to be moderately well developed at the post-primary levels, although it still accounts for a smaller share of enrollments than is average

	Actual	Predicted
Enrollment ratio		
Primary	82	82
Secondary	25	23
Higher	4.6	4.8
	Nepal	*Asia*
Grade attainment	3.6	6.5
Adults literate (%)	26	61

	Nepal	*Asia*
Growth rate*		
School-age		
population	3.1	1.4
Economy	3.8	5.0
Dependency ratio		
1985	49	43
2000	51	36
*projected to 2000 in percent per year		

	Nepal	Asia
Completion rate (%)		
Primary	33	61
Lower secondary	89	77
Upper secondary	81	89
Institutional share of students		
Primary: % private	5	4
Secondary: % private	10	26
Higher: % private	23	30
% distance	1	17
% overseas	2	4
Pupil-teacher ratio		
Primary	36	33
Secondary	28	23
Higher	13	14
Share of females		
Primary	29	44
Secondary	23	39
Higher	20	32

among Asian countries. Females are not well represented throughout the system.

Patterns of cost and financing

Public spending on education as a share of GNP is significantly lower than that in other Asian countries. The structure of unit costs suggests a strong bias in favor of higher education. At this level, unit costs exceed the regional mean by a wide margin, whereas at the two lower levels, unit costs are below the regional means. The extent of cost recovery is reasonably high in secondary and higher education. However, the pattern of costs and structure of enrollments are such that even with this feature in the financing arrangements, public spending on education remains relatively concentrated among a small group of people.

	Nepal	Asia
Public spending on education		
% in GNP	1.8	3.3
% in government budget	9.6	12.6
Index of costliness		
Overall	111	100
Primary	91	100
Secondary	73	100
Higher	167	100
Teacher pay (% of per capita GNP)		
Primary	2.8	2.5
Secondary	5.0	3.3
Cost recovery (%)		
Primary	0	3.6
Secondary	41	18.4
Higher (global)	31.8	33.7
Distribution of resources		
Gini-coefficient	57	43
Share of 10% best-educated	54	36

Papua New Guinea

Overall assessment

Perhaps the most important policy issue is the high costs of education throughout the system. Addressing this issue probably calls for an assessment of teacher salaries, as well as an evaluation of the ways to raise pupil-teacher ratios, particularly in higher education. Beyond this system wide issue, improving completion rates in primary and lower secondary education also warrants attention.

Development of the education system

The education system's coverage is below what might be expected given the country's level of per capita GNP, the gap being wide at all levels of education. The average grade attainment of the school-age population and the rate of literacy among adults compare poorly with the means for Asia.

	Actual	Predicted
Enrollment ratio		
Primary	69	88
Secondary	13	38
Higher	2.0	9.2

	Papua New Guinea	Asia
Grade attainment	4.3	6.5
Adults literate (%)	45	61

Constraints and prospects

The country's school-age population is expected to grow somewhat faster than in most other Asian countries. Thus, although the dependency ratio is likely to drop over the next decade, it will remain relatively high. Because the economy is forecast to grow faster than the school-age population, resources beyond what is needed to maintain current levels of coverage would likely be available for expanding or upgrading education services.

	Papua New Guinea	Asia
Growth rate*		
School-age population	2.0	1.4
Economy	5.1	5.0
Dependency ratio		
1985	50	43
2000	40	36
*projected to 2000 in percent per year		

Operational characteristics

The rate of completion in the education system is not high, particularly in the primary and lower secondary cycles. Private education is not well developed at all levels. At the higher level there is a system of correspondence education that enrolls a fairly sizable share of students. The outflow of students abroad is small but not negligible. In primary and secondary education the pupil-teacher ratio is comparable to the Asian average, but in higher education it is well below the average. Females are under-represented mostly in higher education.

Patterns of cost and financing

	Papua New Guinea	Asia
Completion rate (%)		
Primary	67	61
Lower secondary	63	77
Upper secondary	95	89
Institutional share of students		
Primary: % private	1	4
Secondary: % private	?	26
Higher: % private	6	30
% distance	9	17
% overseas	3	4
Pupil-teacher ratio		
Primary	31	33
Secondary	25	23
Higher (regular)	8	14
Share of females		
Primary	44	44
Secondary	36	39
Higher	23	32

The country's public spending on education as a share of GNP is the highest in Asia, partly because of the exceptional costliness of education throughout the system. Across levels, higher education has the biggest unit costs relative to the regional average. In primary and secondary education the high unit costs reflect mostly the effect of teachers' salaries, which are very high compared with the pay of teachers elsewhere in Asia. The pattern of cost recovery has the unique characteristic of being substantial only in secondary education. For equity, the structure of costs, enrollments, and financing arrangements imply a distribution of public spending that is significantly less equitable than that in most other Asian countries.

	Papua New Guinea	*Asia*
Public spending on education		
% in GNP	6.9	3.3
% in government budget	17.9	12.6
Index of costliness		
Overall	450	100
Primary	294	100
Secondary	352	100
Higher	705	100
Teacher pay (% of per capita GNP)		
Primary	6.8	2.5
Secondary	10.0	3.3
Cost recovery (%)		
Primary	8.7	3.6
Secondary	39.8	18.4
Higher (global)	6.3	33.7
Distribution of resources		
Gini-coefficient	62	43
Share of 10% best-educated	54	36

Philippines

Overall assessment

The education system does not suffer from major structural problems. However, it is currently in transition between two strikingly different policy regimes-from one in which private funding is predominant, particularly at the post-primary levels, to one in which government funding will become larger. At this juncture in the transition, two main concerns are (1) ensuring that public spending on education continues to be equitably distributed, and (2) containing the inevitable rise in costs that often follows nationalization and increased government involvement in financing education. For ensuring continued equity, more attention on improving retention rates in primary education would be appropriate. For containing costs, the focus should be on improving efficiency in secondary education, because it is at this level that public subsidization has increased most dramatically.

Development of the education system

The education system's coverage is extensive, exceeding what might be expected for a country with the Philip-

	Actual	*Predicted*
Enrollment ratio		
Primary	106	87
Secondary	65	37
Higher	38	9
	Philippines	*Asia*
Grade attainment	10.2	6.5
Adults literate (%)	86	61

pines' level of per capita GNP. The average grade attainment of the school-age population surpasses the Asian average by a wide margin, as does the adult literacy rate.

Constraints and prospects

The school-age population is projected to grow modestly, implying a sharp decline in the dependency ratio by 2000. The economy is forecast to grow much faster than the school-age population. Thus, if unit costs and the GNP share of public spending on education remain unchanged, resources beyond what is required to maintain current levels of coverage would probably be available for expansion of the system in quantitative or qualitative terms.

	Philippines	Asia
Growth rate*		
School-age		
population	1.5	1.4
Economy	5.3	5.0
Dependency ratio		
1985	47	43
2000	37	36
*projected to 2000 in percent per year		

Operational characteristics

The system's rate of retention, although comparable to the average for Asian countries, is not high in either the primary or secondary cycles. As documented elsewhere in this report, the low retention rate has led to adverse social selectivity in education. The share of enrollments in the private sector is exceptionally high, exceeding that in all other Asian countries, particularly at the post-primary levels. The pupil-teacher ratio is at the Asian average in primary and higher education, but is much higher at the secondary level. Following the recent nationalization of local secondary schools, however, the trend has been toward a decline in this ratio. Females are exceptionally well represented at all levels, especially in higher education.

		Philippines	Asia
Completion rate (%)			
Primary		66	61
Lower secondary		74	77
Upper secondary		..	89
Institutional share of students			
Primary:	% private	6	4
Secondary:	% private	42	26
Higher:	% private	83	30
	% distance	0	17
	% overseas	0	4
Pupil-teacher ratio			
Primary		31	33
Secondary		32	23
Higher (regular)		16	14
Share of females			
Primary		49	44
Secondary		50	39
Higher		54	32

Patterns of cost and financing

In 1985, government spending on education as a share of GNP was much lower than that in other Asian countries. However, with the dramatic rise in teachers' salaries since 1986, government spending is fast approaching the Asian average. Teachers' salaries are already close to the average for the region. As a result, although unit costs in 1985 were generally on the low side, they have risen steadily in recent years and are now probably comparable to the regional averages.

Sri Lanka

	Philippines	Asia
Public spending on education		
% in GNP	1.8	3.3
% in government budget	11.5	12.6
Index of costliness		
Overall	46	100
Primary	59	100
Secondary	47	100
Higher	34	100
Teacher pay (% of per capita GNP)		
Primary	1.6	2.5
Secondary	1.7	3.3
Cost recovery (%)		
Primary	0	3.6
Secondary	9.3	18.4
Higher (global)	85.8	33.7
Distribution of resources		
Gini-coefficient	19	43
Share of 10% best-educated	14	36

Overall assessment

The education system is well developed at the lower levels in quantitative terms, reflecting the focus of government spending and the fact that unit costs are low. However, there is room for improving retention rates in the primary and, especially, the lower secondary cycle. Higher education appears to be underdeveloped-its coverage is much below what might be expected in a country with Sri Lanka's per capita GNP. Increasing the reliance on private financing at this level is worth exploring as an option for the subsector's expansion. The performance of the open university should be examined, both because its share of enrollments has been dropping sharply in recent years, and because it has a significantly lower pupil-teacher ratio than similar institutions in other countries.

Development of the education system

The system's coverage at the lower levels is more extensive than is predicted on the basis of the country's per capita GNP. However, access to higher education appears to be constrained. The country achieves better-than-average results in the mean grade attainment of the school-age population and in the prevalence of adult literacy.

	Actual	Predicted
Enrollment ratio		
Primary	103	85
Secondary	63	31
Higher	4.6	7.0

	Sri Lanka	Asia
Grade attainment	9.5	6.5
Adults literate (%)	87	61

Constraints and prospects

The school-age population is expected to grow moderately, so that an already low dependency ratio will decline somewhat further during the coming decade. The economy is forecast to grow at about the average pace for Asian countries. Taken together, these prospects

	Sri Lanka	Asia
Growth rate*		
School-age population	1.1	1.4
Economy	4.8	5.0
Dependency ratio		
1985	36	43
2000	31	36
*projected to 2000 in percent per year		

suggest that beyond maintaining the current levels of coverage in the system, public resources would probably materialize for expanding or upgrading education services.

Operational characteristics

The retention rate in primary education is reasonably high, although it could be further improved; in contrast, the rate in the lower secondary cycle is surprisingly low. Private education plays a limited role at all levels in the system. In higher education, the open university accounted for a quarter of total enrollments in 1985, high by Asian standards. However, it is noteworthy that its share had been even larger in past years. The share of enrollments abroad, at 10 percent, is the second highest among Asian countries. At all levels in the system, the pupil-teacher ratio is comparable to the regional average. Females are well represented in the system, particularly at the secondary level.

		Sri Lanka	Asia
Completion rate (%)			
Primary		85	61
Lower secondary		75	77
Upper secondary		99	89
Institutional share of students			
Primary:	% private	1	4
Secondary:	% private	2	26
Higher:	% private	0	30
	% distance	29	17
	% overseas	10	4
Pupil-teacher ratio			
Primary		32	33
Secondary		26	23
Higher (regular)		12	14
Share of females			
Primary		48	44
Secondary		53	39
Higher		40	32

Patterns of cost and financing

Public spending on education as a share of GNP was somewhat below the average for Asian countries in 1985. However, teachers' salaries were raised in 1988, and are now at about the same level as elsewhere in the region. Correspondingly, aggregate government spending on education is now probably close to the regional average. Unit costs in 1985 were only half as high as the Asian averages. Although they probably have risen in recent years, they remain somewhat low by Asian standards.

Their structure across levels implies a bias in favor of the lower levels. The rate of cost recovery is limited in primary and secondary education. In higher education, the global rate is high, but this is due mainly to the relatively high rate of cost recovery in the open university (58 percent); the rate of cost recovery for the regular institutions is very low at less than 4 percent. The distribution of public spending on education does not appear overly inequitable: the best-educated decile in a cohort receives no more than 30 percent of the government's cumulative expenditure on the entire cohort.

	Sri Lanka	Asia
Public spending on education		
% in GNP	2.8	3.3
% in government budget	8.1	12.6
Index of costliness		
Overall	56	100
Primary	62	100
Secondary	50	100
Higher	56	100
Teacher pay (% of per capita GNP)		
Primary	1.6	2.5
Secondary	2.1	3.3
Cost recovery (%)		
Primary	3.1	3.6
Secondary	3.1	18.4
Higher (global)	20.5	33.7
Distribution of resources		
Gini-coefficient	33	43
Share of 10% best-educated	28	36

Thailand

Overall assessment

There appears to be some imbalance in the structure of the education system because secondary education is less well developed than might be expected given the country's per capita GNP. Unit costs in primary education are high, but the retention rate in this cycle is significantly below 100 percent (even though it might be above the Asian average). The mix of schooling inputs probably deserves further investigation. In higher education, the institutional arrangements are unique, with a small, costly, and selective public and private sector (regular institutions) and a large, low-cost, and nonselective system of open universities. There are advantages to such an arrangement, but more information is needed to evaluate performance, particularly for external efficiency.

Development of the education system

The system's coverage is better than predicted in primary and higher education, but worse in secondary education. The adult literacy rate is exceptionally high. However, because of the relative neglect of secondary education, the average grade attainment of the school-age population is only slightly better than the average for Asia.

	Actual	Predicted
Enrollment ratio		
Primary	97	89
Secondary	30	41
Higher	20	10

	Thailand	Asia
Grade attainment	7.0	6.5
Adults literate (%)	91	61

Constraints and prospects

The school-age population is expected to grow very slowly, and the dependency ratio is projected to drop steeply, reaching well below the Asian average by 2000. At the same time, the economy is forecast to expand briskly. These favorable prospects imply that the budgetary constraints on education expansion, in terms of coverage or improved quality, are likely to ease considerably.

Operational characteristics

Completion rates are high throughout the system, although there remains room for improvement in primary education. The private share of enrollments is moderately high only at the secondary level. In higher education, nearly 80 percent of students are enrolled in the open universities; of the remaining students, about 30 percent are in private institutions, and 70 percent in selective public universities. Pupil-teacher ratios at all levels of education are lower than the average for Asian countries, but the gap is large in primary and (regular) higher education. Females are well represented at all levels in the system.

	Thailand	Asia
Growth rate*		
School-age		
population	0.5	1.4
Economy	6.0	5.0
Dependency ratio		
1985	41	43
2000	29	36
*projected to 2000 in percent per year		

	Thailand	Asia
Public spending on education		
% in GNP	3.6	3.3
% in government budget	19.4	12.6
Index of costliness		
Overall	89	100
Primary	157	100
Secondary	83	100
Higher	27	100
Teacher pay (% of per capita GNP)		
Primary	2.5	2.5
Secondary	2.9	3.3
Cost recovery (%)		
Primary	0	3.6
Secondary	18	18.4
Higher (global)	26.9	33.7
Distribution of resources		
Gini-coefficient	33	43
Share of 10% best-educated	23	36

Patterns of cost and financing

The country's public spending on education as a share of GNP is somewhat larger than the average for Asian countries. As a whole, unit costs are lower than elsewhere in the region. In structure, however, the pattern of costs reveals a clear bias in favor of primary education. The below-average unit costs in higher education are due mainly to the predominance of low-cost distance education. In primary education, the high unit costs reflect the effect of a relatively low pupil-teacher ratio. Cost recovery appears to be moderately high at the post-primary levels. However, the rate is much higher in the open universities (28 percent) than in the selective public institutions (5 percent). The distribution of public spending on education is fairly equitable, with the 10 percent best-educated in a generation receiving less than a quarter of the cumulative public spending appropriated to the entire cohort through publicly financed education.

	Thailand	*Asia*
Completion rate (%)		
Primary	80	61
Lower secondary	91	77
Upper secondary	87	89
Institutional share of students		
Primary: % private	9	4
Secondary: % private	20	26
Higher: % private	6	30
% distance	78	17
% overseas	1	4
Pupil-teacher ratio		
Primary	19	33
Secondary	20	23
Higher (regular)	8	14
Share of females		
Primary	48	44
Secondary	48	39
Higher	46	32

Appendix B

Sources of Data

For convenience, the data can be grouped into five main types of indicators, having to do with (1) the education system's macro characteristics (for example, enrollments ratios); (2) the system's operational characteristics (for example, pupil-teacher ratios); (3) the constraints—demographic and economic—acting on the system; (4) the pattern of costs and financing of education services; and (5) the returns to investments in education. (Tables at the end of this appendix are numbered to reflect these categories.) These data come essentially from four sources: the World Bank's computerized databases, BESD and ANDREX[1]; government publications including budget documents; World Bank country reports[2]; and in a few cases, papers by agencies of the United Nations and by individual authors (often government officials).

Data for the more standard indicators—such as enrollment ratios, percentage of females enrolled, population, and GNP growth rates—are readily available through the BESD and ANDREX databases; the other sources were used only to supply the occasional missing number for particular years. The financial data, however, are often not included in the computerized databases, and so were derived primarily from the other three sources. For the sake of completeness, data on either side of a given year were used whenever the statistics for that year are missing. Even so, gaps in the data remain. This shortcoming applies mostly to countries with no active Bank loans for the sector in recent years (such as Thailand) and thus for which no recent sector reports have been issued; or to countries for which no recent macroeconomic report existed at the time of data gathering (such as China). To the extent possible, the required data for such countries were drawn from statistical series issued by the government, supplemented by the reports of informed persons.

Because of the comparative nature of this study, special emphasis was placed on compiling data that share a more or less common definition. This applies particularly to the financial indicators where there is greater scope for differences in definition. To maximize comparability, the statistics were compiled, whenever feasible, from the raw data reported in the sources cited above. As appropriate and possible, the resulting statistics were checked for consistency with other related data.

For data on the macro characteristics of education, note that the length of education cycles reflects the official length of schooling in the system. In some countries, the de facto structure may differ slightly from the official structure. In China, for example, rural schools may have shorter cycles; and in countries where the system has been restructured in recent years (such as India), some pupils may still follow the previous curriculum.

On the share of enrollments in private schools, the public-private distinction is not always the most meaningful one. This is because private schools sometimes receive substantial subsidies from the government. The meaning of the data would be clarified if schools were classified into one of three types: public schools (publicly run and publicly financed), assisted private schools (privately run and partly financed with subsidies from the government), and regular private schools (privately run and privately financed). However, the available data do not permit this breakdown; so the "private" category includes, in most instances, schools that are privately run, regardless of whether or not they receive government subsidies. Where information is available, the extent of public subsidization is indicated in a footnote to the relevant tables.

In the data on the operational characteristics of the education system, note that the pattern of cohort survival and selection may not always coincide exactly with the official structure of the education system—particularly in countries where the current structure is relatively new. In such countries, the old curriculum and the corresponding points of selection in the system may still apply to a significant portion of the students. And for the measurement of excess demand, the number of exam-takers or applicants gives only a rough indication of the demand for higher education. A single examination may serve the dual purposes of certifying completion and screening applicants for the next level, making it hard to distinguish between exam-takers who intend only to obtain the certification and those who intend to proceed further.

For the demographic and financial constraints on the education system, the financial data tend to present more problems because of possible differences in definition. Statistics on government expenditure—overall spending and spending on education—were taken mainly from the statistical appendix of the latest available World Bank country economic memorandum for the country. In most cases the data are presented in standard format across countries and are comparable to data from the IMF Government Finance Statistics Yearbook. Where they differ, the series from the Bank's country economic memoranda were preferred on the assumption that Bank staff use a common definition when constructing the public finance tables. In addition, that source provides the most up-to-date data, often up to 1988. For countries for which the required data are not available through the country economic memoranda, we have taken the data directly from the government's own statistical series (China, Korea, and Myanmar, recent years).

For most countries, "government spending" refers to spending by the central government. However, in countries where local government is fiscally important (as in India), the term refers to the consolidated spending of both the central and local governments. This flexible definition improves the comparability of data on government spending because it reflects more accurately the fiscal size of the government in general, as well as the aggregate public investment effort in the sector.

For government spending on education, the data also include spending by lower levels of government and by non-education ministries where such spending is large. For example, the data for India include the states' spending on education; in China, the data include local authorities' spending on the salaries of primary and secondary school teachers; and in Indonesia, the data include part of the spending of the ministry of home affairs because this ministry is responsible for the salaries of primary school teachers.[3] For the distribution of spending by level of education, the data are for total (capital and recurrent) spending. In theory, it would have been preferable to distinguish between capital and recurrent expenditures because recurrent expenditures better reflect the momentum of spending. However, in many countries, it is not possible to make the distinction; in Bangladesh, for example, the development budget includes significant amounts of recurrent spending; and in Indonesia a large share of the recurrent spending of universities appears in their development budgets.

For the data on costs and financing, unit costs refer to the operating cost per student. In some systems the fees charged to students are kept at the school to defray minor expenditures (such as in Malaysian primary schools) and therefore do not appear in public accounts of government spending on education. Thus, in order to derive unit operating costs, the public cost per student needs to be augmented by the average fee contribution per student to reflect the unit operating cost of education. This adjustment would not be needed, however, in systems where the revenues from fees do not represent extrabudgetary financial flows. In practice, the data were derived in several ways. Where a recent education sector study exists (such as for Bangladesh, the Philippines, Indonesia, and Nepal), the data, when available, were drawn directly from the reports. In other cases, the unit costs were estimated from more basic data on total spending and enrollments. Where possible, all estimates, including those drawn from sector reports, were checked for consistency between the macro statistics on spending and the micro data on both teachers' salaries and distribution of spending between salaries and other education inputs.

Data on teachers' salaries are rare for almost all countries. Only for Indonesia were these data available directly from a sector report. For the other countries teachers' salaries were estimated using one or both of the following techniques (depending on the type of data available): spreading the wage bill for teaching staff (which includes basic pay and allowances) over the total number of teachers (for example, China); reconstructing the average remuneration from the salary scale, applied to the distribution of teachers in the various grades (for example, Sri Lanka and the Philippines). For China, the data refer to the weighted average of teachers employed by the state and by collectives. And for the Philippines, they refer, at the secondary level, to the wages of teachers in national schools.

Finally, for the share of operating costs financed through fees—perhaps one of the most difficult pieces of information to obtain—some of the data were taken from existing education sector reports. The original source in these reports is often official fee schedules, not actual revenues collected. The exceptions are the data for Korea, Sri Lanka (higher education), the Philippines, and Nepal (higher education), which do reflect actual fee revenues; accordingly, these data give a better picture of the extent of financing through fees. For comparisons across levels of education and across countries, one should probably not attach too much importance to small differences in the statistics, say up to 3 to 5 percentage points.

Notes

1. The BESD and ANDREX databases are compiled from statistics supplied by other international agencies. For example, data for education come largely from the United Nations Educational and Scientific and Cultural Organization (Unesco); data for GNP and government finance, from the International Monetary Fund (IMF); and so on. For ease of reference, the name of the relevant file on the BESD database is given in parentheses whenever this source is cited.

2. To keep track of the many World Bank country reports and to simplify additions to the references, the citation for these reports includes the name of the country; thus, a report for China published in 1988 would be cited as "World Bank-China 1988"; this notation distinguishes the report from other World Bank country reports published in the same year. If multiple reports for the same country were issued in a single year, the citation would include an alphabetical suffix after the publication year. World Bank reports that are not country-specific are cited in the usual way (for example, World Bank 1986). Unless otherwise indicated, World Bank country reports and government publications give data only for the country mentioned in the citation. Table sources are listed at the end of each table.

3. Note the case of the Philippines. Until 1986 local governments were partly responsible for financing secondary schools (*barangay* schools), for which revenue was generated through earmarked tax proceeds that were shared with the central government. Mingat and Tan (1988) estimated that local governments' expenditures on education added about 10 percent to the amount spent by the central government. In 1986 the government introduced sweeping changes in education; one of these changes was the nationalization of local schools, under which local school teachers were brought into the civil service. Financial responsibility for education at all levels was shifted largely to the central government. Correspondingly, the revenue from taxes earmarked for education reverted almost wholly to the central government, and spending by local governments disappeared almost completely. Because of these changes, and because local government' spending on education has never been very large, "governments spending on education" reported in the text and appendix tables for the Philippines refers only to central government spending.

Table B1.1 Length of education cycles, selected Asian countries, 1986
(years)

Country	Primary	Secondary		Total	Total primary and secondary
		Lower	Upper		
Bangladesh	5	3	4	7	12
Bhutan	6	2	2	4	10
China	6	3	3	6	12
India	5	3	4	6	11
Indonesia	6	3	3	6	12
Korea	6	3	3	6	12
Lao PDR	5	3	3	6	11
Malaysia	6	3	4	7	13
Myanmar	5	4	2	6	11
Nepal	5	2	3	5	10
Papua New Guinea	6	4	2	6	12
Philippines	6	4	0	4	10
Singapore	6	4	2	6	12
Sri Lanka	6	5	2	7	13
Thailand	6	3	3	6	12

Source: Postlethwaite (1988) for all countries listed except Bangladesh and Myanmar, the sources for which are World Bank-Bangladesh (1988b) and Husen and Postlethwaite (1985).

Table B1.2 Enrollment ratios by level of education, selected Asian countries, selected years, 1970-85

Country	Primary				Secondary				Higher		
	1970	1975	1980	1985	1970	1975	1980	1985	1975	1980	1985
Bangladesh	54	73	62	60	..	19	18	18	..	3.0	5.2
Bhutan	6	9	15	25	1	1	1	4	..	..	0.1
China	89	126	105	118	24	..	..	39	..	1.3	1.7
India	73	79	81	92	26	26	31	41	0.6	..	9.0
Indonesia	80	86	107	118	16	20	29	42	8.6	3.9	6.5
Korea	103	107	109	96	42	56	76	75ᵃ	2.4	15.7	31.6
Lao PDR	53	58	89	94	3	7	17	19	10.3	0.5	1.5
Malaysia	87	91	95	99	34	42	49	53	..	4.3	6.0
Myanmar	83	83	87	107	21	21	22	23	2.8	5.1	5.4
Nepal	22	54	69	82	10	13	21	25	2.1	3.2	4.6
Papua New Guinea	52	56	62	70	8	12	11	13	2.3	1.9	2.0
Philippines	108	107	114	106	46	54	62	65	2.5	27.7	38.0
Singapore	105	110	108	115	46	52	58	71	18.4	7.8	11.8
Sri Lanka	99	77	98	103	47	48	51	63	9.0	2.8	4.6
Thailand	83	83	99	97	17	26	29	30	1.3	13.1	19.6

.. Not available.

a. Figure reflects average for lower and upper secondary education.

Source: BESD (SOCIND) database, supplemented by India (1988); World Bank-Indonesia (1982); Burma (1986) for Myanmar; World Bank-Nepal (1988a); World Bank-Papua New Guinea (1987); and Unesco (1987a) and (1988).

Table B1.3 Percentage of females in total enrolled by level of education, selected Asian countries, selected years, 1970-85

Country	Primary 1970	Primary 1975	Primary 1980	Primary 1985	Secondary 1970	Secondary 1975	Secondary 1980	Secondary 1985	Higher 1970	Higher 1975	Higher 1980	Higher 1985
Bangladesh	32	34	37	40	..	25	24	28	10	10	14	19
Bhutan	5	27	29	34	3	10	..	18	..	..	22	17
China	..	45	45	45	..	39	39	40	..	33	23	30
India	37	38	39	40	28	30	33	34	22	23	26	29
Indonesia	46	46	46	48	34	38	37	43	25	28	31	32
Korea	48	48	49	49	38	41	46	47	24	26	24	30
Lao PDR	37	42	45	45	27	33	39	41	19	28	31	36
Malaysia	47	48	49	49	41	..	48	49	..	..	39	45
Myanmar	47	48	..	..	39	..	..	..	38	49	..	..
Nepal	15	16	28	29	17	17	20	23	..	20	19	20
Papua New Guinea	37	37	41	44	27	28	32	36	..	..	22	23
Philippines	..	..	49	49	..	..	53	50	56	..	53	54
Singapore	47	47	48	47	48	49	50	50	30	40	39	42
Sri Lanka	47	47	48	48	51	51	51	53	3	36	43	40
Thailand	47	47	48	48	42	44	47	48	42	40	44	46

.. Not available.

Source: BESD (UNESCOED) database, supplemented by India (1988); World Bank-Papua New Guinea (1987); and United Nations (1985) for Thailand.

Table B1.4 Share of private enrollments by level of education, selected Asian countries, selected years, 1970-85

Country	Primary				Secondary				Higher		
	1970	1975	1980	1985	1970	1975	1980	1985	1975	1980	1985
Bangladesh	..	4.1	14.6	11.0	..	..	..	93.0[b]	..	..	57.3[b]
Bhutan	..	..	..	..	..	..	..	..	..	..	..
China	..	..	..	0.0	..	..	..	0.0	..	..	0.0
India	..	..	15.9[a]	..	..	..	68.2[a]	..	..	..	57.6[b]
Indonesia	..	15.0	10.0	8.0	..	..	49.1	49.7	..	..	58.3[c]
Korea	1.1	1.2	1.3	1.5	..	45.4	46.4	39.9	..	..	69.3
Lao PDR	11.3	..	0.0	0.0	..	0.0	0.0	0.0	..	..	..
Malaysia	..	..	..	0.3	..	..	..	1.7	..	..	..
Myanmar	..	..	..	..	..	..	..	..	..	..	12.6
Nepal	..	..	..	5.3	..	..	..	10.4	..	..	24.2
Papua New Guinea	63.0	..	2.0	0.5	..	..	..	..	..	..	6.9
Philippines	4.9	5.3	5.2	6.0	..	54.7	46.2	42.4	86.2	84.8	84.7
Sri Lanka	7.3	6.0	1.3	1.4	89.8	..	2.3	2.4	..	..	0.0
Thailand	14.2	11.1	8.4	9.0	..	31.7	18.9	20.0	8.6[d]	5.1	6.4
Average	..	..	..	3.9	..	..	..	26.0	..	..	29.0

.. Not available.

a. Data refer to the total share of aided and unaided schools. The share of enrollments in unaided schools was 42 and 8.9 percent respectively at the primary and secondary levels.

b. Data include enrollments in privately managed institutions.

c. About 29 percent of teachers in private higher education are paid by the government (World Bank-Indonesia 1988).

d. Figure refers to share in 1977.

Source: Computed from data on the BESD (UNESCOED) database for primary education; datafile made available to the World Bank staff from Unesco for secondary education, supplemented by estimates based on ACU (1987), India (1980), Kumar (1985), and World Bank-Bangladesh (1988b), for India; World Bank-Indonesia (1988); Korea (1988); Malaysia (1986); Nepal and USAID (1988), and World Bank-Nepal (1988) for Nepal; World Bank-Papua New Guinea (1987); Mingat and Tan (1988) for the Philippines; and Thailand (1988b), and World Bank-Thailand (1986) for Thailand.

Table B1.5 Percentage of secondary enrollments in vocational/technical education, selected Asian countries, selected years, 1970-85

Country	1970	1975	1980	1985
Bangladesh	..	1	1	1
Bhutan	38	39	..	37
China	0	1	2	7
India	1	1	1	..
Indonesia	22	21	11	9
Korea	14	14	21	17
Lao PDR	14	2	2	6
Malaysia	3	..	2	2
Myanmar	1	1	1	1
Nepal	..	6	..	..
Papua New Guinea	19	23	16	14
Philippines	..	..	..	..
Singapore	8	4	5	5
Sri Lanka	0	0	..	..
Thailand	22	16	15	17

.. Not available.

Source: Computed from data on the BESD (UNESCOED) database.

Table B1.6 Enrollments in higher education by type of institution, selected Asian countries, mid-1980s

	Local institutions			
	Regular institutions		Distance	Overseas
Country	Public	Private	education	institutions
Bangladesh	253,776	340,251[b]	3,211	2,911
Bhutan[a]	1,088	0	0	48
China[a]	2,380,064	0	1,048,090	42,481
India[b]	1,238,088	1,898,898[b]	159,712	17,824
Indonesia	421,521	747,464	113,801	12,850
Korea	316,056	961,769	177,934	22,468
Malaysia	79,443	10,023	1,272	40,493
Myanmar	100,604	0	84,052	425
Nepal	54,475	17,357	1,000	1,450
Papua New Guinea	9,404	697	1,000	286
Philippines	258,485	1,286,040	500	4,540
Sri Lanka	21,424	0	9,851	3,264
Thailand	105,005	45,700	563,823	9,496

a. There were no higher education institutions before 1983.

b. Data include enrollments in privately managed institutions, but exclude enrollments in intermediate colleges and at the *Alim* (higher secondary) level.

Source: For enrollments in local regular public and private institutions, the data are from the same sources as in appendix table B1.4 supplemented by Bangladesh (1986). For enrollments in distance education, the data reflect estimates based on ADB (1987) for Bhutan, Bangladesh, India, Malaysia, Nepal, Papua New Guinea, and the Philippines; China (1986); KEDI (1988); and Thailand (1985b). Data on overseas enrollments are from Unesco (1987b).

Table B1.7 Distribution of enrollments in higher education by field, selected Asian countries, selected years, 1980-85

Country/specialization[a]	Enrollments		Share of total (%)	
	1980	*1985*	*1980*	*1985*
Bangladesh				
Humanities	73,908	147,835	30.8	33.9
Social science	93,978	165,481	39.1	37.9
Medicine	8,347	14,687	3.5	3.4
Science and technology	62,988	105,830	26.2	24.2
Other	951	2,782	0.4	0.6
Total	240,172	436,615	100.0	100.0
China				
Humanities	406,128	572,817	35.0	32.2
Social science	43,551	190,442	3.7	10.7
Medicine	142,737	166,008	12.3	9.3
Science and technology	559,419	835,373	48.2	47.0
Other	9,605	13,968	0.8	0.8
Total	1,161,440	1,778,608	100.0	100.0
India				
Humanities	2,832,302	..	53.0	..
Social science	1,033,385	..	19.3	..
Medicine	146,472	..	2.7	..
Science and technology	1,317,880	..	24.7	..
Other	15,541	..	0.3	..
Total	5,345,580	..	100.0	..
Indonesia				
Humanities	169,738	268,574	30.0	27.4
Social science	244,059	474,065	43.2	48.4
Medicine	22,194	24,855	3.9	2.5
Science and technology	127,173	208,545	22.5	21.3
Other	2,337	4,123	0.4	0.4
Total	565,501	980,162	100.0	100.0
Korea				
Humanities	159,841	438,178	26.0	29.6
Social science	111,685	447,733	18.1	30.2
Medicine	41,420	80,651	6.7	5.4
Science and technology	301,874	488,738	49.0	33.0
Other	632	26,011	0.1	1.8
Total	615,452	1,481,311	100.0	100.0

Table B1.7 (continued)

Country/specialization[a]	Enrollments		Share of total (%)	
	1980	*1985*	*1980*	*1985*
Malaysia				
Humanities	18,894	26,418	32.8	28.3
Social science	15,986	28,689	27.7	30.8
Medicine	1,639	2,920	2.8	3.1
Science and technology	21,052	27,561	36.5	29.6
Other	79	7,661	0.1	8.2
Total	57,650	93,249	100.0	100.0
Nepal				
Humanities	19,045	25,331	49.5	45.6
Social science	11,248	16,612	29.3	29.9
Medicine	1,293	1,130	3.4	2.0
Science and technology	6,864	12,482	17.9	22.5
Other	0	0	0.0	0.0
Total	38,450	55,555	100.0	100.0
Papua New Guinea				
Humanities	538	1136	10.7	22.4
Social science	1,871	1,102	37.1	21.7
Medicine	384	989	7.6	19.5
Science and technology	1,655	1,635	32.8	32.3
Other	591	206	11.7	4.1
Total	5,039	5,068	100.0	100.0
Philippines				
Humanities	102,197	307,753	8.0	15.6
Social science	482,993	714,608	37.9	36.2
Medicine	123,367	125,406	9.7	6.4
Science and technology	503,829	802,924	39.5	40.7
Other	63,630	22,491	5.0	1.1
Total	1,276,016	1,973,182	100.0	100.0
Sri Lanka				
Humanities	..	2,427	..	4.3
Social science	..	21,222	..	37.9
Medicine	..	3,227	..	5.8
Science and technology	..	20,548	..	36.7
Other	..	8,596	..	15.3
Total	..	56,020	..	100.0

.. Not available.

a. Humanities includes courses in education, humanities, fine arts, sociology, and theology; social science includes courses in law, economics, accountancy, commerce, banking, and social science; medicine includes courses in medicine and related sciences, including nursing; science and technology includes courses in science and technology, including agriculture, mathematics, architecture, and other unclassified courses.

Source: Computed from data in Unesco (1987a).

Table B2.1 Estimated education attainment by current population, selected Asian countries, mid-1980s

Country	School-age population[a]	Labor force	Percent increase[b]
Bangladesh	3.9	..	..
Bhutan	1.4	..	..
China	5.1	4.5	13.3
India	4.8	..	..
Indonesia	7.3	3.9	87.2
Korea	11.4	8.0	42.5
Lao PDR	4.8	..	..
Malaysia	9.2	5.0	84.0
Nepal	3.6	..	..
Papua New Guinea	4.3	..	..
Philippines	10.2	7.0	
Singapore	9.9	5.3	86.8
Sri Lanka	9.5	..	..
Thailand	7.0	4.1	70.7

.. Not available.

a. Data reflect the projected future education attainment of the current school-age population, given the present patterns of enrollment and survival in the education system.

b. Figure may be taken as reflecting the inter-generational rise in education attainment of the adult population.

Source: First column estimated from cohort survival rates for current school-age population (appendix table B 2.2); second column from Psacharopoulos and Arriagada (1986).

Table B2.2 Cohort survival rates, selected Asian countries, early to mid-1980s

Country	Primary gross enrollment ratio, 1985	Percentage of population entering grade 1[a]	Percentage of entrants in grade 1 surviving to												
			Gr. 1	Gr. 2	Gr. 3	Gr. 4	Gr. 5	Gr. 6	Gr. 7	Gr. 8	Gr. 9	Gr. 10	Gr. 11	Gr. 12	Gr. 13
Bangladesh	60	100.0	100.0	54.0	41.0	32.4	24.0[b]	22.1	18.8	17.8	12.5	10.7[c]	5.0	4.2	..
Bhutan	25	54.1	100.0	40.0	32.0	27.2	19.6	17.0[b]	8.2	7.4	6.8[c]	3.2	2.8	..	..
China	124	90.0	100.0	84.0	79.0	75.0	67.5[b]	40.5	37.3	30.9[c]	7.4	7.1	6.0	..	..
India	92	83.0	100.0	70.0	56.0	44.8	36.7[b]	30.5	25.6	21.8	17.0	13.4[c]	4.7	2.7	..
Indonesia[e]	118	100.0	100.0	89.0	82.8	75.3	69.3	59.6[b]	36.9	35.1	34.0[c]	18.4	17.7	17.7	..
Korea	96	100.0	100.0	99.0	99.0	97.0	97.0	97.0[b]	95.1	94.1	93.2[c]	46.6	45.2	44.3	..
Lao PDR	94	100.0	100.0	100.0	71.0	50.4	40.3[b]	30.2	23.3	19.6[c]	10.6	8.2	7.2	..	..
Malaysia	99	100.0	100.0	100.0	99.0	99.0	98.0	97.0[b]	77.6	69.9	69.9[c]	41.9	40.2[d]	7.2	6.9
Myanmar	102	..													
Nepal	79	75.0	100.0	48.0	41.8	37.6	33.1[b]	31.8	28.3[c]	25.4	23.7	20.6	..	..	..
Papua New Guinea	69	74.0	100.0	91.0	84.6	79.6	73.2	67.3[b]	24.9	23.2	16.7	15.7[c]	1.9	1.8	..
Philippines	106	100.0	100.0	86.0	80.0	76.0	71.4	66.4[b]	55.8	49.7	44.7	41.1[c]	..	..	..
Singapore	115	100.0	100.0	100.0	100.0	100.0	100.0	100.0[b]	75.0	75.0	75.0[c]	75.0	20.3	19.6[d]	5.7
Sri Lanka	103	100.0	100.0	100.0	100.0	99.0	92.1	84.7[b]	76.2	69.4	63.1	57.4	57.4[c]	18.4	18.4
Thailand	97	100.0	100.0	89.0	88.1	86.3	84.6	80.4[b]	32.2	30.5	29.3[c]	15.0	13.2	13.0	..

.. Not available.

a. The rate of entry to primary education in Bangladesh (and possibly also Lao PDR) may be overestimated due to the presence of "baby" classes that contain underage children. In estimates of the entry rate using enrollment and population data, this factor produced a rate exceeding 100 percent. We have therefore attributed an entry rate of 100 percent here, thus diluting the "baby" class factor to some extent. The result may of course still be overestimated, although to a lesser extent than at first sight.

b. End of primary cycle.

c. End of lower secondary cycle. In the Philippines, the entire cycle is only four years.

d. An additional selection point within upper secondary education.

e. Data from World Bank-Indonesia (1989) suggest that the proportion surviving to the end of primary education may have improved significantly, rising to as much as 75 percent in the second half of the 1980s.

Source: Computed from data on the BESD (UNESCOED) database.

Table B2.3 Excess demand for higher education, selected Asian countries, mid-1980s

Country	Number in last grade of secondary	Number of exam-takers	Number of entrants[a]		
			Local public	Local private	Distance education
Bangladesh	132,580	194,764	156,389	——>	3,288
Bhutan	298	..	..	..	..
China	2,145,000	..	809,960	0	452,344
India	1,136,075	..	843,354	——>	4,456
Indonesia	519,176	983,263	97,416	142,714	40,698
Korea	371,507	790,874	313,640	——>	39,351
Malaysia	146,388	..	24,499	——>	713
Myanmar	133,133	..	25,151	..	21,013
Nepal	54,611	..	13,619	4,339	..
Papua New Guinea	828	..	895	——>	..
Philippines	660,126	595,575	64,621	321,510	..
Sri Lanka	67,714	150,000	5,318	0	3,096
Thailand	290,409	..	15,194	11,425	142,467

.. Not available.

Note: Given the difficulty of measuring excess demand, these data are only suggestive at best, and should therefore be used with extreme caution.

a. Arrows indicate that the numbers in the column for local public education refer to data for entrants to both local public and private institutions.

Source: Data on the number in the last grade of secondary education are from the BESD (UNESCOED) database. Data on the number of exam-takers are from the following sources: Bangladesh (1986); Indonesia and USAID (1986) (the data refer to the number of applicants for university entrance); the Philippines, National Educational Testing and Research Center (1987 personal communication to Jee-Peng Tan);KEDI (1988); and World Bank-Sri Lanka 1986. Data on the intake into higher education are from the following sources: ADB (1987) for India and Papua New Guinea; Bangladesh (1986); Burma (1986); China (1986); World Bank-Indonesia (1988b); KEDI (1988); Malaysia (1986); Mingat and Tan (1988) for the Philippines; Sri Lanka (1988); Thailand (1985) and (1987b). Except for China, India, Indonesia, Sri Lanka, and Thailand (regular institutions), the data on intake are estimated by spreading total enrollments in higher education over an assumed four-year cycle.

Table B2.4 Pupil-teacher ratio in primary education, selected Asian countries, selected years, 1970-85

Country	1970	1975	1980	1985
Bangladesh	46.5	50.7	53.6	47.0
Bhutan	20.7	23.8	25.2	38.5
China	29.1	29.0	26.6	24.9
Hong Kong	33.0	31.1	30.1	27.3
India	41.5	42.1	54.9	57.6
Indonesia	28.9	29.5	32.4	25.3
Korea, Rep. of	56.9	51.8	47.5	38.3
Lao PDR	36.0	26.8	29.8	24.9
Malaysia	31.0	31.9	27.3	24.1
Myanmar	46.6	52.5	51.6	46.4
Nepal	21.7	28.7	38.4	35.5
Papua New Guinea	29.7	31.6	31.4	31.0
Philippines	28.6	29.0	30.4	30.9
Singapore	29.7	30.5	30.8	27.1
Sri Lanka	..	..	..	31.7
Taiwan	41.1	37.7	32.3	31.7
Thailand	34.7	28.0	24.7	19.3

.. Not available.
Source: BESD (UNESCOED) database, supplemented with data from Unesco (1987); China (1984) and (1986); India (1988); Bordia (1988), Mullick (1987), and Britain (1984) for India; Korea (1988); Burma (1986) for Myanmar; and World Bank-Papua New Guinea (1987).

Table B2.5 Pupil-teacher ratio in secondary education, selected Asian countries, selected years, 1970-85

Country	1970	1975	1980	1985
Bangladesh	..	..	23.8	26.2
Bhutan	..	..	..	10.1
China	..	21.0	17.9	17.2
Hong Kong	21.9	24.3	29.3	25.1
India	20.9	20.3	19.4	20.2
Indonesia	13.1	14.4	14.9	15.3
Korea, Rep. of	36.5	37.1	39.1	34.3
Lao PDR	16.9	..	19.2	11.2
Malaysia	25.6	27.3	22.8	22.1
Myanmar	32.1	37.5	34.1	28.5
Nepal	..	24.3	31.3	27.5
Papua New Guinea	..	20.3	22.0	25.4
Philippines	33.1	31.5	34.1	32.3
Singapore	19.9	23.1	19.4	20.4
Sri Lanka	..	..	..	26.1
Taiwan	..	..	..	..
Thailand	15.5	27.2	..	19.6

.. Not available.
Source: As in appendix table B2.4. For Thailand, data for 1985 are from Thailand (1987c).

Table B2.6 Pupil-teacher ratio in tertiary education, selected Asian countries, selected years, 1970-85

Country	1970	1975	1980	1985 Regular	1985 Distance	1985 Private institutions
Bangladesh[a]	16.3	11.7	21.6 (21.6)	15.9 (23.9)	..	..
Bhutan	..	..	8.7	10.9	..	..
China	0.4	3.2	4.7	5.2	36.0	..
Hong Kong	15.2	14.6	12.5	..	..	..
India	18.8	19.6	19.3	15.7	776.5[b]	..
Indonesia	12.4	6.0	9.3	14.0	689.7	46.1
Korea, Rep. of	19.3	20.8	29.1	42.4	414.7	41.1
Lao PDR	..	..	10.1	10.1	..	..
Malaysia	..	..	10.4	11.4	..	..
Myanmar	13.2	..	..	30.3[c]	..	..
Nepal	..	15.5	13.2	..	..	..
Papua New Guinea	..	..	7.9	7.7	..	..
Philippines[d]	22.5	24.2	29.2	16.0 (31.7)	..	48.0
Singapore	11.9	15.6	10.2	..	..	..
Sri Lanka	8.3	7.7	8.9	10.7	84.9	..
Thailand	7.4	14.4	18.4	8.3	618.8	17.6

.. Not available.

Note: Data refer to regular public institutions unless otherwise indicated.

a. Data refer only to universities; figures in parentheses reflect the averages across all types of higher education.

b. Figure reflects data for Andhar Pradesh Open University. Data from the other open university are not available.

c. Figure reflects weighted average for regular and correspondence higher education.

d. The figures for 1970-80 overestimate the true pupil-teacher ratio for tertiary education because many state universities enrolled a large number of primary and secondary level students. Such students were removed from the numerator in James (1988) estimates for 1985; for comparison the unadjusted figure appears in parentheses.

Source: BESD (UNESCOED) for 1970-1980 for all countries and for 1985 supplanted by estimates based on Bangladesh (1986); China (1987a); ACU (1987) for India; James (1988) for the Philippines; Sri Lanka (1988); and Thailand (1985b).

Table B3.1 Dependency ratios, selected Asian countries, selected years, 1970-2000

Country	Population age 0–14 as ratio of population age over 15					Population age 0–14 as ratio of population age 15–64				
	1970	1975	1980	1985	2000	1970	1975	1980	1985	2000
Bangladesh	0.82	0.81	0.71	0.78	0.62	0.55	0.56	0.46	0.49	0.42
Bhutan	0.68	0.68	0.64	0.66	0.71	0.46	0.47	0.44	0.44	0.47
China	0.61	0.52	0.53	0.40	0.36	0.44	0.39	0.44	0.33	0.26
India	0.71	0.69	0.63	0.61	0.49	0.49	0.48	0.45	0.44	0.35
Indonesia	0.75	0.73	0.68	0.63	0.50	0.50	0.50	0.48	0.46	0.35
Korea	0.69	0.58	0.48	0.42	0.34	0.52	0.43	0.37	0.31	0.24
Lao PDR	0.68	0.69	0.90	0.81	0.77	0.45	0.46	0.60	0.53	0.49
Malaysia	0.79	0.72	0.61	0.55	0.45	0.56	0.53	0.44	0.41	0.33
Myanmar	0.64	0.66	0.67	0.70	0.50	0.44	0.45	0.47	0.47	0.35
Nepal	0.69	0.70	0.71	0.71	0.60	0.46	0.48	0.49	0.49	0.51
Papua New Guinea	0.69	0.69	0.70	0.62	0.76	0.47	0.48	0.53	0.50	0.40
Philippines	0.79	0.78	0.70	0.63	0.53	0.53	0.55	0.48	0.47	0.37
Singapore	0.60	0.47	0.40	0.36	0.27	0.48	0.37	0.30	0.26	0.20
Sri Lanka	0.68	0.61	0.56	0.50	0.42	0.49	0.47	0.42	0.36	0.31
Thailand	0.81	0.77	0.64	0.55	0.40	0.56	0.55	0.47	0.41	0.29

Source: Computed from data on the BESD (SOCIND) database for 1970-85; and from Zachariah and Vu (1988) for 2000.

Table B3.2 Population and economic growth rates, selected Asian countries, selected years, 1975-2000

	Annual rate of population growth				Real economic growth (percent per year)		
	Overall Population		*Population (5–14)*				
	1975–85	*1985–00*	*1975–85*	*1985–00*[a]	*1975–85*	*1988*	*1990–00*[a]
Bangladesh	2.4	2.2	1.8	2.0	4.4	1.8	4.9
Bhutan	2.0	2.3	1.6	3.0	6.1	..	..
China	1.3	1.4	0.2	0.4	7.8	7.6	6.6
India	2.2	1.8	1.6	1.3	4.4	7.2	4.8
Indonesia	2.2	1.8	1.8	1.0	6.1	3.6	3.9
Korea	1.4	1.3	-0.8	0.3	7.4	7.8	6.8
Malaysia	2.4	1.9	0.8	1.4	6.3	4.1	5.0
Myanmar	2.0	1.9	2.4	1.0	5.8	5.1	3.5
Nepal	2.5	2.6	2.7	3.1	3.1	5.7	3.8
Papua New Guinea	2.6	2.2	2.6	2.0	1.5	2.0	5.1
Philippines	2.6	2.1	2.1	1.5	2.5	5.0	5.3
Sri Lanka	1.8	1.5	0.1	1.1	4.9	5.5	4.8
Thailand	2.1	1.7	0.6	0.5	5.8	5.8	6.0

.. Not available.

a. Projected.

Source: Computed from population and GNP data on the BESD (SOCIND and UNESCOED) database; data on projected population and economic growth are respectively from Zachariah and Vu (1988) and the World Bank's ANDREX database.

Table B3.3 Literate adults, selected Asian countries, selected years, 1970-85

(percent)

Country	1970	1975	1980	1985
Bangladesh	23	26	29	33
Bhutan	..	..	5	15
China	..	..	66	69
India	34	..	45	43
Indonesia	54	..	67	74
Korea	88	..	..	92
Lao PDR	33	..	..	46
Malaysia	60	..	..	74
Myanmar	71	..	66	..
Nepal	14	19	24	26
Papua New Guinea	32	32	32	45
Philippines	82	..	..	86
Singapore	69	83	..	86
Sri Lanka	77	..	86	87
Thailand	79	..	88	91

.. Not available.

Source: UNICEF (1987) for 1970 and 1985. For 1975 and 1980, BESD (SOCIND), supplemented by World Bank-Bangladesh (1987) for Bangladesh; World Bank-Bhutan 1988b; World Bank-China (1983); and (1988); World Bank-India (1988a); World Bank-Papua New Guinea (1986); and (1988); World Bank-Sri Lanka (1988); and Tilak (1986) for Bangladesh and Bhutan.

Table B3.4 Education attainment of adult populations, selected Asian countries, early 1980s

| | | | | Percentage of population with | | | | | |
| | | | | Primary | | Secondary | | | Mean years of |
Country	Year	Age group	No schooling	Incomplete	Complete	Incomplete	Complete	Higher	schooling
Bangladesh	1981	15–64	66.5	13.8	3.6	9.9	5.1	1.1	2.2
China	1982	15–59	28.7	5.0	27.7	26.5	11.1	1.0	4.8[a]
India	1981	15–59	64.2	8.9	4.3	11.2	8.9	2.6	2.7
Indonesia	1980	15–64	29.2	34.0	23.1	7.5	5.5	0.6	3.9
Korea	1980	15–54	5.3	0.9	27.7	24.3	31.4	10.3	9.4
Malaysia	1980	25–64	34.1	18.4	25.2	12.2	8.5	1.5	4.6
Nepal	1981	15–64	29.5	16.0	16.0	13.8	18.8	5.9	4.3[a]
Papua New Guinea[b]	1980	15–44	62.7	12.4	14.3	9.9	0.4	0.3	2.2
Philippines	1980	15–34	4.0	20.4	23.1	18.1	15.2	19.3	7.7
Singapore	1980	25–59	37.0	2.6	40.0	10.8	5.8	3.8	4.8
Sri Lanka	1981	15–64	11.9	11.5	32.5	39.4	3.9	0.8	5.9
Thailand	1980	15–44	6.1	69.9	5.0	9.8	5.5	3.7	5.0

a. Estimates appear high, particularly for Nepal, but are consistent with the original sources referred to in Unesco (1987a) and Psacharopoulos and Arriagada (1986).

b. Data refer only to nationals.

Source: Data on the distribution of the adult population by level of education is from UNESCO 1987a and data on the length of education cycles is from Unesco (1987b); supplemental data is from China (1985) and Psacharopoulos and Arriagada (1986).

Table B3.5 Distribution of GDP and labor force, selected Asian countries, 1980 and 1986

(percent)

	Share of GDP				Share of labor force		
Country/year	*Agriculture*	*Industry*	*Mfg.*	*Services*	*Agriculture*	*Industry*	*Services*
Bangladesh							
1980	54	13	7	33	75	6	19
1986	47	14	8	39	..	..	..
Bhutan							
1980	45	22	..	33	..	..	..
China							
1980	31	47	..	22	74	14	12
1986	31	46	34	23	..	..	..
India							
1980	37	26	18	37	70	13	17
1986	32	29	19	39	..	..	..
Indonesia							
1980	26	42	9	32	57	13	30
1986	26	32	14	42	..	..	..
Korea							
1980	16	41	28	43	36	27	37
1986	12	42	30	45	..	..	..
Malaysia							
1980	24	37	23	39	42	19	39
1986	20	36	..	44	..	..	..
Myanmar							
1980	46	13	10	41	53	19	28
1986	48	13	10	39	..	..	..
Papua New Guinea							
1980	34	30	8	37	76	10	14
1986	34	26	9	40	..	..	..
Philippines							
1980	23	37	26	40	52	16	33
1986	26	32	25	42	..	..	..
Sri Lanka							
1980	28	30	18	42	53	14	33
1986	26	27	15	47	..	..	..
Thailand							
1980	25	29	20	46	71	10	19
1986	17	30	21	53	..	..	..

.. Not available.

Source: World Bank (1988), supplemented by Malaysia (1986).

Table B3.6 Total government spending as a percentage of GNP, selected Asian countries, selected years, 1970-1980s

Country	1970	1975	1980	1985	Latest data Spending	Year
Bangladesh	..	..	15.4	14.4	16.8	1988
Bhutan	..	..	33.8	52.6	..	..
China	49.9	49.1	48.0	41.7	..	..
India	..	18.7	18.5	22.2	23.6	1988
Indonesia	..	21.0	25.0	25.2	23.7	1986
Korea	..	17.1	20.9	20.4	28.6	1987
Malaysia	..	31.2	41.0	37.9	39.4	1987
Myanmar	..	12.2	13.3	16.7	16.6	1986
Nepal	..	11.4	14.6	18.7	19.3	1987
Papua New Guinea	..	..	41.6	38.2	37.8	1986
Philippines	..	..	15.7	15.5	19.1	1986
Sri Lanka	28.4	24.3	35.8	33.4	30.0	1988
Thailand	18.2	18.9	17.7	18.1	..	..

.. Not available.

Source: BESD (XINCOME) for GDP and GNP data; government spending data from World Bank-Bangladesh (1987) and (1988a); World Bank-Bhutan (1988b); China (1987); India (1985), and World Bank-India (1987), (1988a), and (1988b); World Bank-Indonesia (1988a) and (1988c); Bank of Korea (1988); World Bank-Malaysia (1988); World Bank-Burma (1985), and Burma (1986) for Myanmar; World Bank-Nepal (1988b); World Bank-Papua New Guinea (1988); Mingat and Tan (1988) for the Philippines; World Bank-Sri Lanka (1988); and World Bank-Thailand (1986), and Thailand (1988a).

Table B3.7 Total government spending as a percentage of GDP, selected Asian countries, selected years, 1970-1980s

Country	1970	1975	1980	1985	Latest data Spending	Year
Bangladesh	..	..	15.8	14.7	15.9	1988
Bhutan	..	..	36.1	53.0	..	..
China	..	42.4	41.3	35.1	..	..
India	..	17.3	17.5	20.6	21.6	1988
Indonesia	..	20.5	24.0	24.2	22.7	1986
Korea	..	16.8	20.3	19.7	19.1	1987
Malaysia	..	30.2	39.5	35.1	36.5	1987
Myanmar	..	12.2	13.3	16.5	16.4	1986
Nepal	..	11.5	14.9	20.1	..	..
Papua New Guinea	..	..	40.1	36.4	35.9	1986
Philippines	..	..	15.7	15.1	18.5	1986
Sri Lanka	..	..	..	..	..	..
Thailand	18.2	18.9	17.2	17.5	..	..

.. Not available.

Source: Same as appendix table B3.6.

Table B3.8 Share of public spending on education by level, selected Asian countries, selected years, 1970-1980s

(percent)

Country	1970	1975	1980	1985	Latest data Spending	Latest data Year
Bangladesh						
Primary	..	54.0	44.2	49.2	39.6	1988
Secondary	..	..	..	41.2	51.4	1988
Higher	..	..	..	9.6	8.9	1988
Other	..	..	..	0.0	0.1	1988
China						
Primary	..	..	..	40.6	..	..
Secondary	..	..	..	41.8	..	..
Higher	..	..	..	17.6	..	..
Other	..	..	..	0.0	..	..
India						
Primary	24.6	24.6	27.4	..	..	..
Secondary	45.9	44.4	47.3	..	..	..
Higher	29.5	31.0	19.2	..	..	..
Other	0.0	0.0	6.0	..	..	..
Indonesia						
Primary	..	..	..	61.8	..	..
Secondary	..	..	..	27.1	..	..
Higher	..	..	..	9.2	..	..
Other	..	..	..	2.0	..	..
Korea						
Primary	..	..	..	57.1	..	..
Secondary	..	..	..	33.5	..	..
Higher	..	..	..	9.4	..	..
Other	..	..	..	0.0	..	..
Malaysia						
Primary	..	..	..	37.4	36.3	1988
Secondary	..	..	..	33.3	34.2	1988
Higher	..	..	..	24.7	25.7	1988
Other	..	..	..	4.6	3.8	1988
Nepal						
Primary	..	..	37.2	40.6	51.7	1988
Secondary	..	..	27.1	21.3	16.8	1988
Higher	..	..	34.2	34.7	28.4	1988
Other	..	..	1.5	3.3	3.1	1988

| Country | 1970 | 1975 | 1980 | 1985 | Latest data | |
					Spending	Year
Papua New Guinea						
Primary	..	..	..	44.8	..	
Secondary	..	..	..	18.0	..	
Higher	..	..	..	27.5	..	
Other	..	..	..	9.7	..	
Philippines						
Primary	..	..	66.0	64.0	61.0	1988
Secondary	..	..	13.0	16.0	23.0	
Higher	..	..	21.0	20.0	17.0	
Other	..	..	0.0	0.0	0.0	
Sri Lanka						
Primary	..	..	..	42.5	..	
Secondary	..	..	..	41.2	..	
Higher	..	8.5	16.1	16.3	..	
Other	..	..	..	..	..	
Thailand						
Primary	55.5	52.5	53.9	58.1	..	
Secondary	19.4	18.5	23.0	23.6	..	
Higher	17.8	19.7	17.0	12.4	..	
Other	7.3	9.3	6.2	5.9	..	

.. Not available.

Source: As in table 3.5, supplemented by King 1988 for Bangladesh; World Bank-Bangladesh (1978), (1981), and (1988b); China (1984) and (1986) and World Bank-China (1986); India (1983) and Tilak (1987) for India; Indonesia and USAID (1986); Korea (1988); Laya (1988), Malaysia (1988), and Moock (1985) for Malaysia; Nepal and USAID (1988) and World Bank (1988a) for Indonesia; World Bank-Papua New Guinea (1987); World Bank-Sri Lanka (1986); and Thailand (1985), (1986), and (1987a).

Table B4.1 Unit operating cost of public education, selected Asian countries, mid-1980s

| Country | As percentage of per capita GNP | | | | | Ratio to unit cost of primary education | | | |
| | Primary | Secondary[a] | Higher | | | Secondary | Higher | | |
			Overall	Regular	Open		Overall	Regular	Open
Bangladesh	6.4	30.0	284.6	284.6	..	4.7	44.5	44.5	..
Bhutan	..	..	..	..	..	..	..	..	..
China	6.7	22.6	199.2	269.9	39.0	3.4	..	40.3	..
India	6.0	17.3	231.1	231.1	..	2.9	..	38.5	..
Indonesia	12.6	23.3	91.1	105.7	36.8	1.9	7.2	8.4	2.9
Korea	16.5	23.4	70.6	104.5	10.5	1.4	4.3	6.3	0.6
Malaysia	14.1	21.3	190.3	190.3	..	1.5	13.5	13.5	..
Myanmar	..	..	..	..	..	..	..	..	..
Nepal	9.0	13.5	249.0	249.0	..	1.5	27.7	27.7	..
Papua New Guinea	29.0	65.0	1050.0	1050.0	..	2.2	36.2	36.2	..
Philippines									
1985	5.8	8.6	50.0	50.0	..	1.5	8.6	8.6	..
1988	8.5	11.8	..	..	..	1.4	..	..	..
Sri Lanka									
1985	6.1	9.3	83.3	111.2	22.7	1.5	13.7	18.2	3.7
1988	6.6	9.6	..	..	..	1.5	..	..	..
Thailand	15.5	15.3	39.9	177.9	14.2	1.0	2.6	11.5	0.9

.. Not available.

a. Weighted by distribution of enrollments in the public sector across regular institutions and distance education.

Source: King (1988) for Bangladesh; China (1984), (1986), and (1987); Bordia (1988) and India (1983) and (1987) for India; Indonesia and USAID (1986); World Bank-Korea (1985); Korea (1987) and KEDI (1988); Laya (1988) and Malaysia (1986) and (1988) for Malaysia; Nepal and USAID (1988); World Bank-Papua New Guinea (1987); Mingat and Tan (1988) for the Philippines; Sri Lanka (1986) and (1987), and Smith (1988) for Sri Lanka; World Bank-Thailand (1985) and Thailand (1988b). Data on unit cost in open higher education reflect estimates based on Srisa-an (1987).

Table B4.2 Teacher remuneration as ratio to per capita GNP, selected Asian countries, mid-1980s

Country	Primary	Secondary	Higher
Bangladesh	2.2	..	..
Bhutan	..	..	..
China[a]	1.6	2.8	6.9
India[b]	2.9	3.1	..
Indonesia	2.5	3.2	5.7[c]
Korea[b]	5.0	5.5	..
Malaysia	2.4	3.1	..
Myanmar	..	..	..
Nepal	2.8	5.0[e]	..
Papua New Guinea	6.8	10.0	..
Philippines			
1985	1.6	1.7	..
1988[d]	2.2	2.4	..
Sri Lanka			
1986	1.6	2.1	..
1988[d]	2.0	2.3	..
Thailand	2.5	2.9	..

.. Not available.

a. Data for primary and secondary education reflect the average of salaries of *gongban* and *minban* teachers; the former are employed by the central government, the latter by lower levels of government.

b. Figures reflect estimates based on data on unit costs and pupil-teacher ratios.

c. Figure reflects salaries after the 69 percent increase between 1984 and 1985.

d. Data reflect estimates based on the new salary scales for teachers.

e. Figure reflects the weighted average salaries for lower and upper secondary teachers.

Source: Bangladesh (1984); China (1986) and (1987); Indonesia and USAID (1986); Laya (1988) for Malaysia; Nepal and USAID (1988); World Bank-Papua New Guinea (1987); Mingat and Tan (1988) for the Philippines; Sri Lanka (1986) and (1987); and Thailand (1987c).

Table B4.3 Fees for public education, by education cycle, as a percentage of unit operating costs, selected Asian countries, mid-1980s

Country	Primary	Secondary	Higher education Regular	Open
Bangladesh	7.4	4.0	0.1	..
Bhutan	..	..	..	..
China	4.8	3.2	0.3	..
India[a]	..	11.6	4.9	..
Indonesia	7.1	27.4	18.9	..
Korea	0.0	34.2	45.9	32.0
Malaysia	3.7	4.0	5.8	..
Myanmar	..	..	..	..
Nepal	0.0	40.7	10.4	..
Papua New Guinea	8.7	39.8	0.0	..
Philippines	0.0	9.3[b]	15.3	..
Sri Lanka	3.1	3.1	3.4	57.7
Thailand	0.1	18.3	5.0	27.5

.. Not available.

a. For primary and secondary education, data are estimated from fee schedules; in higher education, the figure is much smaller than the 20 percent figure cited by Kolhatkar (1988) because his data did not include the cost of faculty salaries.

b. Fees for public secondary education, including local schools, were abolished in 1988.

Source: King (1988) and World Bank-Bangladesh (1988b) for Bangladesh; World Bank-China (1986b); ACU (1987) and Kolhatkar (1988) for higher education and India (1987) for primary and secondary education in India; Indonesia and USAID (1986); Korea (1987); Moock (1985) for Malaysia; Nepal and USAID (1988), and Timilsina (1988) for Nepal; World Bank-Papua New Guinea (1987); Mingat and Tan (1988) for the Philippines; Sri Lanka (1986) and (1988); and Thailand (1987). Data on the level of cost recovery in open higher education are from Srisa-an 1987.

Table B5.1 Rates of return to investment in education, selected Asian countries, latest available year
(percent)

Country	Year	Social Primary	Social Secondary	Social Higher	Private Primary	Private Secondary	Private Higher
India	1978	29.3	13.7	10.8	33.4	19.8	13.2
Indonesia	1982	18.0	15.0	10.0	..	..	..
		(14.5)	..	..	..	..	..
Korea	1982	..	10.9	13.0	..	..	..
Malaysia	1983	..	..	7.6	..	..	12.2
Papua New Guinea	1982	19.9	12.0	2.8	29.4	14.7	8.1
Philippines	1985	11.9	12.9	13.3	18.2	13.8	14.0
		(4.4)	(9.3)	(11.6)	(7.2)	(10.2)	(12.5)
Thailand	1975	12.0	24.0	12.8	..	..	..
	1985	..	..	13.3	..	..	17.4

.. Not available.
Note: Figures in parentheses denote rates of return for incomplete education.
Source: Psacharopoulos (1985) for India; Indonesia and USAID (1986); KEDI (1988); Mehmet and Yip (1986) for Malaysia; Gannicott (1987) for Papua New Guinea; Tan and Paqueo (1989) for the Philippines; and Suppachai (1976) and Thailand (1987b) for Thailand.

Table B5.2 Dates of establishment of open universities, selected Asian countries

Country	Date
Bangladesh	n.a.
Bhutan	n.a.
China[a]	1960s
India[b]	1982, 1983
Indonesia	1984
Japan	1985
Korea[c]	1972, 1982
Malaysia	n.a.
Myanmar[d]	1970s
Nepal	n.a.
Papua New Guinea	n.a.
Philippines	n.a.
Sri Lanka	1980
Thailand	1970, 1978

n.a. Not applicable.
a. Reopened in 1979.
b. First date denotes opening of the Andhra Pradesh Open University; the second is for the opening of Indira Gandhi National Open University.
c. First date denotes opening of Korea Air and Correspondence University. The second date denotes the establishment of the first of six open colleges, three of which are private.
d. University correspondence courses offered.
Source: Kolhatkar (1988) for India; World Bank-Indonesia (1988b); Korea (1988); Burma (1986) for Myanmar; World Bank-Sri Lanka (1986); and Chantavanich and Fry in Postlethwaite (1988) for Thailand.

Table B5.3 Rates of return by field of study in higher education, Thailand, 1985

(percent)

Field of study	Rates of return	
	Social	Private
Pure science	13.6	19.5
Agriculture	15.0	19.0
Fine arts/architecture	10.0	17.9
Humanities/social science	14.5	15.9
Medicine	10.4	13.8
Medical technology	7.8	17.5
Accountancy	18.0	17.5
Law	18.0	15.4
Education	10.0	15.9
Engineering	17.9	22.0
Average	13.5	17.4

Source: Thailand (1987b), pages 6–35. Note that the authors report estimates by type of firm in which a graduate is working. For brevity, the estimates selected for reporting are defined: (1) the social rates of return are those calculated from the earnings profile of graduates working in the private sector where wages are more likely to reflect marginal productivity; and (2) the private rates of return are those calculated from the earnings profile of graduates working in all sectors.

Appendix C

Miscellaneous Tables Referenced in Text and Figures

Table C.1 Ordinary least squares regression of the relationship between gross enrollment ratios and per capita GNP, by education cycle, selected Asian countries and world regions, mid-1980s

	Asia			World		
	Primary	*Secondary*	*Higher*	*Primary*	*Secondary*	*Higher*
Per capita GNP x 10E-2	1.44	3.47	1.03	0.57	1.19	0.40
	(0.9)	(2.0)	(1.8)	(3.2)	(8.3)	(5.3)
(Per capita GNP)^2 x 10E-6	-1.40	-0.40	-1.33	-0.32	-0.53	-0.16
	(0.6)	(2.3)	(1.6)	(2.5)	(5.1)	(3.0)
Intercept	79.4	18.2	3.38	82.74	24.31	5.06
Number of observations	16	16	16	100	99	91
R^2	0.46	0.55	0.24	11.5	58.5	43.9

Source: Data on enrollment ratios from Unesco (1987); data on per capita GNP from World Bank BESD database.

Table C.2 Average per capita GNP and gross enrollment ratios, world regions, 1980s

			Gross enrollment ratios (%)		
Region	*Number of countries*	*Per capita GNP (US$)*	*Primary*	*Secondary*	*Higher*
Asia[a]	14	585	90.5	41.0	11.0
Africa	35	517	77.8	19.5	1.5
Latin America	20	1,401	101.8	48.6	16.5
Europe, the Middle East, and North Africa[b]	14	2,902	92.9	46.9	14.2

a. Excludes Hong Kong, Singapore, and Japan.
b. Excludes United Arab Emirates, and Kuwait.
Source: As in appendix table C.1.

Table C.3 Data for text figures

Country	Per capita GNP (1985) US$	Unit cost (US$) of regular higher education	Index of overall costliness	Percent reaching end of primary	Primary education unit costs (percentage per capita GNP)	Index of extent of inter-cycle selection	Unit cost of public regular higher education[a]	Index of private financing in higher education
Bangladesh	159	453	1.36	24	6.4	8	1.57	16.5
Bhutan	151	17	13					
China	273	900	1.32	68	9.2	54	1.82	0.3
India	259	515	1.00	37	6.0	15	1.27	7.1
Indonesia	470	497	1.02	60	12.6	46	0.58	48.7
Korea	2,040	2,132	1.11	97	13.5	87	0.57	76.6
Lao PDR	332	40	21					
Malaysia	1,860	3,540	1.25	97	14.1	79	1.05	15.1
Myanmar	184							
Nepal	142	354	1.07	33	9.0	5	1.37	31.8
Papua New Guinea	621	6,521	4.38	67	29.0	57	5.78	6.3
Philippines	581	291	0.45	66	5.8	18	0.28	85.8
Singapore	7,093	100	99					
Sri Lanka	374	416	0.55	85	6.1	58	0.61	20.5
Thailand	712	1,267	0.87	80	15.5	72	0.89	26.9

Table C.3 (continued)

Country	Per capita GNP (1985) US$	Ratio of unit costs to regional average			Index of overall emphasis on higher education	Share of cumulative resources received by top 10 percent	Deviation from curve in figure 5.3
		Primary	Secondary	Higher			
Bangladesh	159	0.62	1.60	1.86	6	75.8	0.10
Bhutan	151	..	..	..	..	..	..
China	273	0.88	1.47	1.59	1	28.9	-0.40
India	259	0.58	0.92	1.51	5	60.8	0.20
Indonesia	470	1.21	1.25	0.59	-3	21.1	-0.25
Korea	2,040	1.59	1.25	0.46	-3	13.3	0.00
Lao PDR	3,32						
Malaysia	1,860	1.36	1.14	1.24	0	32.1	0.35
Myanmar	184	..	..	..	..	..	..
Nepal	142	0.87	0.72	1.62	1	52.1	-0.40
Papua New Guinea	621	2.79	3.47	6.85	4	55.3	0.50
Philippines	581	0.56	9.46	0.33	-2	14.1	-0.30
Singapore	7,093	..	..	..	..	..	..
Sri Lanka	374	0.59	0.50	0.54	-1	27.0	-0.25
Thailand	712	1.49	0.82	0.26	-2	23.4	0.00

Table C.3 (continued)

Country	Per capita GNP (1985) US$	Females in total enrollments (percent)			Percentage of 1st year entrants surviving to end of cycle		Deviation of unit costs from regional average (percent)		
		Primary	Secondary	Higher	Primary	Secondary	Primary	Secondary	Higher
Bangladesh	159	40	28	19	24	18	-0.38	0.60	0.86
Bhutan	151	34	18	17	17	38	..	..	..
China	273	45	40	30	68	15	-0.12	0.47	0.59
India	259	40	34	29	37	36	-0.42	-0.08	0.51
Indonesia	470	48	43	32	60	49	0.21	0.25	-0.41
Korea	2,040	49	47	30	97	46	0.59	0.25	-0.54
Lao PDR	332	45	41	36	40	23	..	..	..
Malaysia	1,860	49	49	45	97	51	0.36	0.14	0.24
Myanmar	184	..	..	..	..	..	..	..	..
Nepal	142	29	23	20	33	66	-0.13	-0.28	0.62
Papua New Guinea	621	44	36	23	67	8	1.79	2.47	5.85
Philippines	581	49	50	54	66	36	-0.44	8.46	-0.67
Singapore	7,093	47	50	42	100	27	..	..	..
Sri Lanka	374	48	53	40	85	25	-0.41	-0.50	-0.46
Thailand	712	48	48	46	80	41	0.49	-0.18	-0.74

Table C.3 (continued)

Country	Per capita GNP (1985) US$	Avg. teacher pay as ratio to per capita GNP		Number of pupils per teacher	
		Primary	Secondary	Primary	Secondary
Bangladesh	159	2.2	..	47.0	26.2
Bhutan	151	..	..	38.5	10.1
China	273	2.0	3.4	24.9	17.2
India	259	2.9	3.1	57.6	20.2
Indonesia	470	2.5	3.2	25.3	15.3
Korea	2,040	5.0	5.5	38.3	34.3
Lao PDR	332	..	..	24.9	11.2
Malaysia	1,860	2.4	3.1	24.1	22.1
Myanmar	184	..	..	46.4	28.5
Nepal	142	2.8	5.0	35.5	27.5
Papua New Guinea	621	6.8	10.0	31.0	25.4
Philippines	581	1.6	1.7	30.9	32.3
Singapore	7,093	..	..	27.1	20.4
Sri Lanka	374	1.6	2.1	31.7	26.1
Thailand	712	2.5	2.9	19.3	19.6

.. Not available.

Note: All figures refer to early to mid-1980s.

a. Relative to regional average.

Source: See appendix B.

References

ACU. See Association of Commonwealth Universities.

Asian Development Bank (ADB). l986. *Nepal: Education Sector Study.* Manila.

————. 1987. *Distance Education. Proceedings of the Regional Seminar on Distance Education, November 26 – December 3, 1986.* Bangkok.

Association of Commonwealth Universities (ACU). 1987. *Commonwealth Universities Yearbook 1987.* 3 volumes. London.

Bangladesh (Ministry of Education). 1984. *New Life in Education.* Dhaka.

Bangladesh (BANBEIS, Ministry of Education). 1986. *Educational Statistics 1986.* Dhaka.

Bank of Korea. 1988. *Economic Statistics Yearbook 1988.* Seoul.

Behrman, Jere R., and Nancy Birdsall. 1983. "The Quality of Schooling: Quantity Alone is Misleading." *American Economic Review* 73(5): 928–46.

Bordia, A. 1987. "India." In T. Neville Postlethwaite, ed. *The Encyclopedia of Comparative Education and National Systems of Education.* New York: Pergamon Press.

Britain, British Council. 1984. *Education Profile, India.* London: Editorial Section, Central Information Service.

Burma (Ministry of Finance). 1986. *Report to the Phithu Hluttaw on the Financial, Economic and Social Conditions of the Socialist Republic of Burma for l985–86.* Rangoon.

Caldwell, J.C., P.H. Reddy, and P. Caldwell. 1985. "Educational Transition in Rural South India." *Population and Development Review* 11(1): 29–51.

China (People's Education Press). 1984 and 1986. *Achievement of Education in China.* Beijing.

China (Statistical Publishing House). 1985. *1982 Population Census of China.* Beijing.

China (Ministry of Education). 1987a. *Yearbook of Chinese Education Statistics* (in Chinese). Beijing.

China (Statistical Information and Consultancy Service Centre). 1987b. *Statistical Yearbook of China 1987.* Beijing.

Gannicott, Ken. l987. *The Evaluation of Human Capital in Papua New Guinea.* Canberra: Islands/Australia Working Paper, National Centre for Development Studies, Australian National University.

Hanushek, Eric. 1986. "The Economics of Schooling: Production and Efficiency in Public Schools." *Journal of Economic Literature* 24(3):1141–77.

Harbison, Ralph, and Eric Hanushek. 1990. *Educational Performance of the Poor: Lessons from Rural Northeast Brazil.* Baltimore, Md.: Johns Hopkins University Press for the World Bank.

Hartley, Michael J., and Eric V. Swanson. 1984. *Achievement and Wastage: An Analysis of the Retention of Basic Skills in Primary Education. Final report of the International Study of the Retention of Literacy and Numeracy: An Egyptian Case Study.* World Bank, Washington, D.C.

Hinchcliffe, Keith, and R.V. Youdi. 1985. *Forecasting Skilled-Manpower Needs: The Experience of Eleven Countries.* Paris: International Institute of Educational Planning.

*Horn, Robin, and Anna-Maria Arriagada. 1986. "The Educational Attainment of the World's Population: Three Decades of Progress." World Bank, Education and Training Department Discussion Paper EDT 37, Washington, D.C.

Husen, Torsten, and T. Neville Postlethwaite. 1985. *The Encyclopedia of Education.* New York: Pergamon Press.

IEA. See International Association for the Evaluation of Education Achievement.

India (National Council of Educational Research and Training). 1980. *Fourth All-India Educational Survey.* New Delhi.

India (Ministry of Education). 1983. *Analysis of Budgeted Expenditure on Education 1980– 81 to 1982–83.* Planning and Monitoring Unit, New Delhi.

India (Ministry of Finance). 1985. *The Seventh Five-Year Plan.* New Delhi.

India (Ministry of Education). 1987. *Selected Information on School Education in India.* Planning, Monitoring, and Statistical Division, New Delhi.

India (Ministry of Human Resource Development). 1987. *A Handbook of Educational and Allied Statistics.* New Delhi.

India (Ministry of Human Resource Development). 1988. *Selected Educational Statistics 1986–87.* New Delhi.

Indonesia and USAID. 1986. "Indonesia: Education and Human Resources Sector Review." Ministry of Education and Culture of Indonesia with the United States Agency for International Development, Washington, D.C.

International Association for the Evaluation of Education Achievement (IEA). 1988. *Science Achievement in Seventeen Countries. A Preliminary Report.* U.K.: Pergamon Press.

*James, Estelle. 1988. "Philippines Education Sector Review. Higher Education." World Bank, Asia Country Department II, Washington, D.C.

Jimenez, Emmanuel. 1986. "The Structure of Educational Costs: Multiproduct Cost Functions for Primary and Secondary Schools in Latin America." *Economics of Education Review* 5(1): 25–29.

*Jimenez, Emmanuel, Vicente Paqueo, and Ma. Lourdes de Vera. 1987a. "The Relative Efficiency of Private and Public High Schools in the Philippines." World Bank, Population and Human Resources Department, Washington, D.C.

*———. 1987b. "Does Local Financing Make Public Primary Schools More Efficient? The Philippine Case." World Bank, Population and Human Resources Department, Washington, D.C.

KEDI. See Korea Educational Development Institute.

*King, Elizabeth. 1988. "Report on Education Sector for Bangladesh Public Expenditure Review." World Bank, Population and Human Resources Department, Washington, D.C.

Kolhatkar, M.R. 1988. "Country Paper: India." Paper presented at the Regional Seminar on Mobilization of Additional Funding for Higher Education, August, 22–27, 1988. Unesco Principal Regional Office for Asia and the Pacific, Bangkok.

Korea Educational Development Institute (KEDI). 1988. "Education and Economic

Development" (in Korean). KEDI report by Kong En-Bae and others, Seoul.

Korea (Ministry of Education). 1987. *Statistical Yearbook of Education 1977–87*. Seoul.

———. 1988. *Education in Korea 1887–1988*. Seoul.

Korean Council for University Education. 1988. *Equity, Quality, and Cost in Higher Education*. Unesco Principal Regional Office for Asia and the Pacific, Bangkok.

Kumar, Krishna. 1985. "Reproduction or Change? Education and Elites in India." *Economic and Political Weekly* XX(30): 1280–84.

*Laya, Jaime. 1988. "Malaysia: Financing Primary and Secondary Education." World Bank, Asia Country Department II, Washington, D.C.

Lestage, Andre. 1981. *Literacy and Illiteracy*. Unesco, Educational Studies and Documents #42, Paris.

Lockheed, Marlaine, and associates. 1990. *Improving Primary Education in Developing Countries*. Baltimore, Md.: Johns Hopkins University Press for the World Bank.

Malaysia (Office of the Prime Minister). 1986. *Fifth Malaysia Plan 1986–1990*. Kuala Lumpur.

Malaysia (Ministry of Finance). 1988. *Belajawan Persekutuan*. Kuala Lumpur.

Mehmet, Ozay, and Yat Hoong Yip. 1986. *Human Capital Formation in Malaysian Universities*. Institute of Advanced Studies Occasional Papers and Reports KLB #2, Kuala Lumpur.

*Mingat, Alain, and George Psacharopoulos. 1985. *Education Costs and Financing in Africa: Some Facts and Possible Lines of Action*. World Bank, Education and Training Department, Report No. EDT13, Washington, D.C.

Mingat, Alain, and Jee-Peng Tan. 1985. "On Equity in Education Again: An International Comparison." *Journal of Human Resources* 20(2): 298–308.

———. 1986a. *Analytical Tools for Sector Work in Education*, Baltimore, Md.: Johns Hopkins University Press for the World Bank.

———. 1986b. "Public Funding of Education: A Comparison." *Comparative Education Review* 30(2): 260–70.

*———. 1988. "The Cost and Financing of Education in the Philippines: A Documentation and Assessment of Policy Issues." World Bank, Asia Technical Department, Washington, D.C.

*Moock, Peter R. 1985. "Education in Malaysia: A Review of Expenditures and Discussion of Issues." World Bank, Education and Training Department, Report No. EDT11, Washington, D.C.

Mullick, S.P. 1987. "Distance Education in India." In *Distance Education. Proceedings of the Regional Seminar on Distance Education, November 26 – December 3, 1986*. Asian Development Bank, Bangkok.

Murnane, Richard, and D. Cohen. 1986. "Merit Pay and the Evaluation of the Problem: Why Some Merit Plans Fail and Few Survive." *Harvard Educational Review* 56(1): 1–17.

Nepal and USAID. 1988. *Nepal: Education and Human Resources Sector Assessment*. Ministry of Education and Culture of Nepal with the United States Agency for International Development. Washington, D.C.

Paderanga, Cayetano. 1987. "Exploring the PRODED Results: Preliminary Report on the HSMS Project." Government of the Philippines, Department of Education, Culture, and Sports, Manila.

Patwari, A.M. 1987. "The Universities of Bangladesh." In *Commonwealth Universities Yearbook 1987*. London: Association of Commonwealth Universities.

Postlethwaite, T. Neville. 1987. *The Encyclopedia of Comparative Education and National*

Systems of Education. New York: Pergamon Press.

Psacharopoulos, George. 1981. "Returns to Education: An Updated International Comparison." *Comparative Education* 17(3): 321–41.

———. 1984. "The Contribution of Education to Economic Growth. International Comparisons." In John W. Kendrick, ed. *International Comparisons of Productivity and Causes of the Slowdown*. Cambridge, Mass.: American Enterprise Institute/Ballinger Publishing Company.

———. 1985. "Returns to Education: A Further International Update and Implications." *Journal of Human Resources*, XX(4): 584–604.

———. 1988. "Efficiency and Equity in Greek Higher Education." *Minerva* 26(2): 119–37.

Psacharopoulos, George, and Anna-Maria Arriagada. 1986. "The Educational Composite of the Labor Force: An International Comparison." *International Labor Review* 125(5):561–74.

*Smith, W.J. 1988. "Chapter III: Education and Training." Contribution to 1988 Country Economic Report for Sri Lanka. World Bank, Asia Country Department I, Washington, D.C.

Sri Lanka (Ministry of Education). 1986. *Some Indicators and Projections Relevant to First and Second Level General Education*. Colombo.

Sri Lanka (Department of Government Printing). 1987. *1988 New Consolidated Salaries Implementation of Recommendations of Administrative Reforms Committee - Salaries and Cadres*. Colombo.

Sri Lanka (University Grants Commission). 1988. *Statistical Handbook 1986. Statistics on Higher Education in Sri Lanka*. Colombo.

Srisa-an, Wichit. 1987. "Financing and Cost-Effectiveness of Distance Education." In *Distance Education. Proceedings of the Regional Seminar on Distance Education, November 26 – December 3, 1986*. Asian Development Bank, Bangkok.

Srisa-an, Wichit. 1988. "Country Paper: Thailand." Paper presented at the Regional Seminar on Mobilization of Additional Funding for Higher Education. August 22–27, 1988. Unesco Principal Regional Office for Asia and the Pacific, Bangkok.

Suppachai, Panitchapakdi. 1976. "Changes of the Rates of Return to Investment on Education." In *Rak Mueng Thai (Love of Thailand)*. Bangkok: Sciences Society of Thailand.

Tan, Jee-Peng, and Vicente Paqueo. 1989. "The Economic Returns to Education in the Philippines." *International Journal of Educational Development* 9(3):243–50.

Thailand (Ministry of University Affairs). 1985a. *General Information*. Bangkok.

Thailand (National Commission on Education). 1985b. *Statistics Report on Education in Thailand*. Bangkok.

Thailand (National Statistical Office). 1986. *Statistical Yearbook of Thailand 1985–86*. Bangkok.

Thailand (Ministry of Education). 1987a. *The Sixth National Education Development Plan*. Bangkok.

Thailand (National Education Commission). 1987b. *Basic Educational Statistics for Pre-primary and Primary Education*. Bangkok.

Thailand (National Education Commission). 1987c. *Costs and Contribution of Higher Education. A Case Study of Thailand*. Educational Research Division, Bangkok.

Thailand (Bureau of the Budget). 1988a. *Thailand's Budget in Brief*. Bangkok.

Thailand (National Education Commission). 1988b. *A Glance at Educational Statistics during the Fifth Plan (1982–1986)*. Bangkok.

Thomas, R.M. 1987. "Indonesia." In T. Neville Postlethwaite, ed. *The Encyclopedia of*

Comparative Education and National Systems of Education. New York: Pergamon Press.

Tilak, Jandhyala B.G. 1985. "Discriminatory Pricing in Education." NIEPA Occasional Paper. National Institute of Educational Planning and Administration, New Delhi.

———. 1987. "Educational Finances in India." NIEPA Occasional Paper. National Institute of Educational Planning and Administration, New Delhi.

———. 1988. "Educational Finances in South Asia." United Nations Centre for Regional Development Working Paper No. 88-1, Nagoya.

Timilsina, Parthibeshwar. 1988. "Mobilization of Additional Funding for Higher Education in Nepal." Paper presented at the Regional Seminar on Mobilization of Additional Funding for Higher Education, August 22–27, 1988. Unesco Principal Regional Office for Asia and the Pacific, Bangkok.

Unesco. 1984. "Evolution of Wastage in Primary Education in the World Between 1970 and 1980." Paper presented at the International Conference on Education, October 16–24, 1984, International Conference Center, Geneva.

———. 1985. *Development of Education in Asia and the Pacific: A Statistical Review.* Fifth Regional Conference of Ministers of Education and Those Responsible for Economic Planning in Asia and the Pacific, March 4–11, 1985. Organized by Unesco with the cooperation of ESCAP, Bangkok.

———. 1987a. *Statistical Digest 1987.* Paris.

———. 1987b. *Statistical Yearbook 1987.* Paris.

———. 1988. *Education Statistics* (latest year available). Paris.

UNICEF. 1987. *An Analysis of the Situation of Children and Women in the Lao People's Democratic Republic.* Vientianne.

———. 1988. *The State of the World's Children.* New York.

United Nations. 1985. *Selected Statistics and Indicators on the Status of Women.* World Conference to Review and Appraise the Achievements of the United Nations Decade for Women: Equality, Development and Peace, July 15–20, 1985, Nairobi. Report to the Secretary General.

Watson, Keith. 1981. "The Higher Education Dilemma in Developing Countries: Thailand's Two Decades of Reform." *Higher Education* 10: 297–314.

*Winkler, Donald. 1988a. "Decentralization in Education: An Economic Perspective." World Bank, Education and Employment Division, Population and Human Resources Department, Washington, D.C.

*———. 1988b. "Efficiency and Equity in Latin American Higher Education." World Bank Discussion Paper 77, Washington, D.C.

World Bank. 1986. *Financing Education in Developing Countries: An Exploration of Policy Options.* Washington, D.C.

*———. 1988. *World Development Report 1988.* Washington, D.C.: Oxford University Press for the World Bank.

*World Bank-Bangladesh. 1978. "Bangladesh: Education and Training Sector Memorandum." East Asia and Pacific Regional Office, Report 2037a-BD, Washington, D.C.

*———. 1981. "Bangladesh: Education Sector Memorandum." South Asia Projects Department, Report 3548-BD, Washington, D.C.

———. 1987. *Bangladesh: Promoting Higher Growth and Human Development.* Country Studies series, Washington, D.C.

*———. 1988a. "Bangladesh: Adjustment in the Eighties and Short-Term Prospects." Asia Country Department I, Report 7105-BD, Washington, D.C.

*———. 1988b. "Bangladesh: A Review of Selected Issues in Education." Asia Country

Department I, Report 6770-BD, Washington, D.C.

*World Bank-Bhutan 1988a. "Bhutan: Primary Education Project." Asia Country Department I, Staff Appraisal Report 7010-BHU, Washington, D.C.

*———. 1988b. "Bhutan: Development Planning in a Unique Environment." Asia Country Department I, Report 7189-BHU, Washington, D.C.

*World Bank-Burma 1985. "Burma: Policies and Prospects for Economic Adjustment and Growth." South Asia Regional Office, Report 4814-BA, Washington, D.C.

*World Bank-China 1983. "China: Socialist Economic Development. The Social Sectors. Vol. III." Country Study Series, Washington, D.C.

———. 1985. "China: Issues and Prospects in Education." Annex to *China: Long Term Development Issues and Options.* Country Study Series, Washington, D.C.

*———. 1986a. "China: Growth and Development in Gansu Province." East Asia and the Pacific Regional Office, Report 6064-CHA, Washington, D.C.

*———. 1986b. "China: Management and Finance of Higher Education." Country Study Series, Washington, D.C.

*———. 1988. "China: Teacher Training Project." Staff Appraisal Report 7187-CHA, Washington, D.C.

*World Bank-India 1987. "India: An Industrializing Economy in Transition." South Asia Regional Office, Report 6633-IN, Washington, D.C.

*———. 1988a. "India: Recent Developments and Medium-Term Issues." Asia Country Department IV, Report 7185-IN, Washington, D.C.

*———. 1988b. "State Finances in India: The Case of Gujarat." Asia Country Department IV, Washington, D.C.

*World Bank-Indonesia 1982. "Indonesia: Financial Resources and Human Development in the Eighties." East Asia and the Pacific Regional Office, Report 3795-IND, Washington, D.C.

*———. 1984. "General Secondary Education in Indonesia: Issues and Programs for Action." East Asia and the Pacific Regional Office, Report 4954-IND, Washington, D.C.

*———. 1988a. "Indonesia: Adjustment, Growth and Sustainable Development." Asia Country Department II, Report 7222-IND, Washington, D.C.

*———. 1988b. "Indonesia: Higher Education Development Project." Asia Country Department II, Staff Appraisal Report 7085-IND, Washington, D.C.

*———. 1988c. "Indonesia: Selected Issues of Public Management." Asia Country Department II, Report 7007-IND, Washington, D.C.

*———. 1989. "Indonesia Basic Education Study." Asia Country Department V, Report 7841-IND, Washington, D.C.

*World Bank-Korea 1985. "Impact of World Bank Lending for Educational Development in Korea: A Review." Operations Evaluation Department, Report 5950, Washington, D.C.

*World Bank-Malaysia 1988. "Malaysia: Matching Risks and Rewards in a Mixed Economy." Asia Country Department II, Report 7208-MA, Washington, D.C.

*World Bank-Nepal 1988a. "An Assessment of Education in Nepal." Asia Country Department I, Washington, D.C.

*———. 1988b. "Policies for Improving Growth and Alleviating Poverty." Asia Country Department I, Report 7418-NEP, Washington, D.C.

*World Bank-Papua New Guinea 1986. "Papua New Guinea: Country Economic Memorandum." East Asia and the Pacific Regional Office, Report 5967-PNG, Washington, D.C.

*———. 1987. "Papua New Guinea: The Costs and Financing of Education." East Asia and

the Pacific Regional Office, Report 6767-PNG, Washington, D.C.

———. 1988. *Papua New Guinea: Policies and Prospects for Sustained and Broad-Based Growth.* Asia Country Department V, Report 7121-PNG, Washington, D.C.

*World Bank-Philippines 1988. "The Philippines: Country Economic Memorandum." Asia Country Department II, Report 7438-PH, Washington, D.C.

*World Bank-Sri Lanka 1986. "Sri Lanka. Education and Training Sector Memorandum." South Asia Regional Office, Report 5696-CE, Washington, D.C.

*———. 1988. "Sri Lanka: A Break with Past. The 1987-90 Program of Economic Reforms and Adjustment." Asia Country Department I, Report 7220-CE, Washington, D.C.

*World Bank-Thailand 1985. "Completion Report: Thailand Fourth Education Project." East Asia and the Pacific Regional Office, Report 1271-TH, Washington, D.C.

*———. 1986. "Thailand: Growth with Stability. A Challenge for the Sixth Plan Period." East Asia and the Pacific Regional Office, Report 6036-TH, Washington, D.C.

*———. 1988. "Thailand: Building on the Recent Success—A Policy Framework." Asia Country Department II, Washington, D.C.

Zachariah, K.C., and Vu, My T. 1988. *World Population Projections, 1987–88 Edition: Short and Long-Term Estimates.* Baltimore, Md.: Johns Hopkins University Press for the World Bank.

*Za'rour, George. 1988. "Universities in Arab Countries." World Bank PRS Working Paper No. 62, Washington, D.C.

---

*Books preceded by an asterisk are internal documents and for World Bank use only.

LB2826.6.A78 T36 1992   CU-Main

Tan, Jee-Peng, 1954-/Education in Asia : a compara

3 9371 00015 3585

LB 2826.6 .A78 T36 1992
Tan, Jee-Peng, 1954-
Education in Asia

LB 2826.6 .A78 T36 1992
Tan, Jee-Peng, 1954-
Education in Asia

DATE	ISSUED TO

CONCORDIA UNIVERSITY LIBRARY
2811 NE Holman St.
Portland, OR 97211